Emerging Capital Markets and Globalization

THE LATIN AMERICAN EXPERIENCE

Augusto de la Torre and
Sergio L. Schmukler

A COPUBLICATION OF STANFORD ECONOMICS AND FINANCE,
AN IMPRINT OF STANFORD UNIVERSITY PRESS, AND THE WORLD BANK

A copublication of Stanford Economics and Finance, an imprint of Stanford University Press, and the World Bank.

Stanford University Press
1450 Page Mill Road
Palo Alto, Calif. 94304

The World Bank
1818 H Street, NW
Washington, DC 20433

The findings, interpretations, and conclusions expressed herein are those of the author(s) and do not necessarily reflect the views of the Board of Executive Directors of the World Bank or the governments they represent.

The World Bank does not guarantee the accuracy of the data included in this work. The boundaries, colors, denominations, and other information shown on any map in this work do not imply any judgment on the part of the World Bank concerning the legal status of any territory or the endorsement or acceptance of such boundaries.

Rights and Permissions

ISBN-10: 0-8213-6543-6   (World rights except North America)
ISBN-13: 978-0-8213-6544-1   (World rights except North America)
ISBN-13: 978-0-8047-5718-8 (Hardcover)   (North America)
ISBN-13: 978-0-8047-5719-5 (Softcover)   (North America)
eISBN-10: 0-8213-6544-4
DOI: 10.1596/978-0-8213-6544-1

Cover design: Drew Fasick.

Library of Congress Cataloging-in-Publication Data
Emerging capital markets and globalization : the Latin American experience / Augusto de la Torre and Sergio L. Schmukler.
   p. cm.
Includes bibliographical references and index.
ISBN-13: 978-0-8213-6544-1
ISBN-10: 0-8213-6543-6
ISBN-10: 0-8213-6544-4 (electronic)
1. Capital market--Latin America. I. Schmukler, Sergio L. II. Title.

HG5160.5.A3T675 2006
332'.0415098--dc22
                                                      2006028046

Latin American
Development Forum Series

This series was created in 2003 to promote debate, disseminate information and analysis, and convey the excitement and complexity of the most topical issues in economic and social development in Latin America and the Caribbean. It is sponsored by the Inter-American Development Bank, the United Nations Economic Commission for Latin America and the Caribbean, and the World Bank. The manuscripts chosen for publication represent the highest quality in each institution's research and activity output and have been selected for their relevance to the academic community, policy makers, researchers, and interested readers.

Advisory Committee Members

Contents

FIGURES

Foreword

In the early 1990s, most of Latin America enthusiastically embraced the pro-market reforms associated with the "Washington Consensus": market liberalization, deregulation, and privatization.* Much was expected from these reforms, but now we are keenly aware that, relative to their outcome, those expectations often suffered from excess optimism. Views differ widely, however, on the extent and nature of the excess and reasons behind it. For some analysts, the initial optimism was groundless because the reforms themselves were the problem. The pro-market reforms of the early 1990s, they would say, were based on faulty theory and hypotheses and, hence, they did little to alleviate (and may have even helped accentuate) the Latin American problems of low growth, high volatility, and high inequality. In the view of such analysts, countries would have been better off with less reforms of the Washington Consensus type. At the opposite extreme are those who contend that there was nothing wrong with the direction of the reform process itself and that the problem was likely in the poor and incomplete implementation of reforms. In their view, Washington Consensus–type reforms were part of the solution and countries would have been clearly better off with more and better-implemented reforms, particularly if the initial reforms that focused on liberalization and privatization were complemented to a greater extent with the building of market-supportive institutions.

This book is a timely and important contribution to such policy debates. While it focuses on capital markets in emerging economies, particularly Latin America, its empirical results and policy insights are also pertinent to the broader debate on economic development and pro-market reforms.

As for its specific focus, the book is a unique and thorough "stock taking" of securities markets in Latin America. It takes the reader on a grand

---

* The term "Washington Consensus" was coined by Williamson (1990). See World Bank (2005) for a review of the reforms during the 1990s and a discussion of their policy lessons.

tour of relevant historical developments, empirical questions, and policy issues. In contrast with much of the literature on the subject, it analyzes the development of local capital markets as an integral part of the ongoing globalization of financial markets. It then systematically compares Latin American outcomes of pro-market reforms, both in terms of domestic capital market development and integration, with global financial markets and with what happened in other regions in both dimensions. Empirical highlights include inquiries about the factors associated with capital market development and the role of reforms. The book also asks whether Latin America has a shortfall between, on the one hand, institutional and economic fundamentals and the extent of reforms and, on the other hand, the state of development of local capital markets. It establishes the positive effects of reforms and institutional and macroeconomic improvements on capital market development. It examines the interplay between local stock market liquidity and the internationalization of stock trading and issuance. It shows the important role of size (of issuers, issues, and markets) in the development of and access to stock and bond markets. It confirms that exchange rate policy is an important independent factor behind the development of local currency bond markets. It shows that a shortfall exists, i.e., that Latin capital markets have not fully responded to economic and institutional fundamentals and to the extent of the reform effort. And in sharp contrast, the book shows that the degree of integration with international capital markets is larger than expected for Latin American issuers.

The Latin American contrast between the relatively shallow development of local capital markets and their high degree of financial integration in global markets is especially acute when we compare Latin America to East Asia. East Asia shows a higher payoff for reforms in terms of local capital market development, though a lesser impact with respect to integration with global financial markets. Similar reforms have thus produced sharply different results in the two regions. The book suggests some potential reasons for such outcomes (differences in savings rates, degree of macroeconomic volatility, degree of "home bias," time zones, etc.) and leaves these as topics for further inquiry.

These findings deal a blow to the extreme views while adding complications that defy easy categorization. To the chagrin of those who see no redeeming value in Washington Consensus–style reforms, the evidence in the book shows that reforms have indeed spurred capital market development and financial integration. And to the surprise of those who argue that all that is needed is the intensification of the conventionally defined reform agenda, the book shows that the lagging development of Latin American capital markets relative to other emerging markets is not due to lack of reform effort and that the same reforms can have substantially different outcomes in different country environments. The book draws attention to important complexities, particularly that (a) reforms have had unexpected impacts in Latin America (e.g., a bias in favor of internationalization of securities trading and issuance over local trading and issuance) and (b) certain factors (e.g., globalization and size) that have been underemphasized to date need to be taken much more seriously, as they play a decisive role in capital market development.

The book should stimulate a vigorous discussion on how to best revise the reform agenda for capital market development in emerging economies going forward. This effort should involve not only country authorities but also academics and advisers from multilateral agencies such as the World Bank. The complexities highlighted in the book invite intellectual modesty, eclecticism, and constant attention to country specificity. While it does not provide detailed policy prescriptions, the book does point to issues that cannot be ignored and puts forward provocative questions for the policy debate. The policy discussion in the book is particularly interesting with respect to the following aspects:

Internationalization of stock markets. Delisting marks a strong trend in Latin America and in Eastern European countries. Local stock markets appear to be shrinking in this regard. Migration of trading and issuance of stocks abroad seem difficult to stop. Such internationalization appears to impair liquidity in local stock markets. The implicit view that small countries could develop mini Wall Streets appears to have been misguided. This fact, however, does not appear to have limited access to equity markets for large firms, as they have gained enormously in access to global equity markets, which are deeper and more liquid. But it poses a serious problem for the small and medium enterprises (SMEs).

Local currency debt markets. Currency debt markets are very different than stock markets in that local currency debt must have its origin and principal home in local markets. Further, the development of local currency debt markets is crucial for systemic stability—otherwise governments and corporations in nontradable sectors would accumulate major open currency exposures in their balance sheets (a high degree of "liability dollarization"). Contrary to the case of stock markets, developments in local currency debt markets in Latin America (especially in Chile, Colombia, and Mexico) show significant promise. As noted, the book finds that exchange rate regimes matter—pegs promote dollarization and discourage local currency debt market development. The present landscape of low inflation rates, inflation targeting, and exchange rate flexibility has created the right environment for reforms to foster long-term local currency debt markets. More prudent public debt management by governments is also contributing to this result. However, SMEs still are not tapping these emerging markets.

The remaining problem: access for SMEs. Previous expectations that SMEs will have direct access to securities markets appear misguided. The small size of SMEs is a decisive factor preventing direct access, a factor that seems to dominate corporate governance and minority shareholder issues. Transaction costs in fully regulated securities markets become prohibitive for small issues and issuers. Low frequency of issuances further restricts liquidity. An important conclusion of the book is that there is an urgent need to devote significant effort to the analysis and design of creative, out-of-the-box solutions to the problem of SME access to both debt and equity markets. Ongoing efforts by the World Bank (some by the authors of this book) and elsewhere may shed needed light on this problem, a problem that was definitively not solved by the pro-market reforms of the Washington Consensus era.

Guillermo Perry
Chief Economist, Latin America and the Caribbean
The World Bank

Acknowledgments

This book is part of the regional study "Whither Latin American Capital Markets?" conducted at the Latin America and Caribbean Region of the World Bank, under the Office of the Chief Economist and the Financial Sector Unit. We are particularly indebted to Francisco Ceballos, Norbert Fiess, Juan Carlos Gozzi, and Marina Halac, who actively participated in the production of this book and the overall regional study. We also thank Leonor Coutinho and Jurgen Janssens, who helped us in the initial stages of the project. Many authors wrote background papers for the mentioned regional study that are, as a result, incorporated in this book in one way or another. Those papers appear at the regional study's Web site at http://www.worldbank.org/laccapitalmarkets. We are grateful to Guillermo Perry, who encouraged us to undertake the research, disseminate its results, and publish this book, and who provided constructive feedback throughout the entire process. For facilitating the dialogue with financial sector practitioners and for financial support to produce this book we are deeply indebted to Makhtar Diop. For their detailed and useful comments and suggestions, we would also like to thank Christian Broda, Jerry Caprio, Juan José Cruces, Francisco de Paula Gutiérrez, Arturo Galindo, Michael Gavin, Tom Glaessner, Claudio Irigoyen, Miguel Kiguel, Yambeon Kim, Leora Klapper, Anjali Kumar, Jeppe Ladekarl, Danny Leipziger, Giovanni Majnoni, Santiago Pombo, Michael Pomerleano, Luis Servén, Dimitri Vittas, and Sara Zervos, among many others. Dana Vorisek provided excellent editorial assistance. We have also benefited from feedback received at presentations held at the Banco de Mexico (Mexico City, Mexico), the Capital Markets Symposium (Medellin, Colombia), the Central Bank of Chile (Santiago, Chile), the GDN Annual Conference (New Delhi, India), the European Science Foundation Exploratory Workshop at Oxford University (Oxford, United Kingdom), the LACEA Annual Meetings (San Jose, Costa Rica), Séptimo Congreso de Tesorería (Cartagena de Indias, Colombia), the Securities and Exchange Commission (Washington, DC), Stanford University (Stanford, California), the UBS Roundtable (Lima, Peru), the Universidad Torcuato di Tella (Buenos Aires, Argentina), the University of Notre Dame (Notre Dame, Indiana), and the World Bank Finance Forum and LAC Meets the Market (Washington, DC).

About the Authors

Augusto de la Torre has worked for the World Bank since 1997. As senior regional financial sector advisor for Latin America and the Caribbean, he provides technical and conceptual leadership to World Bank financial sector operations and research in the Region and is actively involved in the joint IMF-World Bank Financial Sector Assessment Program. In addition, he works closely with the Office of the Chief Economist for the Latin American and the Caribbean Region, focusing on macroeconomic and financial sector linkages and issues.

He headed the Central Bank of Ecuador from 1993–96. In November 1996, he was chosen by *Euromoney* as the year's "Best Latin Central Banker." He is also a member of the Carnegie Network of Economic Reformers.

From 1986–92, he was an economist with the International Monetary Fund and during 1991–92 was the IMF's resident representative in República Bolivariana de Venezuela.

Sergio L. Schmukler is lead economist in the Development Research Group at the World Bank. He obtained a Ph.D. from the University of California at Berkeley in 1997, when he started working as a young professional and young economist at the World Bank. Since joining the Bank, he has also worked continuously for the Office of the Chief Economist for Latin America and for the East Asia and South Asia regions.

Concurrent with his work for the World Bank, he has been treasurer of LACEA (Latin America and Caribbean Economic Association) since 2004, was associate editor of the *Journal of Development Economics* (2001–04), taught at the University of Maryland (1999–2003), and worked at the IMF Research Department (2004–05). Before joining the World Bank, he worked at the U.S. Federal Reserve, the Inter-American Development Bank, and the Argentine Central Bank.

His research areas are international finance and international financial markets and institutions. He has published many articles in several academic journals and books on emerging markets finance, exchange rate regimes, financial globalization, financial crises and contagion, and financial development.

Abbreviations

ABS	Asset-backed securities
AIOS	Asociación Internacional de Organismos de Supervision de Fundos de Pensiones
ADR	American depositary receipt
BIS	Bank for International Settlements
BM&F	Brazilian Mercantile & Futures Exchange
CNBV	Comisión Nacional Bancaria y de Valores (Mexico)
CPI	Consumer price index
FDI	Foreign direct investment
G-7	Group of Seven
GDP	Gross domestic product
GDR	Global depository receipt
IDB	Inter-American Development Bank
IMF	International Monetary Fund
IPO	Initial public offering
LSE	London Stock Exchange
M&A	Mergers and acquisitions
MBS	Mortgage-backed securities
MexDer	Mexican Derivatives Market
NDF	Non-deliverable forward
NYSE	New York Stock Exchange
OECD	Organisation for Economic Co-operation and Development
OTC	Over-the-counter (market)
Repo	Repurchase agreement
SHF	Sociedad Hipotecaria Federal (Mexico)
SMEs	Small and medium enterprises
UF	Unidad de Fomento (Chile)

1

Whither Capital Market Development?

BACK IN THE EARLY 1990S, economists and policy makers had high expectations about the prospects for domestic capital market development in emerging economies and, particularly, in Latin America. Unfortunately, they are now faced with disheartening results. Though many still hope that securities markets will develop, the reality is that equity and corporate bond markets in most emerging economies remain highly illiquid and segmented, with trading and capitalization concentrated on few firms. Stock markets in many developing countries, particularly in Latin America and Eastern Europe, have seen listings and liquidity decrease, as a growing number of firms have cross-listed and raised capital in international financial centers, such as New York and London. Debt tends to be concentrated at the short end of the maturity spectrum and denominated in foreign currency, exposing countries to maturity and currency risks. Moreover, government debt is crowding out corporate bond markets in many countries.

The state of capital markets in many emerging economies looks particularly poor when considering the many efforts already undertaken to improve the macroeconomic environment and reform the institutions believed to foster financial development. In the case of Latin America, the results appear even more discouraging in light of the better evolution of capital markets in East Asia and their rapid growth in developed economies (especially in international financial centers). This disappointing performance has made the conventional policy recommendations for capital market development questionable, at best. Policy makers are left without clear guidance on how to revise the reform agenda, and many of them do not envision a bright future for domestic capital markets, particularly for the local stock markets or the smaller emerging economies.

The failure to develop deep and efficient capital markets may have important consequences: growing empirical evidence suggests that financial development is not just correlated with a healthy economy; it actually causes economic growth and has a positive impact on poverty alleviation and income distribution as well.[1] Therefore, a better understanding of the drivers of capital market development and the reasons for the perceived failure of reform efforts in many emerging economies can provide useful guidance to policy makers.

This book contributes to the discussion by analyzing where capital market development in emerging economies stands and where it is headed, with a focus on Latin America. The study has three main goals. First, we take stock of the state and evolution of Latin American capital markets and related reforms, over time and relative to other countries, with a joint emphasis on bond and stock markets. Second, we analyze the factors driving the development of capital markets. Third, in light of this analysis, we discuss the prospects for capital market development in Latin America, and in emerging economies in general, and the implications for the reform agenda going forward.

An analysis of the performance of capital markets would nowadays be incomplete without taking into account the recent trends in financial globalization.[2] Thus, we study not only domestic bond and stock market activity, but also the evolution of global capital markets and the participation of developing countries in those markets. Accordingly, we define internationalization as the use of international financial intermediaries and markets by local securities issuers and investors. This definition covers only one of the many possible aspects of internationalization.[3] Other studies concentrate on other facets of the globalization of financial markets, such as the participation of foreign investors in domestic markets and domestic investors in international markets, the level of foreign assets and liabilities held by each country, the extent of capital flows, and the convergence of prices and returns across countries. Though our definition of internationalization is restrictive, we find it to be perhaps the best one to understand the use of domestic and international capital markets, as discussed next.

Several factors make the inclusion of financial globalization in the analysis valuable. First, most of the studies that analyze the development of local capital markets tend to disregard foreign market activity. We believe that this is a major drawback, given the significant participation of emerging economies in international markets. A salient feature of the recent wave of financial globalization has been the internationalization of financial services. An example of this internationalization is the listing and trading of local shares in major international financial centers, such as New York and London. For many emerging economies, stock issuance and trading in international financial markets now exceeds domestic market activity. Therefore, by not taking into account emerging economies' participation in international markets, one misses a substantial part of capital market activity. Second, most papers that analyze the internationalization process do not study its effects on firms that do not participate in international financial markets.[4] This is also an important weakness, since there are contradictory arguments regarding the impact of financial globalization on domestic markets. Some claim that participation in international markets may have positive effects on local markets, because going abroad, among other things, sends positive signals to investors, encouraging them to participate in domestic markets. For example, by raising capital in international markets, governments and firms may choose to abide by stricter accounting and disclosure standards, making them less likely to expropriate investors.[5] On the other hand, others argue that in a context of liquidity agglomeration, internationalization can shift local liquidity to international markets, generating negative spillover effects on local markets.[6] Third, by considering the major developments in financial markets across countries, one can put in perspective the trends in domestic capital markets and may be better able to assess the degrees of freedom available to local authorities to affect these trends. Fourth, despite possible temporary retrenchments, financial globalization may be expected to deepen in the years to come, making it essential in any analysis of financial markets.

This study's focus on Latin America is interesting in several respects. Three stand out. First, Latin American countries have taken major steps over the past decades to reform their institutions and improve their macroeconomic management. Given all these changes, capital markets in the region were expected to develop significantly. Second, many Latin American countries have actively participated in the globalization process. Therefore, one can test the effects of this participation on local capital markets and derive predictions for countries that have not yet embraced the globalization process to the same extent. Third, we are able to present new and interesting data on the evolution of capital markets in Latin America, which is worth studying and could provide useful lessons for other emerging economies. However, despite our emphasis on Latin America, we will discuss, whenever possible, the experiences of other regions, make cross-regional comparisons, and try to draw general lessons for developing countries in general.

The following three chapters of this book describe the current state and the future of capital markets in emerging economies. Chapter 2 documents the main developments in international financial markets and the increasing globalization process. The chapter also describes the influence of these worldwide trends on Latin America, with particular attention to their effects on the policies and reforms adopted. Furthermore, chapter 2 documents the main developments in Latin American capital markets, both in terms of the evolution of domestic securities markets as well as the participation in international financial markets, and compares them with other regions. Chapter 3 evaluates the factors behind the development (or lack of development) of capital markets. The chapter first discusses how different macroeconomic and institutional variables are related to the development of domestic stock and bond markets and analyzes the effects of reforms on those markets. The second part of chapter 3 analyzes the financial internationalization process, focusing on its potential drivers and its impact on local markets. The chapter finishes by examining whether the experience of Latin America has been similar to that of other regions. Finally, chapter 4 discusses the future of capital markets in developing countries and the lessons for the reform agenda going forward.

Three additional clarifications are worth making from the outset regarding the scope and caveats of our analysis. First, this book's primary focus is on capital market development. It does not explicitly address developments and issues in the banking sector, which is an important limitation, considering that financial systems in most emerging countries are dominated by banks. Fortunately, the literature on the banking sector in emerging economies in general, and Latin America in particular, is relatively abundant.[7] Second, throughout the book we measure capital market development using traditional proxies such as stock market capitalization, equity value traded, and bonds outstanding as a percentage of GDP. We do not claim, however, that these measures capture all the relevant dimensions of capital market development. Third, when we seek to empirically establish the relation between those measures and the potential drivers (especially in chapter 3) we are bound to gauge only certain characteristics of the financial system. In particular, by linking typical measures of stock market development with the potential determinants, we leave unanswered some questions that are fundamental to clarify the full implications of capital markets development. The empirical work does not shed light, for example, on the question of whether capital market development is impelled by rising aggregate savings, a reorientation of existing savings toward the financial system, a shift in financial savings away from banks and toward capital markets, or efficiency gains specific to capital markets.[8] Though we recognize the relevance of, and interest in, these topics, we do not assess them in this book. Our empirical analysis is modest in scope, inevitably couched in a partial equilibrium approach. The general equilibrium effects that deal with different sectors of the financial system and the economy are left to be studied in future work. However, all these limitations should not overshadow the relative amplitude and value of our analysis, which covers (unlike most previous studies) key aspects of capital market development from a perspective that takes into account, from the outset and explicitly, salient implications of financial globalization.

This chapter provides a summary of the main issues and results that are developed in greater detail in the following chapters. The rest of this chapter is organized as follows. The next section discusses the role of financial markets and their impact on growth and income distribution. The third section describes the recent process of financial globalization. The fourth section summarizes the main developments in domestic capital markets in emerging economies over the past two decades, with a focus on

Latin America. The fifth section describes the drivers of the capital market development and internationalization processes. The sixth section briefly discusses how the capital market reform agenda for emerging markets might be modified in light of the evidence presented in this book. The final section concludes.

Why Does Financial Development Matter?

The empirical evidence clearly shows that more developed countries have deeper and more efficient financial systems, including capital markets (Beck, Demirgüç-Kunt, and Levine 2001b). However, the direction of causality between financial development and economic growth is difficult to determine. On the one hand, financial development may increase efficiency in the mobilization and allocation of resources, allowing countries to grow faster. On the other hand, some authors argue that finance responds almost automatically to the changing demands from the real sector, and therefore financial development simply follows economic growth and has very little effect on it.[9]

From a theoretical perspective, financial development can boost growth through several channels.[10] First, financial intermediaries may reduce the costs of acquiring and processing information, as a consequence improving resource allocation and fostering growth. Without intermediaries, each investor would face the large and (mostly) fixed costs of evaluating business conditions, firms, managers, and so forth in order to allocate the savings. Financial intermediaries arise to undertake the task of researching investment opportunities and to sell this information to investors. By economizing on information acquisition costs, these intermediaries improve the assessment of investment opportunities, with positive ramifications on resource allocation and growth.[11] Financial intermediaries may also boost the rate of technological innovation by helping identify entrepreneurs that are more likely to successfully carry out profitable projects and launch new products.[12] This view lies at the core of the Schumpeterian argument, compellingly restated by Rajan and Zingales (2003b), that financial development causes growth because it fuels the process of "creative destruction" by moving resources to the hands of efficient newcomers.

Risk amelioration through diversification is another mechanism through which financial development may positively affect growth. Financial intermediaries can help investors to mitigate the idiosyncratic risk associated with individual projects, firms, industries, and so forth by providing mechanisms for trading, pooling, and diversifying risks. Investors typically dislike risk; however, higher-return projects tend to be riskier. By making it easier for investors to diversify risks and allocate them to those willing to bear them, financial intermediaries may induce a portfolio shift toward riskier higher-return projects, thus altering resource allocation and increasing long-term growth.[13] Financial markets may also help investors deal with liquidity risk. Some investment projects require a long-term commitment of capital, but investors typically are not willing to relinquish control of their savings for long periods. Financial markets allow investors to hold liquid assets, such as equities, bonds, and demand deposits, and transform those liquid instruments into long-term and more illiquid capital investments.[14]

Another channel through which financial development may influence economic growth is by improving corporate governance. Financial intermediaries may help reduce monitoring costs, thereby providing additional means for investors to effectively, even if indirectly, supervise managers and induce them to maximize firm value, with positive ramifications on both savings and investment decisions. Financial development may also affect economic growth by reducing the transaction costs associated with collecting savings from disparate investors, thereby increasing savings, exploiting economies of scale, and overcoming investment indivisibilities. Better savings mobilization may also improve resource allocation and boost technological innovation by facilitating access to multiple investors and therefore allowing projects to achieve economically efficient scales.

Since the beginning of the 1990s, a growing body of empirical work, including broad cross-country and panel studies, time series analyses, individual country case studies, and firm- and industry-level analyses, has provided evidence supporting the view that financial development is not just correlated with economic growth, it is actually one of its drivers. Cross-country studies tend to find that financial depth predicts future economic growth, physical capital accumulation, and improvements in economic efficiency, even after controlling for initial income levels, education, and policy indicators.[15] Several papers have extended the analysis by using country-level panel data, exploiting both the time series and cross-country variations in the data.[16] These studies find that both stock markets and banking systems have a positive impact on capital accumulation, economic growth, and productivity. This evidence is confirmed by time series analyses and country case studies, which tend to find that the evolution of financial systems over time is positively related with a country's growth pace.[17] Alternatively, some researchers have employed both industry- and firm-level data across a broad cross-section of countries in order to resolve causality issues and to document in greater detail the mechanisms, if any, through which finance affects economic growth. For instance, Rajan and Zingales (1998) show that industries that rely relatively more on external financing grow faster (compared to industries that do not rely so heavily on external capital) in countries with well-developed financial systems. Similarly, Demirgüç-Kunt and Maksimovic (1998) show that firms in countries with deeper financial systems tend to grow faster than they would be able to if their financing were restricted to internal funds and short-term debt.[18]

In recent years, the literature has extended the analysis beyond the finance-growth nexus to study the impact of financial development on other relevant variables, such as income distribution and poverty. Financial market imperfections generate credit constraints that are particularly binding on lower-income households and small entrepreneurs who lack collateral, credit histories, and political connections.[19] By reducing informational asymmetries, transaction costs, and contract enforcement costs, financial development facilitates access to capital for the outsiders and the poor, helping them to overcome the limitations that would otherwise arise from their lack of wealth and connections.[20] Therefore, financial development should disproportionately benefit lower-income households and small entrepreneurs. Consistent with these arguments, the empirical evidence suggests that financial development is associated with lower poverty and reduced income inequality. For instance, Beck, Demirgüç-Kunt, and Levine (2006) find that in countries that experience financial-sector deepening, the income of the poorest 20 percent of the population grows faster than average GDP per capita and income inequality falls at a higher rate. There is also some evidence, albeit still limited, that the expansion of access to finance may reduce poverty.[21] Burgess and Pande (2005), for instance, find that a 1 percent increase in the number of rural bank locations in India reduces rural poverty by 0.34 percent (see also Department for International Development, 2004, and references therein).[22]

An important question that has elicited significant debate in the literature is whether the financial structure—that is, the mix of financial markets and banks operating in the economy—matters. Compared with capital markets, banks may have some advantages in researching firms, monitoring managers, and financing industrial expansion. Because these markets disseminate information very quickly, investors may not have enough incentives to invest in information acquisition. In contrast, banks can make investments without revealing their decisions immediately, enabling them to build up private knowledge on projects and debtors through a "know your client" approach, and appropriate the returns from those research activities. At the same time, banks with close ties to firms may be able to exert pressure for repayment and to monitor managers more effectively than atomistic markets. On the other hand, proponents of market-based financial systems argue that banks may acquire too large an influence over firms and might be able to extract rents from them, increasing the costs of accessing capital. Also, banks may not be effective gatherers and processors of information in situations involving innovative products and processes. Furthermore, banks may collude with firms against other creditors and investors.

Other authors reject the importance of the bank versus markets debate and argue that what matters is the overall level of financial development, not the particular mix of capital markets and banks in the economy.[23] Also, markets and banks may provide complementary growth-enhancing financial services. For instance, by offering alternative means of financing investment, securities markets may reduce the potentially harmful effects of excessive bank power. Also, the development of securities markets can help banks to better manage their risk exposures, by facilitating hedging activities through the use of derivatives and by reducing their vulnerability to liquidity risks through bond issuance. From a broader perspective, having both well-functioning banks and securities markets can increase the stability of the economy, as shocks to one particular sector of the financial system can be, at least partially, compensated by others.

The evidence shows that there is a tendency for financial systems to become more capital market–based as income levels increase (Demirgüc-Kunt and Levine 2001). However, most empirical studies find that there is not one optimal mix of banks and capital markets for providing growth-enhancing financial services to the economy. In fact, after controlling for the level of financial development, financial structure does not seem to explain differences in growth rates across countries and industries or to affect access to external finance.[24] This evidence suggests that what matters in financial development is the access to efficient financial services more than the particular structure of the financial system that provides such services.

Evolution and Globalization of Capital Markets

As mentioned above, the recent developments in domestic capital markets, as well as their prospects, would be difficult to understand without considering the trends in global capital markets. Studying how international capital markets have evolved helps not only for setting a benchmark to assess the performance of domestic markets, but also for understanding the degree to which local developments are the result of changes in international capital markets. This section first outlines the main developments in international capital markets and then describes how Latin American countries have responded to these worldwide developments.

An important message from this section is that financial globalization has expanded to a degree that it has become difficult to ignore. Moreover, many new developments have taken place in the last three decades, bringing about significant changes to capital markets in both developed and developing nations. However, despite the perception of widespread financial globalization, the international financial system is far from being perfectly integrated, and there is evidence of persistent capital market segmentation both across and within countries.[25]

Main Developments in International Capital Markets

Capital markets in developed countries have grown substantially over the past three decades, experiencing a large boom in the 1990s. As part of this process, companies raised more capital in bond and equity markets, while both retail and institutional investors increased their participation in those markets. Financial markets experienced such a robust expansion that by 2004 the combined credit to the private sector by financial institutions, stock market capitalization, and private bonds outstanding reached an average of over 260 percent of GDP for G-7 countries, compared with about 100 percent in 1975.

The development of capital markets in rich countries has been accompanied by an increasing financial integration across nations. This globalization is not new. International capital flows have existed for a long time.[26] In fact, according to some measures, the extent of global capital mobility and capital flows a hundred years ago—especially during the gold standard era (roughly from 1880 to 1914)—is comparable to today's level. At that time, however, few countries and sectors participated in financial globalization. Capital flows tended to follow migration and were generally directed toward supporting trade flows and infrastructure investment in the then developing world (including, for instance, North America). For the most part, capital flows took the form of bond flows and were long term.

The advent of World War I represented the first blow to this wave of financial globalization, which was followed by a period of instability and crises that ultimately led to the Great Depression and World War II. After these events, governments reversed financial globalization, imposing capital controls to regain monetary policy autonomy. This depressed capital flows, which reached very low levels during the 1950s and 1960s. The international system was then dominated by the Bretton Woods arrangement of fixed but adjustable exchange rates, limited capital mobility, and autonomous monetary policies. The 1970s witnessed the beginning of a new era in the international financial system. As a result of the oil shock, rising capital mobility operating through the Eurodollar market (that is, bypassing official capital controls), and the subsequent breakup of the Bretton Woods system, a new wave of globalization began. With the disintegration of the Bretton Woods arrangement of fixed exchange rates, countries were able to open up to greater capital mobility while keeping the autonomy of their monetary policies.

Although globalization at the beginning of the 20th century mainly entailed flows from rich countries (mostly the United Kingdom) to emerging economies, most of the action in the more recent globalization phase has taken place among developed economies. In this phase, capital flows across developed countries have increased sharply. At the same time, capital market activity has concentrated in a few large international financial centers, mainly in Frankfurt, London, New York, and Tokyo.

Different forces have fostered the recent wave of capital market development and financial globalization. These forces can be grouped into three categories: government policies, technological and financial innovations, and demand and supply-side factors.

First, governments have fostered capital market development by liberalizing the financial sector. As discussed in greater detail in chapter 3, the rapid growth of the offshore Eurodollar market played a key role in this regard, as it led to a surge in capital mobility that skirted the capital controls that had been erected by nation states under the Bretton Woods era. This rise in capital mobility through offshore markets put increasing pressure on developed countries to liberalize and open up their national financial markets, which in turn further boosted cross-border capital flows. The liberalization process entailed many measures. Typical policies included the elimination of interest rate controls, the scaling down of directed credit programs, the liberalization of stock markets, and the opening of the capital account of the balance of payments. These measures were intended to enable market forces to operate with greater freedom, make the financial sector more efficient, promote the emergence and use of securities markets, and allow cross-country risk diversification.

Second, technological advances have eased the use of capital markets by reducing transaction costs and making trading, clearing, and settlement activities more efficient. Also, financial innovation has helped in the development of new instruments that enable investors to diversify and hedge risks. A significant financial innovation has been the securitization of illiquid assets, most notably of mortgage and consumer loans, to transform them into liquid securities that trade in capital markets. The process of technological and financial innovation has been aided by the emergence of large international financial conglomerates, which operate worldwide and offer a wide range of financial services.

Third, changes in the demand side have also provided an important boost to capital markets. Investors have found new ways to diversify their portfolios by holding securities instead of bank deposits. The emergence of institutional investors such as mutual and pension funds has enabled retail investors to purchase securities at low cost and, at the same time, diversify their investments in an array of assets and even across countries.

Developing Countries and the Globalization Process

Although most of the capital market development and globalization portrayed above have taken place in financial centers and in developed economies, developing countries have also been affected by the same underlying trends and were able to participate to some extent in these processes. The global trends affected developing countries in at least two ways. First, new capital became available in international financial markets, with developing countries trying to attract it to their domestic markets. Second, developing countries tried to emulate the increasing use of capital markets that characterized developed economies by reforming their local markets.

The efforts to attract international capital to developing countries were in part a result of the increased availability of liquidity in global markets.

New capital became available following the oil shock of 1973, which provided international banks with fresh funds to invest in developing countries. These funds were used mainly to finance sovereigns through syndicated loans. The boom in capital flows of the 1970s and early 1980s was followed by the debt crisis that started in Mexico in 1982. Eventually, to solve this crisis within an internationally agreed-upon framework for debt restructuring—the Brady Initiative—the so-called Brady bonds were created starting in the late 1980s, leading to the reentry of emerging countries into international capital markets and the development of liquid sovereign bond markets for these countries.

The more recent wave of capital flows to the periphery differs markedly in at least two ways from the 1976–82 period of capital inflows: first, in terms of magnitude; second, in terms of flow composition. Capital flows to emerging economies during the 1990s peaked in 1997, reaching nearly US$340 billion, then decreased sharply in the following years as a consequence of the financial crises in East Asia and the Russian Federation. Since then, capital flows have recovered, experiencing a strong growth and reaching about US$412 billion in 2004. The composition of capital flows to developing countries has also changed significantly. Official flows declined by more than half, and private capital flows became the major source of capital for a large number of countries. The nature of private capital flows also changed markedly. Foreign direct investment (FDI) has grown continuously since the early 1990s. Mergers and acquisitions (M&As) were the most important source of this increase, especially the ones resulting from the privatization of state-owned companies. Portfolio flows also became important.

A salient feature of the recent wave of financial globalization has been the internationalization of financial services, that is, the use of international financial intermediaries by local issuers and investors. This internationalization has been achieved through two main channels. The first channel is an increased presence of international financial intermediaries in local markets. Along with the capital flows, international financial institutions went to operate in developing countries. The second channel involves the use of international financial intermediaries and markets located outside the country, by local issuers and investors. One example of the latter channel is the listing and trading of shares in major world stock exchanges, mostly in the form of depositary receipts.[27]

Developing countries have tried in different ways to attract the new capital available in international markets. One way to attract this capital was financial liberalization, which mostly took place in the late 1980s and early 1990s in developing countries, some years after developed countries had liberalized their financial systems. As a consequence of the liberalization process, governments and firms have actively raised capital in international financial markets and foreigners have invested in domestic markets. Financial liberalization also implied that international financial institutions were allowed to enter developing countries to purchase local banks and establish local branches or subsidiaries. Another way to attract foreign capital was through the privatization process, initiated by Chile and the United Kingdom, and then followed by most countries. Privatization proceeds were substantial; in developing countries, they climbed from US$2.6 billion in 1988 to US$66.6 billion in 1997. Furthermore, as several privatizations were conducted through public offerings on local stock exchanges, the process also had a direct impact on domestic stock market capitalization and trading. As mentioned above, the boom in equity flows and FDI is partly explained by cross-border acquisitions of state-owned enterprises. Finally, developing countries tried to improve the climate for capital to flow in by pursuing macroeconomic stabilization, better business environments, and stronger economic fundamentals.

Besides these efforts to attract foreign capital, developing countries also tried to emulate in their local market the burgeoning performance observed in the capital markets of the developed economies. To this end, they implemented a rather aggressive reform agenda. The reforms had a logic that is easier to understand in the context of globalization. At the early stages, the reforms had primarily a development focus. The main idea was that capital markets would provide relatively cheap financing, mobilizing savings efficiently to their most productive use and offering investors attractive investment opportunities. The intention of fostering capital markets squared well with the global trend of moving toward a market-oriented system and emulating the functioning of capital markets in developed economies. Among other things, capital markets would exert competition on domestic banking systems, which in many developing countries charged high intermediation spreads. After the East Asian crisis of 1997–98, some regarded the development of local capital markets as a way to make the financial systems of developing countries more stable.[28] The rationale was that financial markets, especially bond markets, could be the "spare tire" of the system, sustaining finance when the "main tire" (banks) is flattened by a crisis. Moreover, capital markets could help absorb shocks by passing on to investors—in real time—changes in asset values. Additionally, capital markets would provide local currency and long duration debt securities as well as more derivatives products, which could help better manage and even reduce systemic risk.

The ensuing barrage of reforms can be grouped into first- and second-generation ones. First-generation reforms focused on stabilizing the macroeconomic environment, setting up the basic legal and regulatory frameworks, liberalizing domestic financial markets, and opening up the capital accounts. Second-generation reforms tended to focus on building better institutional and market infrastructures to increase market activity and liquidity, broaden investor participation, and expand the universe of instruments traded.

Apart from the liberalization and privatization mentioned above, reform efforts were complemented in a number of cases by structural pension system reforms, shifting from publicly administered defined-benefit, pay-as-you-go systems to privately administered defined-contribution systems of individual pension accounts. Among other things, the new pension systems were expected to boost the availability of long-term finance for the private sector. Chile was the first country to adopt this system in 1981, and many other countries implemented similar reforms over the past 15 years.[29]

Enticed by the potential benefits of having a well-functioning, market-oriented financial system, governments also approved new legislation aimed at creating the proper legal frameworks and market infrastructures and institutions for capital markets to flourish. In particular, countries created domestic securities and exchange commissions, developed considerably the regulatory and supervisory framework, and took important strides toward establishing and improving the basic environment for market operations. The latter included new policies related to centralized exchanges, securities clearance and settlement systems, custody arrangements, and varying degrees of improvements in accounting and disclosure standards. More recently, new laws and regulations intended to protect creditors and investors have enhanced this infrastructure, including improvements in the general legal framework and property rights, minority shareholders rights, bankruptcy laws, and insider trading regulations.

Main Developments in Domestic Capital Markets

This section describes the main developments in domestic capital markets and is intended to portray how local capital markets have performed over the past decades, where they stand, and how they differ across regions.

Although capital markets in many developed countries have witnessed a boom in the past decades, the picture is more mixed when focusing on developing countries, with wide heterogeneity across nations.[30] Some countries experienced growth of their domestic capital markets, but in most cases this growth was not as significant as that witnessed by industrialized nations. Other countries experienced an actual deterioration of their domestic capital markets. Noticeable differences arise when comparing the development of domestic capital markets across regions. Among emerging economies, capital markets in East Asia have developed relatively well. On the other hand, markets in Latin America have lagged behind, with many of them characterized by high dollarization, short-termism, and illiquidity.

Domestic bond markets have grown significantly since the mid 1990s. The rise in debt issuance was especially pronounced in East Asia, where governments and firms increasingly switched to bond financing after the

1997 crisis. Latin America also witnessed a substantial growth in domestic bond markets, but these tend to be dominated by public sector debt. Efforts to develop corporate bond markets in Latin America have, so far, not been very fruitful, perhaps with the exception of Chile and, more recently and to a much lesser degree, Mexico. Bond markets also differ across regions along other dimensions. Compared with East Asian and Eastern European bond markets, Latin American domestic bonds are, on average, more short term, with many floating-rate bonds. Governments of some countries (for example, Chile, Colombia, and Mexico) have made important strides toward lengthening local currency or CPI-indexed debt maturities to reduce rollover risk in times of crises; however, short-term debt remains relatively high throughout the region. Available evidence suggests that the short-term maturity structure can be explained by capital market factors that make long-term borrowing relatively expensive (Broner, Lorenzoni, and Schmukler 2004). Latin America has on average a higher share of foreign currency–denominated bonds, which exposes issuers to currency risk. In recent years, partly as a result of improved domestic fundamentals and partly as a consequence of favorable international financial conditions, some Latin countries have increasingly issued domestic currency bonds, both at home and in international markets.[31] However, it is still too early to tell whether this positive trend constitutes a durable change that would eventually expand and be sustainable throughout the region.

The performance of stock markets in many emerging economies has also been disappointing. Although stock market activity increased in most of these countries, this increase has differed substantially across regions. Market activity in Latin America has grown at a slower pace, with markets being much smaller than those in East Asia. For example, stock market capitalization relative to GDP was just under 42 percent in Latin America at the end of 2004, compared to 94 percent in G-7 countries and 146 percent in East Asia. Regional differences are more striking when comparing trading activity, a good proxy of liquidity. Value traded relative to GDP in Latin American stock markets was only 6 percent during 2004. On the other hand, the value traded in East Asian and G-7 stock exchanges over the same period reached 105 and 92 percent of GDP, respectively. Another feature of the poor development of stock markets in many countries is the high concentration of trading and capitalization in very few firms. This lagging development in Latin American stock markets has also been manifested in the delisting of firms and migration of large companies to major international stock exchanges, as described below. These latter trends have been pronounced in Latin America and Eastern Europe; in contrast, several East Asian countries have seen an increase in the number of companies listed in their domestic stock markets.

Other securities markets have attracted some attention in recent years, including those for derivatives, structured finance operations, and "repo" transactions (repurchase agreements).[32] Despite the rapid growth of global derivatives markets over the past decades, derivatives markets in emerging economies are generally underdeveloped, illiquid, and limited to certain instruments, especially when compared with developed countries. For example, emerging market derivatives account for only 1 percent of total outstanding notional derivatives in global markets. Notwithstanding their small size, derivatives markets—mainly for currencies—have started to appear in some Latin American countries, such as Argentina, Brazil, Chile, Colombia, and Mexico. These markets have gained some momentum, not only domestically, but also internationally. For example, the non–deliverable forward market—which in the case of Mexico, for instance, is larger than the domestic market—has allowed international investors to hedge various currency risks. In the case of structured finance operations, while markets in developed countries have experienced a strong growth, not only in terms of issuance volume but also in terms of the assets that are securitized, markets remain notably underdeveloped in most emerging economies. In Latin America, issuance has grown significantly in recent years, with Brazil and Mexico being the largest markets. In contrast with the relative underdevelopment of derivatives and structured finance markets, repo markets in emerging economies are much more liquid and typically used for liquidity management. In many cases, and perhaps most noticeably in the case of Brazil, the value of repo transactions exceeds the value traded of the underlying assets.

The contrast between the large number of policy initiatives and reforms and the poor performance of capital markets raises several questions. Are capital markets in emerging countries truly underdeveloped, or are they where they would be expected to be, given these countries' macroeconomic and institutional fundamentals? To what extent have capital markets responded to reforms? Were the reforms misconceived? Were expectations too optimistic? Are other factors affecting domestic stock markets and driving out the impact of reforms? Is more time needed to see the full fruits of reforms? Does the reform agenda need to be rethought? These are difficult questions to answer, but the analysis in the rest of this chapter and the remainder of this book helps to shed light on these issues.

Factors behind the Development and Internationalization of Capital Markets

What are the driving factors behind the processes of domestic capital market development and internationalization? In chapter 3 we address this question in extensive detail, from different angles. Here, we summarize our approach. First, it is useful to analyze cross-country, time series evidence to understand the role of macroeconomic and institutional factors such as monetary stability, overall economic development, and the legal environment on the development of both bond and stock markets. Second, we study how capital markets have responded to the wide array of reforms that governments undertook during the past two decades. In other words, we ask whether capital markets have responded as expected to the reform process. These reforms are basically improvements in the institutional and macroeconomic conditions. The motivation for this analysis comes from the popular argument that reforms do promote domestic capital market development and that if markets in some countries have not developed sufficiently, it is owing to the lack of reforms. This type of study is complementary to the analysis of economic fundamentals. Third, we analyze the fundamentals that drive stock markets' internationalization process. Our main interest is to understand whether the factors that drive domestic capital market development also affect the internationalization process and, if so, in what direction. In addition, we are concerned about the effects that this internationalization process may have on domestic stock markets' activities. Finally, we analyze whether Latin American countries have responded differently than countries in other regions to economic fundamentals and reforms. Namely, we study if the underdevelopment of Latin American capital markets can be explained by poor fundamentals.

In recent years, prompted by the increasing evidence of the financial sector's relevance as a fuel for economic growth, interest in understanding the determinants of financial market development has grown. The literature has highlighted the role of several factors, including fiscal and monetary policies, income levels, and the institutional and legal environment. The income level has been shown to be important: more developed countries tend to have larger and deeper capital markets. Better fiscal and monetary policies, together with a more stable macroeconomic environment, help to reduce uncertainties and positively affect the size of capital markets. Well-functioning and well-designed legal and institutional environments improve investors' confidence and contribute to the growth of capital markets. The size of an economy appears to be an important factor for the development of these markets, because it generates economies of scale and scope as well as network externalities and provides a more fertile ground for the achievement and sustainability of sufficiently liquid markets.

Though most of these factors affect both stock and bond markets, differentiating between the two types of instruments can underline the existence of some variables that may affect only one of them.[33] The intrinsic characteristics of bonds make them dependant on factors such as bankruptcy laws and currency regimes, factors that do not exert as large an effect on stocks. In this respect, the currency composition of government debt has lately received much attention related to the vulnerability to exchange rate risk that arises in a foreign-currency–denominated debt portfolio, which might increase the probability of financial crises. This study investigates which are the relevant factors that potentially affect currency composition of debt, reviewing the evidence on the role of institutional and economic factors. Overall, the evidence suggests that countries with larger economies, larger fiscal burdens, and lower inflation rates have a higher share of domestic currency debt (Claessens, Klingebiel, and Schmukler forthcoming). Conversely, countries that follow more fixed exchange rate regimes and those with a larger foreign investor demand tend to have a higher share of foreign currency bonds.

Another aspect of bond markets that has received attention has been the maturity structure of government debt. A broad concern is related to the risks associated with excessive reliance on short-term borrowing, an aspect usually associated with the recurrent financial crises in developing countries. But why do emerging markets borrow short term in spite of the associated risks? One answer could be that short-term debt reflects an optimal risk allocation between lenders and borrowers, which arises from the balancing decision between the higher cost of borrowing long term and the higher risks associated with short-term debt. In particular, the cost of long-term issuance is normally much higher than short-term issuance, and the larger this excess the higher the incentives for countries to rely on short-term debt (Broner, Lorenzoni, and Schmukler 2004).

Though cross-country analyses are very informative, they also present some shortcomings that can be important for the policy debate in developing countries. The relevant question for many countries is how an improvement in their macroeconomic and institutional environment will affect capital markets. Cross-country analysis that highlights that capital market development is positively associated with the quality of institutional fundamentals may not offer practical help in this regard, since a poor country cannot replicate the environment that exists in rich countries in the short to medium run. Moreover, time series analysis would hardly throw light on the matter, as there is little time variation in the institutional environment—that is, institutions change slowly and over the long term. As a consequence, panel results are likely to be driven by cross-country differences and not by the evolution of the institutional variables over time. Finally, the institutional data available across countries might be too general and not very relevant for capital market development.

An alternative to overcome some of the shortcomings of the panel estimations is to conduct event studies to measure the effects of "reforms" (changes in the macroeconomic and institutional environment) on capital markets' development. This analysis, which is also presented in detail in chapter 3, helps examine new variables that are not generally included in panel estimations because of limitations in data coverage. The reforms of interest are financial liberalization, market infrastructure reforms (those related to the trading environment and with clearing and settlement processes), institutional reforms (associated with law and order and corruption), enforcement of insider trading laws, pension reforms, and privatizations. The evidence from the event studies suggests that reforms are indeed positively associated with the development of domestic stock markets. Stock market capitalization, value traded domestically, and capital raised in domestic markets all increase as a percentage of GDP following the introduction of reforms (de la Torre, Gozzi, and Schmukler 2006b).

Besides these domestic developments, what are the factors behind the growing internationalization activities of domestic firms in developing countries? Firms are said to internationalize when some of their exchange activities (listing, capital raising, or trading) take place abroad. As with the case of domestic markets, it is also important to understand how the internationalization process responds to changes in several macroeconomic and institutional factors. In this respect, at least two competing views can be found. The first view argues that international markets will be used relatively less in response to an improvement in fundamentals, because they would increase reliance on domestic stock markets. The second view, by contrast, predicts an increase in international investors' confidence following domestic institutional improvements, which can result in greater willingness to provide access for local firms, with international market activity growing faster than local activity.

The evidence discussed in chapter 3 suggests that internationalization is affected in the same direction and by the same economic fundamentals that drive the development of stock markets. Higher income levels (per capita and in absolute terms), greater macroeconomic stability with lower fiscal deficit, stronger legal systems, and more financial openness increase both domestic stock market development and internationalization relative to GDP (Claessens, Klingebiel, and Schmukler 2006). In other words, better economic fundamentals help develop local markets, but they also increase the internationalization of stock exchange services. The evidence also indicates, however, that internationalization accelerates as fundamentals improve. These findings are at odds with the hypothesis that countries with worse fundamentals are the ones that see more stock exchange activities in international markets. Rather, the findings support the view that better fundamentals facilitate the access to foreign markets, with firms tapping new investor bases as their countries become more attractive.

What is the impact of internationalization on the trading activity and liquidity of domestic firms, those that rely only on domestic market financing? How does migration of firms to developed country stock markets affect the emerging stock markets they leave behind? Theoretically, the answer could go either way. On one hand, internationalization may negatively affect domestic stock market activity through two main channels: the migration of trading activities from domestic to foreign markets and the negative spillovers that arise as a result of increased transaction costs in a context of the local market's fixed costs. On the other hand, domestic activity might be spurred by internationalization as a result of broader market integration, plus have positive spillover effects related to the greater transparency induced by this process. The answer to the questions therefore has to be found empirically.

The evidence we present in chapter 3 indicates that as more firms become international (obtain financing and trade in international markets), the turnover of firms that stay in the local stock market is lowered. Moreover, this effect operates through the channels described above. There is evidence of migration: as the fraction of international firms rises, the trading of international firms shifts from domestic markets to international markets. Furthermore, there are spillovers: the domestic trading of international firms is strongly and positively related to the turnover of domestic firms. Hence, as the turnover of international firms in the domestic market dries up because of migration, the turnover of domestic firms diminishes because of spillovers. The migration and spillovers channels, however, are not the only mechanisms linking internationalization and the local market turnover. The data also suggest that as firms internationalize, the domestic market intensifies its trading of the internationalized shares, while trading of firms that do not internationalize wanes. In other words, there is evidence of trade diversion. The trade diversion channel is consistent with theories that emphasize that when a firm internationalizes, this enhances its reputation, transparency, and shareholder base in ways that make it more attractive overall and relative to domestic firms.[34]

As in the case of domestic capital markets, reforms can also affect the internationalization process. The evidence discussed in chapter 3 suggests that not only do domestic measures respond to reforms, these also have a positive impact on the internationalization of stock market activities. Furthermore, consistent with the evidence derived from cross-country, time series estimations, the data suggest that reforms accelerate internationalization. Most reforms are associated with higher ratios of market capitalization of international firms to total market capitalization and of value traded abroad to value traded domestically (de la Torre, Gozzi, and Schmukler 2006b).

Finally, where does Latin America stand in capital market development and internationalization? Why have Latin American capital markets grown less than expected? Is the poor performance of domestic markets in Latin America the result of poor fundamentals and lack of reforms? Or is there a shortfall between the extent of reform in Latin American countries and the actual outcomes? The evidence suggests that stock markets in Latin America exhibit a relative underdevelopment, both in size and in trading activity, when compared with the rest of the regions. These results survive even after controlling for the possibility of unaccounted-for factors such as macroeconomic volatility, quality of the institutional environment, size of the economy, or the average savings rate of the analyzed countries.

Policy Implications

The evidence discussed in previous sections shows that the state of securities markets in many emerging economies, and especially in Latin America, is disheartening. Despite the intense reform effort of the past two decades, local capital markets in most emerging economies remain underdeveloped. Although some developing countries' domestic markets grew, this growth in most cases has not been as significant as the growth witnessed by industrialized nations. Other countries experienced an actual deterioration of their capital markets as a growing number of firms have cross-listed and raised capital in international financial centers. In the case of Latin America, the results appear even more discouraging, given the intensity of reform efforts in the region, the better evolution of capital markets in East Asia, and their rapid growth in developed economies. Furthermore, the evidence summarized in the preceding section (and discussed in detail in chapter 3) indicates that capital markets in Latin America are below what can be expected, after controlling for relevant factors, including per capita income levels, economic size, macroeconomic policies, and the degree of legal and institutional development. The evidence also shows that the relation between globalization and domestic market development is complex and in many cases differs from what was expected at the beginning of the reform process. In particular, the empirical results indicate that improvements in fundamentals and capital market reforms have a pro-internationalization bias, especially for stock markets—that is, they lead to a higher internationalization of stock issuance and trading, relative to similar activities in the local market.

Drawing policy implications for the reform agenda from the foregoing evidence is not as simple a task as often believed. Assessing the evidence is a process that, by nature, involves significant resorting to judgment calls. The same evidence could lead to different interpretations and, hence, to contrasting policy conclusions. There is, for instance, ample scope for differing yet reasonable explanations for the gap between expectations and outcomes. In effect, in chapter 4 we illustrate in detail how contrasting policy views evolve from the evidence and the experience of capital market development in emerging markets. In particular, to provide a flavor of the range of perspectives, we identify three typological views. The first two views are general characterizations of two different diagnoses that have emerged repeatedly in the debate. The third view is essentially our reevaluation of the first two views, based on how we interpret the evidence presented throughout this report. Each of the three views emphasizes distinct aspects of the evidence, reaching different diagnoses and drawing different lessons; therefore, they are not necessarily incompatible.

The first view, encapsulated in the message "be patient and redouble the effort," contends that past reforms were essentially right, that the reforms needed in the future are mostly known, and that reforms—especially second-generation ones—have long gestation periods before producing visible dividends. It thus recommends letting market discipline work, while forging ahead patiently with further reform implementation efforts. The second view, encapsulated in the message "get the sequence right," draws attention to problems that arise when some reforms are implemented ahead of others. Its central prescription is that key preconditions should be met—including the achievement of a minimum institutional strength—before fully liberalizing domestic financial markets and allowing free international capital mobility.

Despite their important contributions and insights, we argue that these two views do not properly address some relevant aspects of the evidence. We thus propose a third view, which arises from the identification of some of the shortcomings of the previous two views. This third view can be encapsulated in the message "revisit basic issues and reshape expectations." It contends that perhaps the most questionable aspect of the first two views is their implicit assumption that domestic capital market development in emerging economies should be measured against the benchmark of capital markets in industrialized countries. Indeed, for the first two views, the reform path may be long and difficult, but the expected outcome is, in most cases, only one—to look increasingly like a mini-Wall Street. But it is difficult to accept this premise, given the evidence, which suggests that certain characteristics of emerging markets in general, and Latin American countries in particular, traditionally have not been fully considered in the analysis and policy debate. These characteristics include the small economic size, limits to risk diversification, presence of weak currencies, prevalence of systemic risk, and the impact of financial globalization, among others. The third view thus invites a serious analysis of the implications of these characteristics, in particular for the reform agenda going forward. The implications are paramount, as we illustrate in chapter 4 by discussing in some detail issues pertaining to the interaction of economic size, globalization, and segmentation of access with capital market liquidity and risk diversification. The third view therefore calls for a more varied reform agenda, as a one-size-fits-all approach is destined to fail. The third view emphasizes that a key step in designing country-specific reforms should be a determination of whether the emerging economy in question can sustain an active domestic market for private sector equity securities. It also argues that, ultimately, any reform agenda for capital markets needs to be couched within a broader vision of financial development for emerging markets in the context of international financial integration.

Conclusions

This book yields important lessons for the debate on the future of capital markets in emerging economies and in Latin America in particular. Three main messages stand out from the analysis.

First, it is very difficult to understand where domestic capital markets stand today without analyzing them in the context of globalization. For many countries, a significant part of the capital market activity takes place abroad. Domestic capital market development and internationalization are closely related, therefore any evaluation of capital markets that focuses just on domestic markets is likely to have severe limitations.

The increasing use of international capital markets is having both positive and negative effects on domestic markets. In terms of positive effects, the financing obtained by firms and governments in international markets tends to be of longer-term nature than that obtained in domestic markets. Also, when firms go to international capital markets, they become more transparent, providing domestic investors with better investment opportunities. As governments and the largest firms obtain financing abroad, there is a potential for a "crowding in" effect, increasing the domestic financing for other issuers. Aside from these positive effects of internationalization on domestic markets, there are also some negative ones. For instance, the listing of large local firms in international markets can have a negative impact on domestic market trading and liquidity, as trading activity migrates abroad. Moreover, financing in international markets is volatile, with the risk premium increasing substantially during crisis periods. Foreign bond financing tends to be denominated in foreign currency, exposing issuers to currency risk. These factors have led many to link financial globalization with crises.

One important feature of the current globalization process is that it is characterized by segmentation across countries and firms. This is relevant because if countries and companies benefit from access to foreign capital, only a small group of countries and firms are the ones reaping most of the benefits. For example, although the flow of net private capital to developing countries increased in recent years, private capital does not flow to all countries equally. Some countries tend to receive large inflows, while other countries receive little foreign capital. And within those developing countries that do receive capital flows, not all agents are equally able to reap, at least directly, the benefits of financial globalization. The evidence suggests that the largest companies are the ones able to tap international financial markets. This segmentation might increase the gap between those countries and firms that are able to internationalize and the rest.

The second big message from the study is that expectations about the reform process and policy options need to be revisited. This view contrasts with the other explanations as to why capital market reforms did not work as expected. Those explanations argue either that reforms need more time to produce the expected effects or that the sequencing of reforms was incorrect. Here, we claim that the reform process did not take into consideration important aspects related to the nature of globalization and emerging economies.

According to the evidence, capital market reforms and improvements in fundamentals have indeed had a positive impact on domestic capital markets. But this process has also helped countries to obtain financing in international capital markets, sometimes at the expense of domestic market development. Future policies will need to take into account more explicitly the effects of globalization on capital markets. To the extent that full integration is not possible, future policies might need to consider ways in which globalization can have spillover effects on all sectors of the economy, including those that are not directly linked to the international financial system.

Capital market development policies need to take into account the intrinsic characteristics of developing countries (such as small size, illiquid markets, lack of risk diversification, presence of weak currencies, and prevalence of systemic risk), and how these features limit the scope for developing deep domestic capital markets. These limitations are difficult to overcome by the reform process. In other words, even if countries carry out all the necessary reforms, they might not obtain the domestic capital market development that many expected in the early 1990s.

The third big message from this study is that, although securities markets in Latin America have grown substantially since 1990, capital markets in the region remain underdeveloped when compared with markets in industrial and East Asian countries. Furthermore, the evidence also shows a shortfall in domestic stock market activity in the region, after controlling for many factors, including per capita income, macroeconomic policies, and measures of the legal and institutional environment. In other words, Latin American countries have lower domestic stock market development than countries in other regions with similar fundamentals and extent of reforms. Although there are different possible explanations as to why Latin America has performed worse, it is difficult to reach a definite answer with the available evidence. Future work is necessary to shed more light on this issue.

Given the evidence discussed in this study, we can now be more certain about the state of capital markets in emerging economies, and particularly in Latin America. However, the conclusions from this study do not lead to simple policy recommendations. On the contrary, the evidence from our work opens a new array of questions that might prompt future policy discussions. In this sense, the contribution of this book—particularly chapter 4—is to raise new issues that cannot be easily ignored when redesigning the reform agenda going forward.

2

Developments in Capital Markets

THE WORLD'S FINANCIAL LANDSCAPE UNDERWENT significant changes during the past few decades. The global financial system grew substantially after the early 1970s and boomed during the 1990s. Financial intermediation through both financial institutions and securities markets expanded at a remarkable pace, and the spectrum of financial services and instruments reached new dimensions.

Developing countries were not immune to these global developments, and what happened in domestic capital markets across regions was to a large extent a reaction to global forces linked to financial globalization and innovation. Latin America is a clear example of this. Nevertheless, capital markets in the region today are not simply a smaller-scale replica of markets in developed countries. In fact, domestic capital market developments in Latin America have differed in some major aspects from developments not only in industrialized countries, but also in other emerging markets, most notably East Asia.

To provide a better understanding of the current state of domestic capital markets, this chapter first documents the developments in international financial markets and the increasing globalization process. The chapter then describes how developing countries, and in particular Latin American economies, responded to these worldwide changes. We describe the extensive reform agenda that policy makers pursued in an effort to match developments in international markets and to turn their domestic capital markets into an attractive destination for international capital flows.

To assess the development of domestic capital markets, this chapter documents the evolution of Latin American markets over time and compares them with other regions, especially East Asia and developed countries. Because capital markets across the region show a high degree of heterogeneity, we also highlight country differences and provide a closer look at Chile and Mexico, which are often perceived as regional success stories in terms of domestic securities market development.

This chapter does not attempt to quantify the impact of specific policy choices or market trends on capital market development, nor does it explain why domestic securities markets developed the way they did or what needs to be done to further improve the situation. These tasks are left for chapters 3 and 4.

The rest of the chapter is organized as follows. We (a) document developments in international financial markets, (b) describe Latin America's policy response to financial globalization and describe the reforms undertaken in Latin America to develop capital markets, (c) document the evolution of Latin American domestic securities markets relative to other regions of the world and describe their main features, (d) analyze the participation of firms and governments in international markets, and (e) conclude.

The Global Context

International financial markets have changed dramatically over the past several decades. Financial sector depth and activity in the largest developed economies started to increase sharply in the early 1970s and boomed during the 1990s. Financial intermediation through both financial institutions and securities markets expanded at a remarkable rate. The spectrum of financial services and instruments widened substantially. The sum of credit from financial institutions, stock market capitalization, and private bonds outstanding reached, on average, approximately 260 percent of GDP for G-7 countries in 2004, compared to about 100 percent in 1975 (see figure 2.1).

The main factors behind the strong increase of securities markets in the world's main financial centers during the past decades can be bundled into three major driving forces: financial liberalization and deregulation, groundbreaking technological and financial innovations, and a growing dedicated investor base.

In the aftermath of World War II, policy makers came to a consensus view that the preexisting free movement of capital around the globe had destabilized national economies and set in motion the competitive devaluations that proved harmful to international trade and, ultimately, contributed to the Great Depression in the 1930s. To simultaneously ensure free trade in goods and services, stable exchange rates, and a significant degree of monetary policy autonomy, policy makers agreed to restrict free capital mobility. The system that emerged was cemented in the postwar Bretton Woods agreement and guarded by the International Monetary Fund (IMF), which was created precisely for that purpose.

Capital controls under the Bretton Woods system, however, were not watertight. As discussed in Rajan and Zingales (2003b, chapter 11), small cracks appeared, particularly because the system did not obligate member countries to help enforce capital controls in another country—for example, by returning to the country of origin the capital that had fled from it, breaching the controls. Because of these types of cracks, the Bretton Woods system

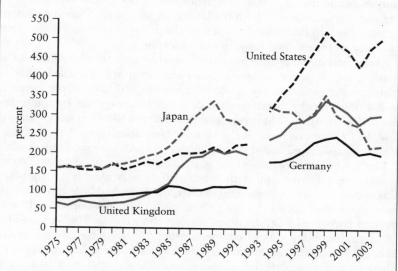

Figure 2.1 Capital Market Development in Selected Developed Countries, 1975–2004

Source: BIS; IMF; World Bank; S&P Emerging Markets Database.
Note: The series represents the sum of credit to the private sector by financial institutions and stock market capitalization (after 1993, the amount outstanding of private sector bonds is also included) over GDP. The value for 1993 is not reported to highlight the break in the time series.

had to yield eventually to the growing pressure of international capital mobility. The emergence of the Eurodollar market, a market free of government control and regulation, played a central role in this process. This market originated when the British government, in order to protect the value of the British pound and to avert a currency crisis, restricted capital mobility in 1957. British banks, fearful of losing their stake in the international lending market, circumvented the restrictions by using their dollar deposits to provide loans in U.S. dollars via the (offshore) Eurodollar market. This market further grew during the Cuban crisis, when Russian banks shifted their dollar reserves from American accounts to London. However, the biggest growth impulse for the Eurodollar market came when, in the late 1960s, the U.S. administration imposed capital controls in an effort to reduce its growing balance-of-payments deficit and to restore the gold backing of the dollar required under the original Bretton Woods system.[35] As British banks had done before, U.S. financial interests turned increasingly to the Eurodollar market to circumvent the actions of their own government.

British and U.S. authorities had an ambivalent attitude toward the Eurodollar market. While eroding the capital controls they had established for their national system, the Eurodollar market had located in London, boosting the city's role as a major international financial center. In the end, the incentives in both the United States and the United Kingdom favored the Eurodollar market—it used the dollar as the main transaction currency and the United Kingdom as a location.

As capital mobility rose in tandem with the growth of the Eurodollar market, the scope for monetary policy autonomy was curtailed. That in turn increasingly limited the developed countries' ability to pursue domestic policy objectives by delinking their domestic business cycle from international developments. The pressures on the Bretton Woods system mounted and, in 1971, it collapsed as the United States abandoned the gold backing of the dollar and ended its commitment to restrict capital movements. "With the largest economy of the world [the United States] not willing to control capital flows and with substantial activity already taking place across their borders with the Euromarket, countries had little choice but to open themselves up. By the late 1980s, much of the developed world was open to cross-border capital flows" (Rajan and Zingales 2003b, p. 263).

Capital mobility was of course boosted following the demise of the Bretton Woods system, and this raised further pressures on countries to liberalize and deregulate their domestic financial sectors. Financial deregulation, in turn, stimulated the growth of securities markets, in particular by paving the way to financial innovation.

. Financial markets have in effect been transformed by various waves of financial innovation over the last three decades. The fast pace of financial innovation enabled international securities markets to dynamically transform themselves. Merton (1992) coined the term "financial innovation spiral" to describe how innovative financial products satisfy previously unmet market demand and generate calls for further innovation and new markets. New financial instruments allowed investors to benefit from portfolio diversification and risk management through advanced hedging practices involving derivatives. Structured finance is another financial innovation that boosted securities markets. In its simplest form, structured finance is a process in which assets are pooled and transferred to a third party, which in turn issues securities backed by this asset pool. Typically, several classes of securities with distinct risk-return profiles are issued.[36] This process transforms illiquid assets into tradable securities. The upsurge in mortgage and consumer lending in many industrialized nations during the 1990s is an example of how structured finance can lead to increased financial intermediation.

Important technological advances that further reinforced the expansion of international securities markets assisted financial innovation. Advances in communication technologies brought more efficient and faster transmission of financial information around the globe. This reduced information gaps and rendered geographic distance less relevant for investors. Technological innovations further influenced trading (for example, shifts from floor to electronic trading systems, and online brokerage services), custody, clearing, and settlement (for example, real-time gross settlement systems). This lowered transaction costs, improved liquidity in many securities markets, and provided the tools for around-the-globe and around-the-clock trading.

Clearly, financial and technological innovations would not have occurred at the same pace if market demand had not kept up. Demand-side factors, therefore, also played a crucial role in the securities market boom in developed countries. Greater individual financial wealth and good economic prospects brought about changes in the saving and investment habits and risk-taking behavior of households. The search for higher returns encouraged a major shift from bank deposits to investment in securities. The emergence of privately managed pension funds further stimulated securities demand. In addition, a fast-growing mutual funds industry enabled a broad base of retail investors to partake in the expansion of international securities markets.

All these forces contributed to a rapid transformation of capital markets over the past few decades. These developments were most pronounced in industrialized countries, which attracted the largest share of international capital flows.[37] The volume of capital flows to industrialized countries has increased sharply since the 1970s. At the same time, financial services expanded across borders, as investors also looked increasingly for foreign securities. Financial intermediaries, moreover, increasingly established physical presences abroad, especially through mergers and acquisitions. In addition, international financial conglomerates soared, seeking to operate through a global network of international branches and subsidiaries that would serve both multinational and local clients. All of this accentuated the international integration of the local securities markets of developed countries. For example, foreign holdings of U.S. securities increased sharply. According to recent IMF statistics, in 2004 more than 30, 20, and 10 percent of U.S. Treasury bonds, corporate bonds, and stocks, respectively, were foreign owned.[38]

Reflecting the developments mentioned above, stock market capitalization more than doubled during the 1990s in G-7 countries, reaching a peak in 1999 (figure 2.2). That growth was marked by the fallout from the 1998 global economic shock induced by the Russian crisis and the bursting of the high-tech sector's bubble in early 2000. The stock market boom of the 1990s was accompanied by a strong increase in corporate bond issuance, both domestically and abroad (figure 2.3). With equity issuance on the decline in the early 2000s, the corporate sector in industrial countries continued issuing bonds as an alternative source of financing. At the end of 2004, the amount of private bonds outstanding in G-7 countries represented, on average, about 47 percent of GDP.

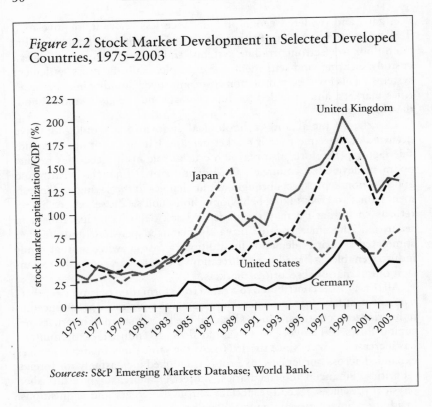

Figure 2.2 Stock Market Development in Selected Developed Countries, 1975–2003

Sources: S&P Emerging Markets Database; World Bank.

Financial globalization has also contributed to the concentration of market capitalization and liquidity in few international financial centers, such as Frankfurt, London, New York, and Tokyo. Financial activity in these centers vastly overshadows market activity elsewhere.

Developing Countries in the Global Context

The wave of financial globalization and internationalization that swept the world over the past decades did not leave Latin America and other emerging markets unaffected; in fact, it generated forces for change. As noted, for many decades and as part of the Bretton Woods arrangement, most emerging markets had imposed tight controls on their financial sectors. Domestic capital markets prior to the 1990s were predominately bank-based, and securities markets were virtually nonexistent. Governments heavily regulated interest rates, intervened directly in the operation of financial institutions, and orchestrated the allocation of credit by

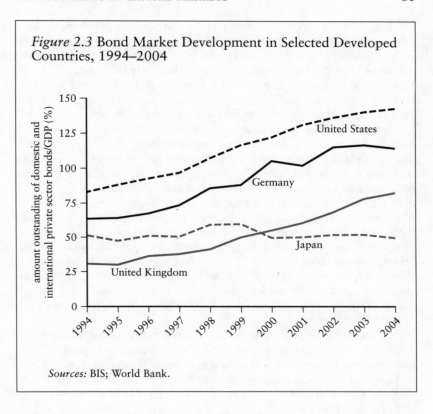

Figure 2.3 Bond Market Development in Selected Developed Countries, 1994–2004

Sources: BIS; World Bank.

private banks. This section describes the ways in which global trends in international financial markets affected Latin America and other developing countries and how policy makers responded.

How Global Trends Have Affected Developing Countries

Financial globalization affected capital flows to emerging markets in at least two ways: first, through changes in the volume and composition of capital flows, and second, through the internationalization of financial services.

The greater availability of liquidity in international capital markets led to various booms in capital flows to developing countries. The first wave reflected the recycling through the international banking system of the petrodollars accumulated by oil exporters during the petroleum price boom of the 1970s. Awash in liquidity, international commercial banks used the funds mainly to finance—through syndicated loans—governments in emerging markets, notably Latin America. The binge in bank-originated capital flows of the 1970s and early 1980s led to the debt crisis that started in Mexico in 1982. Although first treated as a liquidity problem, the debt crisis in developing countries was eventually seen as it was—a major sovereign solvency problem that had to be dealt with through an internationally agreed-upon debt reduction protocol. The Brady Initiative, which was launched in this context, provided a framework for indebted countries to negotiate, within IMF-supported programs, reductions of debt and debt service with their commercial bank creditors. The negotiated Brady "packages" resulted in the restructuring and transformation of old and distressed bank loans into the new so-called Brady bonds. As a result, and in a relatively short time, a deep market for the sovereign bonds of emerging economies developed, paving the way for the "reentry" of these economies into the booming international capital markets.

With the establishment of this new Brady bond market, initiated in 1989, investor confidence in developing countries started to recover gradually, and with a growing demand for emerging-market bonds, governments soon seized the opportunity to issue debt outside the Brady market. Private issuers soon followed.[39] Thus, emerging-market bond issuance increased from US$4 billion in 1990 to US$99 billion in 1997. In the aftermath of the East Asian and Russian crises of 1997–98, issuance decreased significantly, but it has recovered strongly in recent years, reaching a peak of US$183 billion in 2005.

The wave of capital flows to emerging markets that started in the 1990s differs in at least two ways from the 1976–82 period of capital inflows: first in terms of magnitude and second in terms of flow composition. Capital flows to developing countries in the 1990s dwarfed those of the 1980s, reaching a peak of US$353 billion (at 2000 prices) in 1997, compared to US$158 billion in the peak prior to the debt crisis in 1982 (figure 2.4). As a result of the financial crises in East Asia and Russia, capital flows decreased significantly after 1997, but they have recovered strongly in recent years, surpassing the previous peak and reaching US$379 billion (at 2000 prices) in 2004. The composition of capital flows to developing countries has also changed significantly. Although capital flows prior to the 1990s were predominately official flows and commercial bank loans, the 1990s brought not only a strong decline in the significance of official flows, but also a shift from commercial bank loans to bond- and equity-related flows. In particular, foreign direct investment (FDI), fueled in part by large-scale privatization schemes, experienced a strong expansion. The shift toward equity-related flows, and FDI in particular, has been even stronger in recent years (World Bank 2006). Whereas equity flows represented about 53 percent of total capital flows to developing countries between 1990 and 2000, they reached 67 percent between 2001 and 2004.[40] The trend toward an increased share of equity flows after 2000 has been particularly pronounced for Latin America and East Asia.

Even though private capital flows to developing countries have increased significantly during the recent wave of financial globalization, private cap-

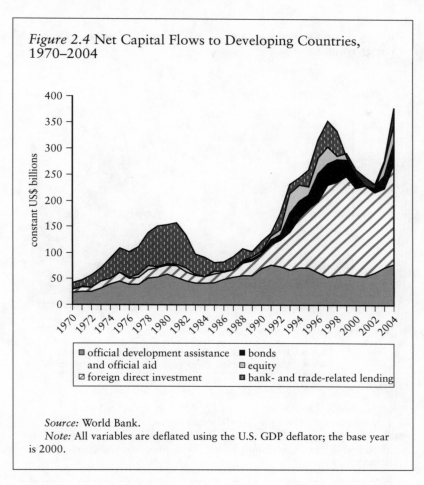

Figure 2.4 Net Capital Flows to Developing Countries, 1970–2004

Source: World Bank.
Note: All variables are deflated using the U.S. GDP deflator; the base year is 2000.

ital does not flow to all countries equally. Some countries tend to receive large amounts of private inflows, while others receive little foreign capital. The top 10 countries in terms of private capital flows between 1990 and 2004 concentrated about 68 percent of these flows (figure 2.5).[41] Most of the remainder went toward middle-income countries, with low-income countries receiving only a marginal amount of private foreign capital. The high concentration of capital flows may have significant implications, to the extent that countries benefit from access to foreign capital.

A salient feature of the recent wave of financial globalization has been the internationalization of financial services, that is, the increasing use by local issuers and investors of financial products provided by international financial intermediaries. This trend is partly explained by a greater presence

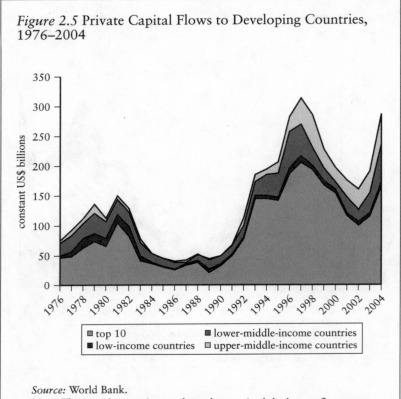

Figure 2.5 Private Capital Flows to Developing Countries, 1976–2004

Source: World Bank.

Note: The top 10 countries are those that received the largest flows over the 1990–2004 period. Those countries are (in decreasing order of magnitude) China, Brazil, Mexico, Argentina, Poland, India, Malaysia, Chile, Turkey, and Hungary.

of international financial intermediaries in local markets, but also by the fact that issuance and trading of local securities continues to migrate to international markets. The impact of the internationalization of financial services is described in more detail in the section "Participation in International Capital Markets."

Finally, the recent wave of financial globalization coincided with a high degree of instability of both capital flows and domestic financial systems. Sudden shifts in the availability of external finance due to abrupt changes in investor sentiment toward emerging markets have exposed the vulnerability of these countries. In particular, the East Asian crisis of 1997–98 and the Russian crisis of 1998 raised awareness about the need to better cope with capital flows, as sudden reversals in international flows forced painful macroeconomic adjustments in the domestic front. Contagion, one of the by-products of financial globalization, further ensured that the pain was felt not only by countries at the epicenter of the crises but also throughout global capital markets.

The Policy Response: Attract, Emulate, and Manage

The global trends outlined above affected developing countries in at least three ways. First, new capital became available in the international financial markets, with developing countries trying to attract it to their domestic markets. Second, developing countries tried to emulate the increasing use of capital markets that characterized developed economies by instituting a series of reforms. Third, the boom-and-bust pattern of capital inflows, particularly in the second half of the 1990s, made policy makers increasingly aware of the need to properly manage the risks of global financial integration.

Attracting International Capital Flows Developing countries have tried in different ways to attract the new capital available in international markets. Financial liberalization was the most direct route toward this goal. Most developing countries liberalized their financial systems in the late 1980s and early 1990s, some years after financial liberalization in developed countries (figure 2.6). As part of this liberalization process, governments and firms have actively raised capital in international financial markets, and foreign investors were granted access to domestic markets. The liberalization of financial systems also implied that international financial institutions were allowed to move to developing countries, purchasing local banks and establishing local branches or subsidiaries.

Privatization was another way to attract foreign capital. In the early 1980s, Chile and the United Kingdom were the first to launch extensive privatization initiatives. Soon after, countries around the world followed. Privatization revenues in developing countries climbed from nearly US$3 billion in 1988 to a peak of US$67 billion in 1997, amounting to a cumulative total of US$413 billion over the 1988–2003 period. Because many emerging countries conducted privatization sales through public offerings on the local stock exchange, privatization also had a direct impact on the growth of local stock market capitalization.[42] As mentioned above, the boom in equity flows and FDI is partly explained by cross-border acquisitions of former public enterprises.

Finally, developing countries tried to improve the climate for capital inflows by pursuing macroeconomic stabilization, better business environments, and stronger institutional and economic fundamentals. This was, most likely, also encouraged by the fact that those Latin American countries that liberalized aggressively, reduced inflation, and maintained an

Figure 2.6 Financial Liberalization Index, 1973–2001

Source: Kaminsky and Schmukler (2003).

Note: The liberalization index is calculated as the simple average of three indices (liberalization of the capital account, domestic financial sector, and stock market) that range between 1 and 3, where 1 means no liberalization and 3 means full liberalization. These data are then aggregated as the simple average between countries of each region. G-7 is the average of Canada, France, Germany, Italy, Japan, the United Kingdom, and the United States. Latin America is the average of Argentina, Brazil, Chile, Colombia, Mexico, Peru, and República Bolivariana de Venezuela. Asia is the average of Hong Kong (China), Indonesia, Korea, Malaysia, the Philippines, Taiwan (China), and Thailand. Europe is the average of Denmark, Finland, Ireland, Norway, Portugal, Spain, and Sweden. Figures correspond to annual averages calculated from monthly data.

open trading and financial system attracted a larger share of capital flows than those that did not (see Gavin, Hausmann, and Leiderman 1995). This helped overcome a history of poor macroeconomic policies, which had hampered financial sector development in the past.

Emulating the Performance of Capital Markets in Developed Countries
Besides these efforts to attract foreign capital, developing countries also tried to emulate the performance of capital markets in developed economies by undertaking a series of reforms thought to foster development of

domestic securities markets. These reforms had their own logic and are easy to understand in the context of globalization.

At the early stages, reforms had primarily a development focus. McKinnon (1973) and Shaw (1973) pioneered the view that financial liberalization and financial sector development are essential for growth. They argued that the deregulation of capital markets increases economic growth through higher savings rates and improved resource allocation. King and Levine (1993a) later redefined the financial sector growth nexus by arguing that capital markets play a crucial role in the processing of information. The ability of financial institutions to select profitable innovations and projects that increase productivity and, hence, growth, was seen as the key contribution of capital markets to economic development.[43]

The intention to develop domestic capital markets squared well with the global trend of moving toward a market-oriented system. Capital markets would enhance financial sector efficiency by introducing competition to the commercial banking sector, which in many developing countries charged high intermediation spreads. Securities markets would further provide a mechanism for the efficient valuation of assets. Well-functioning securities markets would create liquidity in financial claims and allocate and diversify risks efficiently. In the process, securities markets would reduce the cost of capital, enabling larger economywide savings and investment. Domestic capital markets were also often seen as the missing bridge to long-term financing in local currency.

Managing Volatile Capital Flows Financial liberalization, privatization, and reforms jointly ushered considerable amounts of external capital into emerging market economies. However, the rise of global capital inflows coincided with a turbulent period of financial crises in several emerging economies.

A major policy lesson of the 1990s was that most domestic financial systems in emerging economies were not strong enough to withstand major capital flow shocks. Two opposing views emerged with respect to financial stability and financial sector development. On the one hand, some considered that financial liberalization had gone too far, that it was unwisely and prematurely introduced, before the needed macro, regulatory, and institutional underpinnings were in place. This view thus concluded that to enable the safe development of a well-functioning domestic capital market, financial opening would have to be slowed down, halted, or even scaled back. On the other hand, others argued that liberalization and related reform efforts must be, if anything, deepened and infused with additional momentum to ensure financial stability.

These two views are discussed in greater detail in chapter 4, where we note that the question of whether financial stability is best served by strengthening reform efforts or by delaying further liberalization is still an ongoing topic in the debate. Here, the point we wish to highlight is that, against the backdrop of financial instability and crises, emerging markets began to see part of the solution as the development of local securities markets, particularly debt securities.

Following the Asian crisis, in effect, many advanced the thesis that the vulnerability of emerging markets was in no small measure linked to lack of diversification in their financial systems, which relied excessively on bank-based intermediation. It was argued in particular that local currency bond markets, which were mostly missing in the region prior to 1997, would have made emerging economies less vulnerable to financial crises.[44] Greenspan (1999) propelled this view to greater visibility by stressing the importance of having multiple avenues for financial intermediation. Capital market alternatives in financial intermediation had served the United States well during two banking crises—the Latin American debt crisis and the savings and loans crisis—which seriously affected banking institutions. In that context, Greenspan made the now often quoted statement that "Before the [Asian] crisis broke, there was little reason to question the three decades of phenomenally solid East Asian economic growth, largely financed through the banking system, so long as the rapidly expanding economies and bank credit kept the ratio of non-performing loans to total bank assets low . . . The failure to have backup forms of intermediation was of little consequence. The lack of a spare tire is of no concern if you do not get a flat" (1999).

Thus, efforts to improve the performance of capital markets were quickened by the perception that well-functioning capital markets were important shock absorbers in times of turbulence, as investors take in gains and losses through changes in asset prices. Capital markets would not only help avoid shifting risk to the government, but would also help mitigate the adverse consequences of bank runs and enable hedging. Local currency bonds with long maturities and well-developed derivatives markets were expected to provide substantial insurance by helping overcome chronic currency and maturity mismatches and by injecting liquidity into secondary markets (see, for example, Herring and Chatusripitak 2000; IFC 2001; and Batten and Kim 2001). More recently, the case has been made that domestic bond markets are likely to present a less risky alternative to borrowing abroad, as they are a form of self-insurance against costly capital flow reversals (Häusler, Mathieson, and Roldos 2004).

The Reforms

A barrage of reforms was implemented in emerging economies to foster the development of local capital markets. These reforms can be grouped in four categories: (a) reforms aimed at creating the enabling environment for capital markets—such as the strengthening of macroeconomic stability and the enforcement of property rights; (b) reforms aimed at enhancing efficiency and market discipline in the entire financial system through greater competition—such as capital account liberalization; (c) reforms indirectly supportive of capital market development—such as pension reforms and privatization programs; and (d) capital market–specific reforms—such as the development of the regulatory and supervisory framework and improvements in securities clearance and settlements systems.

Figure 2.7 illustrates the logic of some of the interactions between most common financial sector reforms, the supply and demand of funds in the economy, and expected outcomes in terms of capital market development. The establishment of the regulatory supervisory framework and improvement of investor protection are the keys to enhancing the enabling environment to sprout investment in securities. These reforms can also help mitigate information and agency problems through improved transparency, enhanced market integrity, and more reliable contract enforcement. Capital market–specific reforms, such as the modernization of trading, custody,

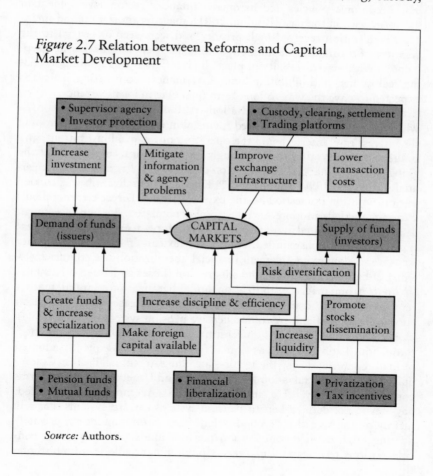

Figure 2.7 Relation between Reforms and Capital Market Development

Source: Authors.

clearing, and settlement systems, can considerably reduce transaction costs. Privatization schemes directly increase the availability of investable assets. Financial liberalization fosters discipline and efficiency in the system, while making available foreign capital to local firms and foreign assets to local investors. Altogether, these reforms can allow investors to diversify their portfolios within a much broader universe of assets and at lower transaction costs, which further encourages participation in capital market activities, raising the available supply of funds. This virtuous circle can be strongly complemented by pension system reforms—which bring retirement-related savings to the capital markets—and by the expansion of the mutual fund industry, which is the key to offering investors attractive alternatives to traditional bank deposits.

In the context of this type of reasoning, policy makers in Latin America took on the task of introducing reforms with enthusiasm. Because poor macroeconomic policies had hampered financial sector development in Latin America in the past (Roubini 2001), macro stabilization and financial liberalization received high priority and were seen as crucial to the creation of a suitable enabling environment for capital market development.[45] With macro stability in place, high inflation was no longer eroding real savings and inhibiting long-term financial contracting. This was expected to pave the way to long-term financing in local currency.

Financial liberalization ended a long period of financial repression, in which governments had restricted financial intermediation by controlling the interest rate, interfering in the operation of financial institutions, and influencing credit allocation. Though Latin America lagged behind the global wave of financial liberalization of the 1980s, liberalization accelerated during the 1990s (figure 2.6).[46] Financial liberalization was carried out on both the domestic and the external fronts. Direct credit controls were abandoned, and interest rates were deregulated. Foreign investment restrictions were lifted, and most controls on foreign exchange and capital transactions were dismantled. After the Mexican crisis of 1994, further steps were taken to complement financial liberalization with the strengthening of banking regulation and supervision (Loser and Guerguil 2000).

Apart from macro stabilization and liberalization, capital market reforms were also complemented in a number of cases by privatization efforts (figure 2.8) and by comprehensive pension system reforms. Chile's pioneering example in pension reform had a major demonstration effect throughout Latin America, as similar reforms were subsequently adopted by many countries during the 1990s—including Argentina, Bolivia, Colombia, Costa Rica, El Salvador, Mexico, Peru, and Uruguay.[47] These reforms consisted, basically, of a shift away from government-administered, pay-as-you-go, defined-benefit pension systems toward systems that rely mainly on the so-called "second pillar," that is, on mandatory, privately administered, defined-contribution pension funds. These types of pension reforms gave capital markets a predominant role in administering

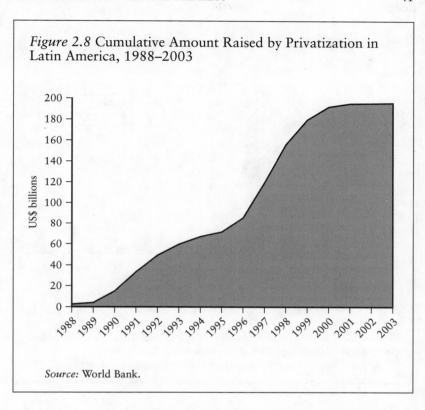

Figure 2.8 Cumulative Amount Raised by Privatization in Latin America, 1988–2003

Source: World Bank.

retirement-related savings and providing old-age income security. Pension reforms were perceived as conducive to local capital market development by making available long-term funds to the private sector.[48]

Experience from Chile indicates that pension reform can indeed have a significant impact on capital market development and economic growth. In a comprehensive macroeconomic study, Corbo and Schmidt-Hebbel (2003) conclude that Chile's pension reform allowed the economy to grow by an additional one-half percentage point on average, during the 21-year period of 1981–2001. They identify increases in capital market depth and efficiency as one of the main channels through which pension reform contributed to economic growth. Pension funds' demand for financial assets not only resulted in deeper markets and greater variety of financial instruments, but also led to improvements in financial regulation, corporate governance, and transparency. Figure 2.9 shows that mandatory pension funds in the region have grown very quickly. The significant size of pension funds in Chile is explained by the fact that it was the first country to reform its pension system, in 1981.

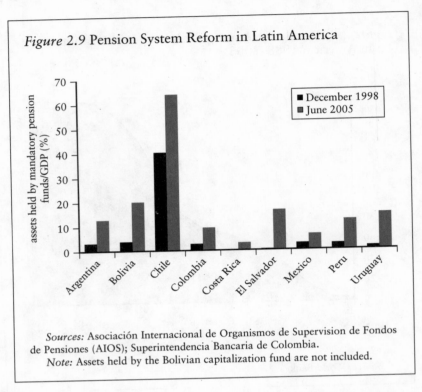

Figure 2.9 Pension System Reform in Latin America

Sources: Asociación Internacional de Organismos de Supervision de Fondos de Pensiones (AIOS); Superintendencia Bancaria de Colombia.
Note: Assets held by the Bolivian capitalization fund are not included.

Governments also approved legal reforms aimed at creating the proper infrastructure and institutions for capital markets to flourish. In particular, countries created domestic securities and exchange commissions, developed considerably the regulatory and supervisory framework, and took important strides toward establishing and improving the basic environment for market operations. The latter included new policies related to centralized exchanges, securities clearance and settlement systems, custody arrangements, and varying degrees of improvements in accounting and disclosure standards (figure 2.10).

More recently, new laws and regulations, intended to protect the rights of investors, have enhanced this basic infrastructure (Capaul 2003). These include improvements in the general institutional framework, property rights, minority shareholders' and creditors' protection, and deterrence of insider trading. As figure 2.11 shows, between 1990 and 1997 there was a strong improvement in the legal and institutional framework in Latin America. The institutional environment subsequently worsened following the Asian (1997) and Russian (1998) crises. The financial crisis in Argentina and a deteriorating political environment in Colombia and República Bolivariana de Venezuela contributed to further declines in institutional quality after 2000.

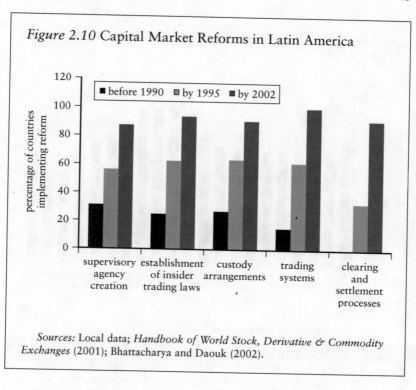

Figure 2.10 Capital Market Reforms in Latin America

Sources: Local data; *Handbook of World Stock, Derivative & Commodity Exchanges* (2001); Bhattacharya and Daouk (2002).

The emergence of a number of international standards and codes relevant to financial sector development further boosted and guided additional reforms efforts.[49] The assessment of country observance with these standards turned into a major program, strongly endorsed by the major developed countries and actively embraced by emerging markets. Such assessments help identify vulnerabilities and gaps in financial system development and are instrumental in setting reform objectives and priorities. Even in Chile, which may be considered the front runner in many aspects of capital market development in the region, a recent assessment of compliance with international standards identified shortcomings in various dimensions of securities market infrastructure.[50]

Developments in Domestic Capital Markets

This section describes the evolution of domestic capital markets since the early 1990s and their main features. The first part presents a brief description of the main trends in stock and bond markets in Latin America

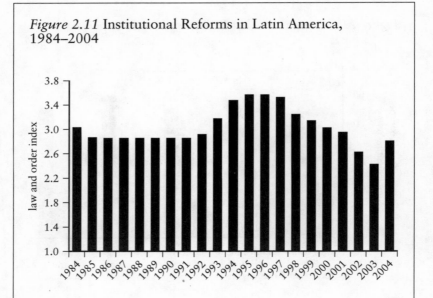

Figure 2.11 Institutional Reforms in Latin America, 1984–2004

Source: International Country Risk Guide.

Note: The data are averages of the law and order index for Argentina, Brazil, Chile, Colombia, Ecuador, Mexico, and Peru. The index is a qualitative variable that ranges from zero to six, with higher values representing higher levels of law and order. Law and order are evaluated separately, with each subcomponent comprising zero to three points. The law subcomponent is an assessment of the strength and impartiality of the legal system, and the order subcomponent is an assessment of popular observance of the law.

compared with other regions, especially developed and East Asian countries. The second part describes in more detail the salient characteristics of local capital markets in Latin America. And the last part provides a closer look at Chile and Mexico, which are often perceived as regional success stories.

Comparative Trends in Domestic Capital Markets

Although financial development in the largest industrial economies started to increase sharply in the 1970s, Latin American financial markets remained stagnant until the early 1990s. From that period to the present, however, capital markets in the region have grown considerably. The average domestic stock market capitalization in terms of GDP in the seven largest markets in Latin America (Argentina, Brazil, Chile, Colombia,

Mexico, Peru, and República Bolivariana de Venezuela) more than tripled over this period, growing from 12 percent in 1990 to 32 percent in 1995 and to 42 percent in 2004. Value traded in domestic stock markets also increased significantly, from 2 percent of GDP in 1990 to 7 percent in 1995, and standing at 6 percent of GDP in 2004 (figure 2.12).

Domestic bond markets in Latin America have also experienced a significant growth spurt, especially after 1994. The amounts outstanding of public and private sector domestic bonds increased from 14 and 7 percent of GDP in 1994, respectively, to 21 and 11 percent of GDP in 2004 (figure 2.12). Bond markets in the region are clearly dominated by the trading and issuance of public sector debt, with the notable exception of Peru. The development of government bond markets was fostered by a general shift from monetary to debt financing of public sector deficits during the 1990s and the need to sterilize large capital inflows. In the last six years or so, local government bond markets have been further boosted, despite the reduction in borrowing requirements of public sectors (reflecting stronger fiscal positions), by a rather widespread shift by government funding from external sources to local markets.

As noted in the previous sections, the recent evolution of capital markets in Latin America needs to be placed in the global context that provided the general tenor for regional market development. Once placed in this context, the observed growth in domestic capital markets in Latin America appears dwarfed, not only by outcomes in industrial countries, in particular the major financial centers, but also by developments in other emerging markets, notably East Asia.

In effect, the tripling of stock market capitalization in Latin America since 1990 still leaves the region at a very modest level when compared with other regions. At 42 percent of GDP in 2004, stock market capitalization in Latin American countries pales in relation to levels of 94 percent and 146 percent in G-7 and East Asian countries, respectively (figure 2.13). Differences are more striking when comparing trading activity across regions. Though trading has grown exponentially in developed countries and East Asia, Latin American countries appear to be caught in a low liquidity trap. In terms of GDP, the current value traded in Latin America's stock exchanges corresponds roughly to the amount of trading observed in East Asian and G-7 countries at the beginning of the 1980s. Since then, value traded in these countries has significantly increased, reaching 92 percent of GDP in G-7 countries and 105 percent in East Asia in 2004 (figure 2.13).[51]

Domestic bond markets in both developed and developing countries have also experienced a significant increase in recent years. This growth was especially pronounced in East Asia, where (as mentioned above) after the 1997 crisis governments and the corporate sector increasingly switched to bond financing. In Latin America, most progress has been made in domestic markets for government bonds. Public sector bond

Figure 2.12 Capital Market Development in Latin America

a. Stock Market Development

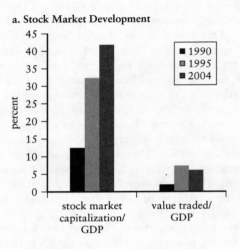

b. Bond Market Development

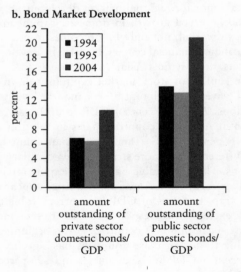

Sources: BIS; S&P Emerging Markets Database; World Bank.

Note: The data on stock market development are averages for Argentina, Brazil, Chile, Colombia, Mexico, Peru, and República Bolivariana de Venezuela. The data on bond market development are averages for Argentina, Brazil, Chile, Mexico, and Peru.

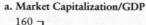
Figure 2.13 Stock Market Development in Selected Regions, 1978–2004

a. Market Capitalization/GDP

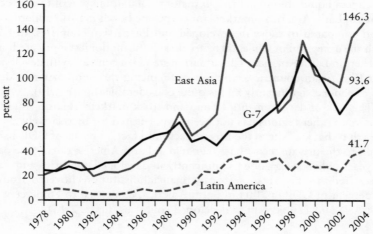

b. Value Traded Domestically/GDP

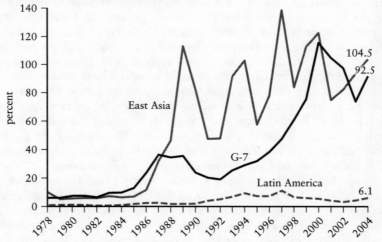

Sources: S&P Emerging Markets Database; World Bank.

Note: G-7 is the average of Canada, France, Germany, Italy, Japan, the United Kingdom, and the United States. East Asia is the average of Hong Kong (China), Indonesia, Republic of Korea, Malaysia, the Philippines, Taiwan (China), and Thailand. The data for Latin America is the average of Argentina, Brazil, Chile, Colombia, Mexico, Peru, and República Bolivariana de Venezuela.

markets in some of the largest markets in the region present a development level similar to that of East Asian countries, although they are typically much less liquid (figure 2.14). On the other hand, in spite of their recent growth, Latin America's markets for corporate bonds are still underdeveloped compared to those in developed and East Asian countries. In fact, with the exception of Chile, there are no significant domestic private bond markets in Latin America. This situation stands in contrast with developed and East Asian countries, where firm financing through corporate debt has expanded significantly and is quite considerable (figure 2.14).

The lack of development of bond and stock markets in Latin America relative to other regions has not been compensated for by relatively faster growth of bank credit to the private sector. In fact, in terms of GDP, bank credit to the private sector has stagnated in Latin America during the past 15 years, while it expanded significantly in developed countries and East Asia. Credit to the private sector by financial institutions hovered around 25 percent of GDP in 2004 in Latin America, compared to 76 percent in East Asia and 126 percent in developed countries (figure 2.15).

Main Features of Domestic Capital Market Development

Latin American financial markets continue to be dominated by banks and are characterized by short-termism, illiquidity, and, in a good number of countries, dollarization. Stock and private bond markets have failed to develop as a serious alternative to bank loans. As noted, the increase in the size and turnover in local bond markets is mostly accounted for by government paper. Even though many countries have made efforts to extend bond maturities and develop meaningful yield curves for government bonds, maturities have remained fairly short, except in a few countries, notably Chile, Mexico, and Colombia. Illiquidity is another serious constraint of Latin American securities markets. This is clearly the case for nearly all listed private debt and equity securities, but even liquidity for public debt in several Latin American countries is insufficient.

Even where capital markets for private securities are reasonably deep (as Chile), they are highly concentrated. Only a handful of high-grade companies actively participate in domestic bond and stock markets. In Chile and Argentina, for example, three companies account for almost 50 percent of domestic market capitalization. In Mexico, one firm (Telmex) represents about 25 percent of market capitalization and between 20 and 40 percent of trading (Yermo 2003). As figure 2.16 shows, in most countries in Latin America the top 10 companies account for more than 50 percent of value traded, compared to less than 10 percent in the United States. Furthermore, as described later in this section, local stock markets appear to be shrinking in the face of a persistent migration of corporate issuers to international financial centers.

Figure 2.14 Bond Market Development in Selected Regions, 1990s to 2004

a. Amount Outstanding of Public Sector Domestic Bonds/GDP

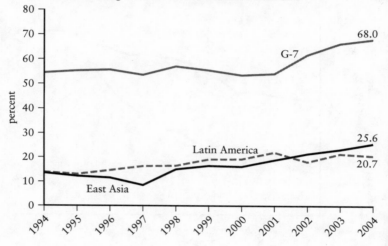

b. Amount Outstanding of Private Sector Domestic Bonds/GDP

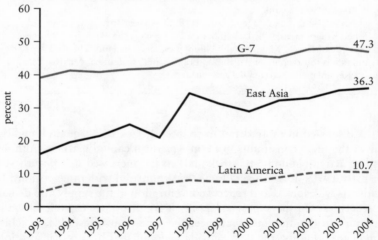

Sources: BIS; World Bank.

Note: G-7 is the average of Canada, France, Germany, Italy, Japan, the United Kingdom, and the United States. East Asia is the average of Hong Kong (China), Republic of Korea, Malaysia, Taiwan (China), and Thailand. Latin America is the average of Argentina, Brazil, Chile, Mexico, and Peru.

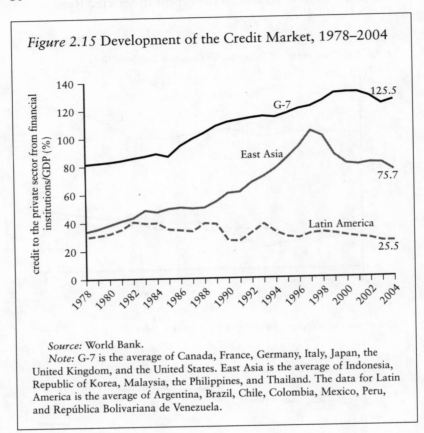

Figure 2.15 Development of the Credit Market, 1978–2004

Source: World Bank.
Note: G-7 is the average of Canada, France, Germany, Italy, Japan, the
United Kingdom, and the United States. East Asia is the average of Indonesia,
Republic of Korea, Malaysia, the Philippines, and Thailand. The data for Latin
America is the average of Argentina, Brazil, Chile, Colombia, Mexico, Peru,
and República Bolivariana de Venezuela.

As discussed in more detail in chapter 4, lack of adequate liquidity is
one of the main constraints in Latin American capital markets. Although
trading activity in domestic stock markets has increased significantly since
the early 1990s, it is still very low when compared with other regions. Illiquidity is widespread and reflects concentration in the supply and demand
of securities. On the supply side, only a few firms are capable of issuing
securities in the amounts that meet the minimum thresholds to achieve
significant liquidity; the demand side is dominated by a few institutional
investors, which tend to follow buy-and-hold investment strategies and
concentrate most of their holdings in government debt. Illiquidity in secondary markets hampers price revelation, which is often considered the
most distinctive function of securities markets relative to banks. Illiquidity
weakens the reliability of marking to market and fair value accounting
(chapter 2 annex). Furthermore, it magnifies the effects of shocks on asset
price fluctuations.

Figure 2.16 Stock Market Concentration of Top 10 Firms in Selected Markets, 2004

a. Top 10 Firms, Share of Total Market Capitalization

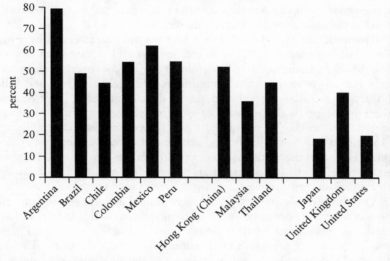

b. Top 10 Firms, Share of Total Trading

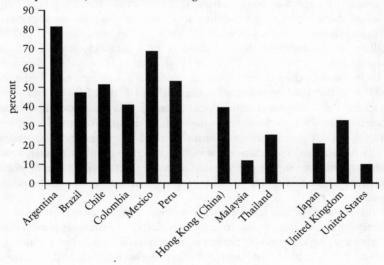

Source: World Federation of Exchanges.

Despite a significant deepening in the markets for government debt securities, these markets are fragmented and relatively illiquid, with the few mentioned exceptions of Chile (where public sector debt is mainly central bank debt), Mexico, and Colombia. Illiquidity in public bond markets is particularly widespread in smaller countries. In fact, often what is called "securities markets" in these countries is almost exclusively a repo-based money market in the centralized exchange, where public sector paper is used as the most common underlying security.[52]

Domestic bond markets in Latin America are characterized by a high degree of short-termism. While in recent years efforts have been made to lengthen debt maturities to reduce rollover risk in times of crisis, short-term debt remains relatively high. According to Mihaljek, Scatigna, and Villar (2002), in 2000, 37 percent of domestic debt securities in Latin America were short-term (with a maturity of up to one year), down from 53 percent in 1995, but still higher than in East Asia (22 percent) and Central Europe (15 percent). Although public and private sector bond issuers can achieve relatively longer maturities in international markets (see figure 2.17), most emerging economy bonds issued abroad are denominated in foreign currency, exposing governments and firms to exchange rate risk.[53]

Only in the most recent period have some Latin American countries been able to issue domestic currency–denominated bonds in international markets. This is in part a reflection of improved fundamentals and partly a consequence of favorable international financial conditions. This has attracted the attention of policy makers and the academic community, as it raises the hope that countries could indeed break free from the "original sin" curse—that is, the inability to issue long-duration local-currency debt in foreign markets. Between 2003 and 2004 Uruguay issued US$540 million in global bonds denominated in local currency, while Colombia raised US$825 million in two issues of local currency debt that were mostly purchased by international investors. More recently, in September 2005, the Brazilian government successfully placed US$1.5 billion worth of global bonds denominated in local currency. It is worth noting that two common features of these issues were their medium-term maturity and the significant participation of international investors.[54] These experiences have raised expectations about a changing trend in foreign investors' eagerness to invest in domestic currency instruments from emerging markets, which could help to reduce Latin American economies' exposure to currency risk.[55]

It is still too early to tell whether this positive trend constitutes a durable change in investors' appetite for domestic currency instruments or is just a temporary phenomenon (Borensztein, Eichengreen, and Panizza 2006). On the one hand, many Latin American countries have significantly improved their macroeconomic fundamentals, maintaining fiscal surpluses, reducing their debt to GDP ratios, and improving their solvency positions. Also, most Latin American countries currently hold much larger reserves

Figure 2.17 Average Bond Maturities in Latin America, by Jurisdiction

a. Average Maturity of Corporate Dollar Bonds, by Jurisdiction

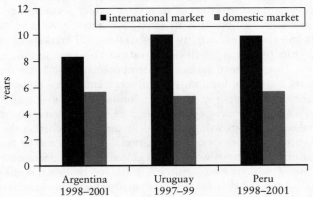

b. Average Maturity of Government Dollar Bonds, by Jurisdiction

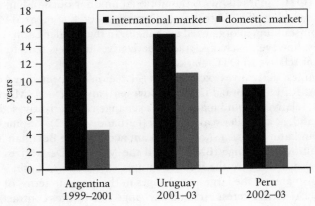

Source: Bloomberg.

Note: Bonds of maturity shorter than one year are excluded from the sample. Different time periods are displayed due to limitations in data availability.

than during the 1990s and tend to have less short-term debt. Moreover, there has been significant progress in adopting flexible exchange rate regimes and credible inflation targeting schemes throughout the region. All these factors should make local currency instruments more attractive to investors, local and international alike. On the other hand, one could reasonably argue that the increased appetite for local currency instruments among international investors is to a large extent a consequence of the current international juncture. In effect, low interest rates in developed countries and abundant liquidity in global financial markets have encouraged investors to search for riskier investment opportunities in emerging economies. The sustained exchange rate appreciation in Latin America in recent years has made local currency instruments more attractive. Also, part of the improvement in economic fundamentals in Latin American countries is a consequence of external factors, such as better terms of trade and global economic growth. It is not clear, therefore, whether the appetite for local currency bonds among international investors will be maintained if international conditions worsen and global liquidity decreases.

Derivatives markets have exploded in the international scene over the past few decades, but they lag behind in many emerging countries. Emerging market derivatives account for only 1 percent of the total notional amount outstanding in derivatives markets worldwide (IMF 2002). Most of the global derivatives market activity is carried out through over-the-counter (OTC) markets, with the notional amount outstanding in those markets reaching US$252 trillion in December 2004, compared to US$47 trillion outstanding in organized exchanges. In the smaller Latin American countries, however, exchange-traded derivatives markets tend to be more significant relative to OTC markets.

The largest derivatives exchanges in the region are located in Argentina (MATBA, ROFEX), Brazil (BM&F, Bovespa), and Mexico (MexDer). In addition, relatively liquid markets for exchange rate derivatives also exist in Chile and, at a smaller scale, in Peru (Fernandez 2002).[56] Some of these markets in Latin America show significant activity. The Brazilian Mercantile & Futures Exchange (BM&F) and the Mexican Derivatives Market (MexDer) not only are the leading futures exchanges in Latin America, but are also among the largest exchanges in the world in terms of the volume of short-term interest rate and exchange rate futures contracts traded (figure 2.18).[57] The Brazilian Mercantile & Futures Exchange presents a paradox: liquidity at the BM&F is very high, despite an illiquid underlying cash market.

For the larger Latin American countries, the OTC derivatives markets have gained impressive momentum, often exceeding the growth of exchange-based derivatives markets, not only domestically but also internationally.[58] In Mexico, for example, the domestic OTC derivatives market—which trades in currency options, forwards, cross-currency swaps, and peso-denominated interest rate swaps—is six times larger in trading

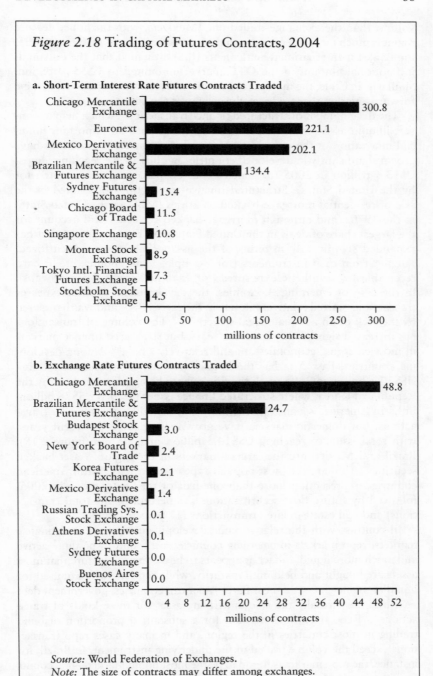

Figure 2.18 Trading of Futures Contracts, 2004

a. Short-Term Interest Rate Futures Contracts Traded

Chicago Mercantile Exchange — 300.8
Euronext — 221.1
Mexico Derivatives Exchange — 202.1
Brazilian Mercantile & Futures Exchange — 134.4
Sydney Futures Exchange — 15.4
Chicago Board of Trade — 11.5
Singapore Exchange — 10.8
Montreal Stock Exchange — 8.9
Tokyo Intl. Financial Futures Exchange — 7.3
Stockholm Stock Exchange — 4.5

millions of contracts

b. Exchange Rate Futures Contracts Traded

Chicago Mercantile Exchange — 48.8
Brazilian Mercantile & Futures Exchange — 24.7
Budapest Stock Exchange — 3.0
New York Board of Trade — 2.4
Korea Futures Exchange — 2.1
Mexico Derivatives Exchange — 1.4
Russian Trading Sys. Stock Exchange — 0.1
Athens Derivatives Exchange — 0.1
Sydney Futures Exchange — 0.0
Buenos Aires Stock Exchange — 0.0

millions of contracts

Source: World Federation of Exchanges.
Note: The size of contracts may differ among exchanges.

volume than the exchange-traded one (MexDer), with the added feature that it is much more integrated into the international market. By end-2005, the Bank for International Settlements (BIS) estimated that the outstanding notional amount in the OTC market amounted to US$530 billion. Similarly, in Chile, the market for currency derivatives is a non–deliverable forwards market that trades exclusively over the counter.

The development of structured finance transactions, which help to convert illiquid assets into tradable securities, has been an important financial innovation of the past decades. Structured finance transactions have grown significantly in developed countries, with issuance reaching almost US$3.6 trillion in 2005 (of which about 85 percent was accounted for by the United States). Structured finance transactions originated in the sale of residential mortgage-backed securities (MBS) in the United States in the 1970s, and although mortgage-backed securities still account for the largest share of deals in the United States and Europe, the market has expanded significantly in terms of the assets that are now securitized, ranging from cash instruments (for example, loans, bonds, credit card receivables) to synthetic exposures (for example, credit default swaps). In the case of emerging economies, the development of these types of transactions started relatively slowly in the early 1990s and was hampered by the lack of an adequate legal structure.[59] The volume of transactions has increased significantly in recent years, but structured finance markets in most emerging economies are still relatively small.[60] Among developing countries, East Asia has the largest markets, with issuance totaling US$30.1 billion in 2005, with the lion's share being accounted for by the Republic of Korea, where structured finance issues reached US$26 billion. In Latin America, issuance was initially dominated by cross-border transactions, but domestic markets have grown significantly in recent years, with total issuance reaching US$14.5 billion in 2005 (see figure 2.19). Brazil and Mexico are the largest markets in the region. Asset-backed securities (ABS) are the most popular type of contract in Latin American countries, representing more than one-half of the transactions in 2005, followed by future flow securitizations (22 percent of the total transactions) and real estate–related transactions (17 percent).[61]

In contrast with the relative underdevelopment of structured finance markets, repo markets in emerging countries are found to be quite active and much more liquid. In fact, it appears to be a common feature that most assets are bought and held until maturity, while repo markets are used for liquidity management. In most Latin American countries, government debt securities are virtually the sole underlying asset for these kinds of transactions.[62] Repo operations account for a substantial proportion of bond trading in most countries in the region, and in many cases repo transactions exceed the volume traded of the underlying instrument. In Brazil, for instance, the repo market is found to be the most liquid market—it accounts for 60 percent of average daily value traded in all markets, followed by

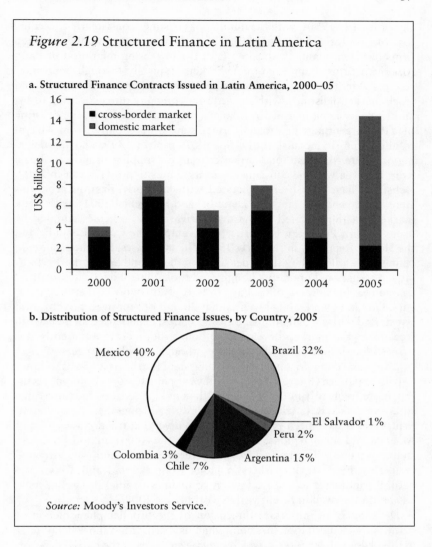

Figure 2.19 Structured Finance in Latin America

a. Structured Finance Contracts Issued in Latin America, 2000–05

b. Distribution of Structured Finance Issues, by Country, 2005

Source: Moody's Investors Service.

swaps and futures, which represent 20 percent (Glaessner 2003). As mentioned above, in some of the smaller countries in the region, such as Costa Rica, El Salvador, and Guatemala, trading in what is called the "securities market" is almost exclusively a repo market (with government paper typically the only underlying asset) where transactions, for legal and regulatory reasons, are obligatorily carried out through a centralized exchange.

A significant trend in Latin America over the past decade has been the delisting of large issuers from the domestic stock markets. The number of listed firms in the largest stock markets in the region has decreased since the early 1990s, with the number of delistings consistently exceeding that of new listings (figure 2.20). This reduction in the number of listed firms has been mainly associated with the increasing migration of Latin American firms to international markets, typically through depositary receipts. Merger and acquisition activity is another explanation behind stock market delistings, with the acquirer company often choosing to list and trade its stock in a major financial center. For example, the delisting of YPF (Argentina's privatized former state oil company) from Merval resulted from its acquisition by Spain's Repsol in 1999, and the delisting of White Martins (South America's largest supplier of industrial gas) from Bovespa was the consequence of its acquisition by Praxair in 2000. Delistings have also been associated with how privatization programs were implemented (Claessens, Djankov, and Klingebiel 2001), with stock market delistings related to the mass privatization schemes adopted by some Eastern European countries (for example, the Czech Republic and the Slovak Republic) in the early 1990s. In such cases, the initial surge in listings was followed by sharp delistings in the second half of the 1990s as large international operators bought and took control over the privatized companies. In contrast, other Eastern European countries (Estonia, Hungary, Latvia, Poland, and Slovenia) that did not opt for mass privatization but started with a small number of listed shares, experienced an increase in stock listings as markets developed, although they have more recently also witnessed a decline in listed companies, though at a slower pace.

A regional comparison of stock listings data for the past 15 years shows a striking pattern (figure 2.20). Delistings are much more common, occurring more frequently in Latin America than in East Asia. At the same time, stock markets in East Asia have been recording a listings increase. Different explanations have been presented for this diverging trend between Latin America and other regions. For one, unlike the American and European stock markets, which performed well over the 1990s and thus attracted issuers to them, stock markets in Hong Kong (China) and Tokyo, the natural candidates to attract foreign companies to migrate within Asia, have not done well in recent years (World Bank 2004a).

Delisting is an important dimension of the broader phenomenon of stock market internationalization, which is discussed in more detail later in this chapter. In chapter 3, we investigate empirically the partial determinants of this internationalization phenomenon and its impact on domestic stock markets' trading and liquidity.

In addition to falling stock market listings, there has also been a significant drop in equity issuance in Latin America since 1998. The 1998 global economic shock, induced by the Russian crisis, severely restricted corporate access to capital markets both at home and abroad. Given the initial tightness of bank credit and the dearth of equity markets globally, firms increasingly shifted to bond issuance as an alternative source of financing. With falling interest rates after 2000, private corporate bond

Figure 2.20 Stock Market Listings between 1990 and 2004

a. Domestic Stock Markets in Latin America

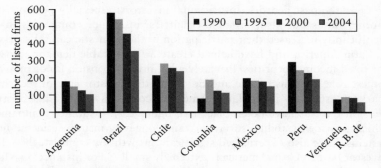

b. Domestic Stock Markets in South East Asia

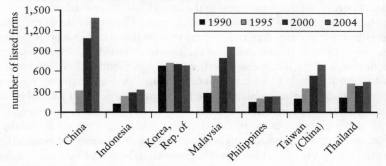

c. Domestic Stock Markets in Eastern Europe

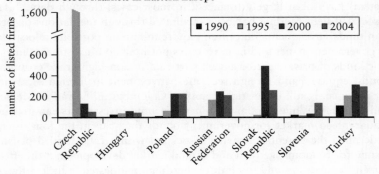

Source: S&P Emerging Markets Database.

Note: The figures are year-end values. Data for 1990 for Hungary, Poland, and the Russian Federation correspond to 1991.

issuance has increased, notably in Chile and Mexico. In recent years, there has been some activity in terms of local equity issuance in the region, with nearly US$6 billion raised through domestic stock markets in 2005, but capital-raising activity is still relatively low in the region overall (World Bank 2006).

Over the past decades, institutional investors (especially pension and mutual funds but also, in some countries, insurance companies) have significantly increased their participation in the domestic capital markets in Latin America and have helped create a more stable demand, mostly for fixed-income securities. Privately administered pension funds play the largest role in terms of size and dominate the investor side of securities markets, especially in the Latin American countries where Chilean-style pension reforms have taken place (see figure 2.9). Insurance companies, which provide disability, survivors', and longevity insurance in the new systems, have also experienced significant growth. By contrast, the retail investor base in Latin America is extremely small.[63] For instance, in Mexico retail investors in securities markets were estimated to represent less than 1 percent of the population in the late 1990s, compared to 44 percent in the United States and 27 percent in France. The small size of the retail investor base in Latin America in part reflects the fact that a large part of the population in the region lacks the financial wealth for investments in securities markets, while individuals with high net worth have direct access to foreign (typically U.S.) investment instruments. Furthermore, the local mutual funds industry, which is crucial for the emergence of a retail investor base, remains underdeveloped in most Latin American countries.

A striking feature of institutional investors in Latin America is that their asset holdings are predominately concentrated in government bonds (figure 2.21). This is in part because the transitional costs of pension reforms (i.e., the transition from a pay-as-you-go system to a privately funded system) have been largely financed, in most cases, through debt.[64] The associated debt funding has been facilitated through regulations on pension funds' investments that often require minimum portfolio allocations to government paper and in most cases put limits on investments in specific kinds of private sector assets, particularly non-high-grade corporate bonds, equities, and foreign securities. Investment in foreign securities, for instance, is still under tight limits in Colombia, El Salvador, Mexico, and Uruguay. While the limits on pension fund investments can produce a guaranteed market for government bonds they can in the longer-term undermine the potential benefits associated with a fully funded pension system for economic growth and capital market development.[65] In effect, current regulations tend to reinforce herding (manifested in little differentiation across pension fund portfolios) as well as the preference for "buy and hold" investment strategies, which can be detrimental to securities markets liquidity (Gill, Packard, and Yermo 2005). Investment regulations also reinforce capital market concentration, by unduly biasing invest-

Figure 2.21 Composition of Mandatory Pension Fund Investment Portfolios in Latin America, Year-end 2005

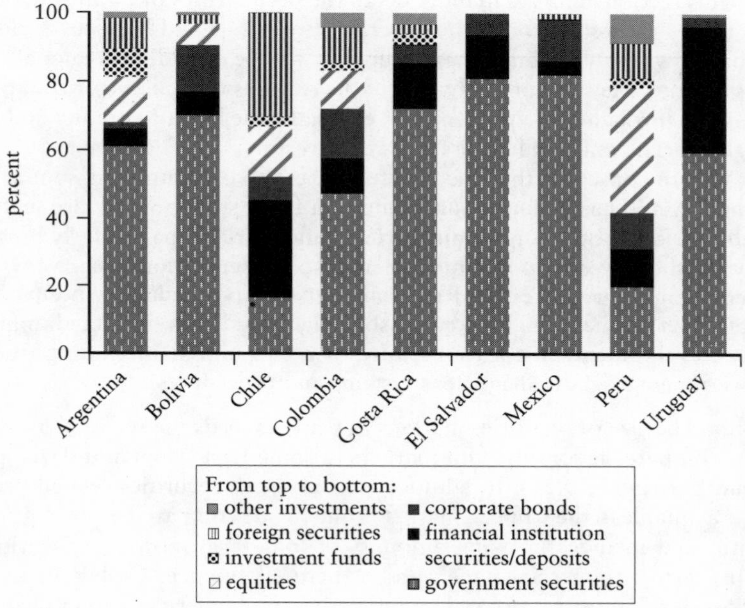
100
80
60
40
20
0
percent
Argentina
Bolivia
Chile
Colombia
Costa Rica
El Salvador
Mexico
Peru
Uruguay
From top to bottom:
other investments
foreign securities
investment funds
equities
corporate bonds
financial institution securities/deposits
government securities

Sources: AIOS; International Federation of Pension Fund Administrators (FIAP).

ments in favor of the highest rated securities, as shown by Zervos (2004) for the cases of Chile and Mexico. It must be noted, however, that even in countries with less restrictive portfolio limits, pension funds appear to favor government papers over private securities. This is arguably due to the fact that, during the 1990s, yields on sovereign emerging market bonds outperformed other asset classes in many markets, even when measured in risk adjusted terms (Broner, Lorenzoni, and Schmukler 2004).

Country Experiences: Chile and Mexico

Although capital markets across Latin America share some common features and present an overall disheartening state, as described above, some countries, most notably Chile, have been rather successful in developing their domestic securities markets and have gone further than the regional average in terms of capital market development. Another regional success story in the more recent period is Mexico, where capital markets, especially the fixed-income market, have been experiencing significant growth, even if they still remain underdeveloped relative to comparable middle-income countries.

This section analyzes in more detail the peculiarities of Latin American securities markets through the experiences of Chile and Mexico. A closer look shows that, although these countries may be considered regional success stories, they still present some of the features that characterize capital markets throughout Latin America, especially the lack of liquidity and the high concentration of both issuers and investors.

We are conscious that the choice of these two countries is somewhat arbitrary and has its limitations. Indeed, a fuller study should also feature a discussion of other important Latin capital markets, particularly Brazil's (by far the largest regional market in absolute terms, and where government bond, derivatives, and repo markets are particularly vibrant) and Colombia's (where the market for sovereign bonds has registered impressive development, not least because of a substantial upgrading of the government's debt management systems and procedures).

Chile The size of securities markets in Chile exceeds the regional average and compares favorably with markets in some East Asian and developed countries (figure 2.22). In addition, the range of securities-related products available in the Chilean market is quite wide compared to the regional norm and includes growing amounts of long-term mortgage securities, short-term commercial paper, and structured finance. Chile's financial sector development is not only a reflection of a higher per capita income, sound institutions, and macroeconomic policies, but also the result of substantial financial sector reforms. The greater financial development in Chile compared to the rest of the region is arguably not independent from the fact that, while most Latin American countries implemented macroeconomic and capital market reforms during the 1990s, in Chile many of those reforms were undertaken much earlier, during the 1980s.[66]

The Chilean primary market for private fixed-income securities is relatively well developed. The private sector bond market in Chile is the largest in Latin America, with the amount outstanding of private sector bonds reaching 23 percent of GDP in 2004, and there has been increased financial innovation in the form of securitization of receivables and future cash flows. This development of the private fixed-income market was fostered not just by macroeconomic stability but also by the government's debt management strategy. The Chilean government has maintained a fiscal surplus since 1986 (with the sole exception of 1999, when a fiscal deficit equivalent to about 1.5 percent of GDP was recorded), and therefore has not needed to issue debt instruments to finance its expenditures. Nonetheless, it has followed an explicit strategy of issuing bonds in both international and local markets in order to develop a sovereign risk benchmark

Figure 2.22 Development of Domestic Capital Markets of
Selected Countries, Year-end 2004

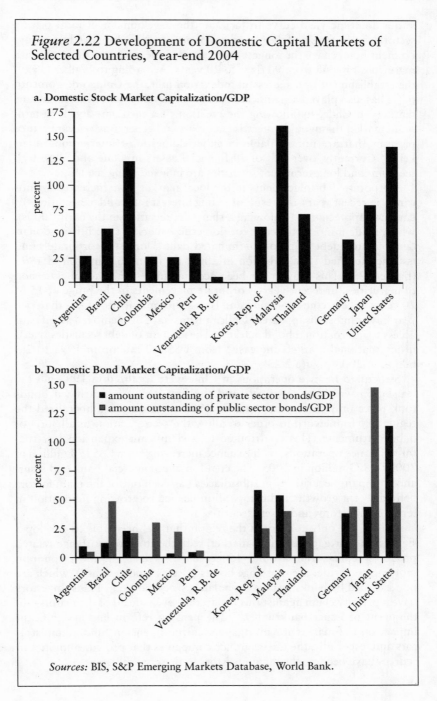

a. Domestic Stock Market Capitalization/GDP

b. Domestic Bond Market Capitalization/GDP

■ amount outstanding of private sector bonds/GDP
■ amount outstanding of public sector bonds/GDP

Sources: BIS, S&P Emerging Markets Database, World Bank.

and a domestic yield curve to facilitate the development of local private sector debt markets and the placement of private debt abroad. Chilean government bonds have the longest average maturities in Latin America, with maturities ranging from 90 days to 20 years. According to Walker (1998) the establishment of a successful indexation unit, the Unidad de Fomento (UF), has also played a significant role in the development of fixed-income markets in Chile, by allowing the creation of a medium- and long-term bond market that would otherwise not exist and generating relevant return patterns that are not available in either domestic or international markets.[67] Currently, over half of all financial assets in Chile and almost all medium- and long-term debt securities are indexed using the UF.

Corporate debt placements in the local market have increased significantly in recent years as a result of falling interest rates and expectations of currency appreciation (following a sharp depreciation in the early 2000s), which made it more attractive for domestic issuers to switch from dollar-denominated debt to peso-denominated debt. Domestic corporate bond issuance reached US$2.5 billion in 2003, up from 70.5 million in 1995 (figure 2.23). This growth has been accompanied by a gradual extension of maturities. In recent years, corporate placements in the range of 15 to 20 years have become common and issues with maturities of less than one year have almost disappeared. Chilean firms have also enjoyed significant access to international bond markets. The amount of debt securities issued in international markets increased from US$300 million in 1995 to 2.3 billion in 2003 (figure 2.23).

Structured finance operations in Chile were legalized in 1993 but the legislation was very restrictive and the first issue of securitized bonds took place only three years later. In 1999 the authorities liberalized the regulatory framework in order to allow the securitization of all sorts of debt instruments. This contributed to a significant expansion in structured finance operations, with issuance increasing from US$173 million in 2000 to 873 million in 2005. The creation of commercial bank and insurance company securitization subsidiaries has been one of the main factors behind recent growth, and competition has led to growing innovation in terms of structures and assets securitized.

Chile is the only country in the region that has been able to develop a significant mortgage securities market, with the stock of mortgage-related products representing around 15 percent of GDP. The most common mortgage securities are mortgage bonds ("letras hipotecarias"), which are bonds issued by banks against on-balance sheet mortgage loans. Investors have a priority claim against this collateral—even ahead of depositors—in the event of issuer bankruptcy.[68] The pension reform had a significant impact on the market for mortgage securities; pension fund administrators and, especially, the life insurance companies that provide annuities to retirees have become the main investors in these securities.

Figure 2.23 Bond Issuance by Chilean Firms, 1995–2003

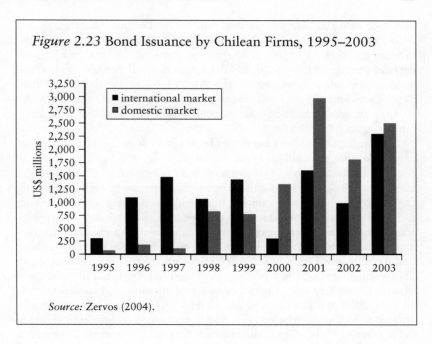

Source: Zervos (2004).

As noted, the size of Chile's stock market compares favorably not only with markets in other emerging economies but also with markets in developed countries. Market capitalization stood at 124 percent of GDP at year-end 2004. Despite its significant size, the Chilean stock market has experienced a decline in the number of listed firms over the last decade, from 284 firms in 1995 to 246 in 2005. This reduction has been associated with the increasing migration of Chilean firms to international markets, with 25 of the top 40 local companies being listed in U.S. markets through American depositary receipts (ADRs), and the dearth of new equity issues after 1998. In recent years, increased interest in local equity issuance and initial public offerings (IPOs) has been registered, with US$951 million having been raised through equity issues during 2004. The largest IPO in the history of the Santiago Stock Exchange took place in 2004, when Cencosud (a local retailer) listed 20 percent of its shares, raising US$332 million.[69]

The use of derivatives in Chile, with the notable exception of foreign exchange forwards, remains limited. Following the adoption of a flexible exchange rate regime in 1999, the local market for foreign exchange forwards expanded rapidly and has now become quite deep.[70] An important factor driving the growth of this market in recent years has been the increasing foreign investment by pension funds. In line with regulatory requirements, pension funds must hedge 80 percent of the resulting exchange rate risk. Hence, pension funds have become major players in selling forward contracts (i.e., they sell foreign exchange for pesos in the forward market). As of July 2005, pension funds held nearly US$3 billion in these contracts. The use of other derivatives is still limited or nonexistent. In particular, there is no market for interest rate derivatives, which complicates interest rate risk management, especially for life insurance companies, whose asset-liability matching is highly sensitive to interest rate changes.

Chile has embarked on a series of legislative reforms in recent years to overcome some of the limitations of its securities markets. The Law on Tender Offers and Corporate Governance ("Ley de OPAs"), enacted at the end of 2000, improved minority shareholder protection by regulating the market for corporate control, requiring that transactions involving a change of control of more than 25 percent of the shares of a public company be performed through a tender offer to all shareholders in equal terms, and increasing disclosure requirements and sanctions for insider trading. The law also guaranteed equal treatment to ADR holders, especially regarding voting procedures, and required large listed firms to form a board committee with a majority of members unrelated to the controller.[71] In 2001 the government introduced a reform package (generally referred to as Capital Markets I) aimed at promoting competition in financial markets and reducing financial costs. Capital gains on transactions in widely traded stocks became tax-exempt, and various tax and administrative barriers to voluntary savings and the development of securities and credit markets were removed. Also, mutual fund management and investments by insurance companies were liberalized. Moreover, a stock market for emerging companies within the Santiago Stock Exchange, with less stringent registration requirements, was created, although it has had little success so far. A second legislative reform package, aimed at deepening corporate governance reforms and strengthening regulation and supervision, was prepared by the government in 2003 and is now being discussed by Chile's congress.

Despite their large size and the relatively wide range of available securities-related products, capital markets in Chile present some important limitations. In the first place, although there has been some progress in recent years, liquidity is quite low in most securities markets, with the notable exceptions of the exchange rate forward market and the repo-based money market. Trading in public sector bonds has increased substantially in recent years, as a result of government efforts to facilitate the emergence of a yield curve, but remains below that of other countries.[72] Liquidity in mortgage bonds is very limited, and practically no secondary market exists for corporate bonds. The stock market is extremely illiquid, despite its large capitalization. Second, access to the Chilean market is quite segmented and with limited credit risk diversification. In particular, the set of firms that can access local capital markets through debt or equity issues is quite limited. Bond issuance is concentrated in the largest firms, and most issues correspond to highly rated issuers (in the AAA to A rating category). In fact, there is currently no active high-yield market in Chile.

Although low liquidity is to some extent the result of gaps in market infrastructure, structural factors play a significant role.[73] Illiquidity is in part a reflection of concentration in supply and demand. On the supply side, concentrated firm ownership results in a low free float of shares.[74] Controlling shareholders own about 70 percent of the shares of the 60 most traded firms, and the concentration level is even higher among less actively traded companies.[75] The real free float of some of the largest firms has been estimated at between 7 percent and 16 percent. On the demand side, the vast majority of investable funds are channeled mainly through pension funds and life insurance companies, which tend to follow "buy and hold" strategies. As pension funds have grown, achieving a dominant position in the domestic capital markets, these strategies have become institutionalized, since large block sales can have a negative impact on prices. Additionally, as already noted, there has been a significant migration of securities issues and trading abroad, which has adversely affected liquidity in the domestic stock market (see chapter 3 for general evidence on this). In 2000, almost 50 percent of the total trading activity (measured by value traded) of Chilean stocks took place in U.S. exchanges.

The lack of breadth in terms of debt and equity issuers is also explained by special supply and demand factors. On the supply side, only a few firms and issues meet the minimum size thresholds necessary to achieve adequate liquidity. Ownership concentration hinders the willingness to "go public," as this entails a dilution of control. Also, large, creditworthy firms are able to raise capital in international markets, in many cases on better terms than in the local market, reducing the supply of domestic securities. On the demand side, mandatory pension funds are subject to investment regulations, particularly credit rating regulations, that limit their ability to invest in lower rated issuers. Also, the overall regulatory and supervisory framework and the significant reputational costs associated with incurring losses may have led fund managers to avoid riskier investments, concentrating on large, well-known firms.

Mexico The development of Mexico's capital markets, especially its fixed-income markets, in recent years can be considered a success story in many respects. After the 1994–95 crisis the government adopted several measures to develop the local bond market, including macroeconomic and structural reforms and the introduction of a clear debt management strategy, that have proven quite effective.[76] The government reformed the primary market for public sector debt by gradually opening auctions of government securities to a wider range of investors and introduced a market-making scheme for government debt in order to increase secondary market liquidity. Predictability and transparency in debt management have been increased by announcing annual debt management strategies and using quarterly auction calendars that specify the particular issues to be auctioned each week. All these efforts, together with a more stable macroeconomic environment, have allowed the government to increase issuance in the domestic market, thus reducing its dependence on foreign financing. Since 2001 the entire fiscal deficit has been financed in the local market. In 2004 domestic borrowing was used to repay US$1.8 billion in external debt. This has resulted in a significant increase in the amount outstanding of domestic government bonds, from 8 percent of GDP in 1994 to over 22 percent in 2004.[77] The Mexican government has also been able to extend domestic market maturities, successfully issuing 3-, 5-, 10-, and 20-year fixed-rate bonds. This has helped to develop a benchmark yield curve, which has opened a significant source of long-term financing for the private sector.

Capital market growth has also been fostered by the 1997 pension reform, which created a fast-growing institutional investor base, and the 2001 financial sector reform, which, among other things, eliminated legal hurdles and inconsistencies, increased minority shareholder protection, and granted stronger inspection and enforcement powers to the securities regulator (Comisión Nacional Bancaria y de Valores, CNBV). This reform also included amendments to the mutual funds law, permitting the development of a wide variety of collective investment vehicles and allowing funds to offer different fee and commission structures to different kinds of investors. Historically, Mexican corporate governance practices have exhibited serious shortcomings in the areas of conflicts of interest, director responsibilities, and shareholder rights, which led to a perception of extensive insider dealing.[78] The 2001 reform addressed many of these issues, improving minority shareholders' protection by reducing the ownership required to appoint a statutory auditor to 10 percent and allowing private shareholders holding 15 percent of equity to file derivate suits, irrespective of voting rights. Nonvoting shares were limited to a maximum of 25 percent of the public float of a company, and firms exceeding this limit have been given a limited time frame during which they must exchange nonvoting shares.[79] Further legislative reforms to improve investor protection were implemented in 2005, including requiring firms to create independent audit and corporate governance committees, allowing minority shareholders to name board members with only 10 percent of votes, and mandating firms to inform investors when they ignore independent board advice.

The local corporate bond market, although still relatively small, has experienced significant growth in the last few years. Peso-denominated corporate debt issuance reached about US$12 billion in 2004, up from only US$593 million in 1999. This growth has been accompanied by a lengthening of maturities—a growing number of companies issuing fixed-rate debt in pesos with a maturity of more than three years. The rapid development of the corporate bond market has been fostered not only by the government's efforts to establish a benchmark yield curve and the pension reform that created a stable demand for these securities (about 20 percent of pension funds' portfolios are invested in corporate bonds), but also by the creation of new debt instruments (IMF 2005). The 2001 securities laws introduced a new instrument (Certificados Bursatiles, CBs) that combines the attractive features of instruments already available in the market (medium-term notes and debentures) in order to accommodate the needs of issuers and investors.[80] CBs offer the speed and ease of issuance of medium-term notes, plus the flexible amortization schedules and covenants of debentures, and have become the dominant instrument in the market, accounting for over 90 percent of total corporate debt issuance in 2004.

Structured finance operations in the local market, once extremely rare, have experienced significant growth in recent years. Mexican companies with dollar-denominated income have typically tapped international markets through cross-border structured deals, particularly the securitization of export receivables. This type of deal allows them to exceed their foreign-currency rating and therefore access foreign capital in better terms. However, in recent years, cross-border structured finance transactions have decreased, because improvements in international financial conditions and the achievement of investment-grade status by the Mexican government have allowed firms to increasingly tap international bond markets directly.[81] The development of the domestic fixed-income market has also offered an alternative source of financing. The local structured finance market has experienced strong growth in recent years, and Mexico has become the largest market in Latin America for this type of transaction, representing over 40 percent of total domestic issuance in the region in 2005 (see figure 2.19). The volume of transactions has increased from only US$65 million in 2000 to US$4.9 billion in 2005, with most of the activity being concentrated in securitized accounts receivables, toll roads, and the mortgage and home-building sector. Several reforms to the housing finance system, which is dominated by the public sector, have generated a rapid growth of real estate–related transactions.[82] In 2001 the government created Sociedad Hipotecaria Federal (SHF), a housing development bank that provides second-tier financing to banks and nonbank financial firms (Sociedades Financieras de Objeto Limitado, or Sofoles) and also has the mandate to develop the secondary mortgage market.[83] SHF has played a significant role in the growth of residential mortgage–backed securities, by providing mortgage insurance and partial credit guarantees and helping to standardize mortgage origination. The development of the MBS market has also been fostered by the securitization of mortgages originated by INFONAVIT (Instituto del Fondo Nacional de la Vivienda para los Trabajadores), Mexico's low-income housing agency.[84] Apart from the MBS market, there is also an active market for the securitization of loans to construction developers.

Derivatives markets have also experienced significant growth in recent years. Instruments to hedge against exchange rate risk, such as currency futures and forwards, have become increasingly popular following the move to a flexible exchange rate regime. The largest derivatives market in Mexico is the OTC market. The most traded instruments in this market are currency options and forwards, cross-currency swaps, and peso interest rate swaps. The outstanding notional amount in the OTC market reached US$530 billion at year-end 2005. As mentioned above, there is also an active market for interest rate derivatives on the Mexican Derivatives Exchange (MexDer).[85] Interest rate derivatives have been popular for hedging risks taken in the forwards markets. Some banks also use these instruments to meet regulations requiring a balance between short-term liabilities and assets. Activity in MexDer grew rapidly between 2001 and 2004 but experienced a strong reduction (with the notional outstanding amount falling over 50 percent) in 2005 when one of the market makers shifted its operations offshore.

Mexico's stock market is the second largest in the region by absolute size, after the Brazilian market, but market capitalization represents only 25 percent of GDP. The market has attracted significant interest among foreign, especially U.S., investors, who owned more than half of the market as of March 2005, up from only 19 percent in 1996. Foreign investor interest has also resulted in a significant migration of Mexican firms to international markets, and about 50 percent of firms listed in the local market have listed abroad or raised equity capital in international markets. This migration, together with the dearth of new equity issues, has resulted in a reduction of domestic listed firms from 199 in 1990 to 152 in 2004.[86]

Despite their significant growth in recent years, Mexico's securities markets are still relatively underdeveloped and present many of the shortcomings of capital markets throughout the region. Market access is confined to a few high-grade issuers, and secondary market liquidity is limited. Institutional investors, notably pension funds, dominate the demand side, and their holdings are concentrated in government debt.[87]

Mandatory pension funds have strict rating restrictions, being allowed to invest only in debt securities rated AA and above. This has led to a high concentration of bond issues among highly rated securities and issuers, with more than 90 percent of total corporate bond issuance in the 2001–03 period lying in the AA to AAA rating range (figure 2.24). The set of firms that can access local capital markets through debt or equity issues is quite limited. For instance, only nine firms accounted for almost 90 percent of the total amount outstanding of corporate bonds in the domestic market as of October 2003. In the stock market, only 10 firms represented nearly 70 percent of value traded during 2004.

Although there has been some progress in recent years, liquidity remains quite low in most securities markets.[88] Trading activity in the public sector bond market has increased, mainly as a result of the introduction of primary dealers who have an obligation to make continuous bid-ask offers, but market depth is still reduced, and liquidity remains concentrated in

Figure 2.24 Mexican Corporate Bond Market Concentration

a. Cumulative Amount of Corporate Bonds Issued in the Local Market, by Credit Rating, 2001–03

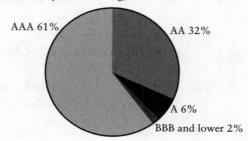

AAA 61%

AA 32%

A 6%

BBB and lower 2%

b. Amount Outstanding of Corporate Bonds in the Local Market, by Issuer, October 2003

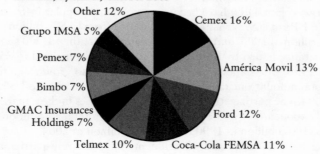

Other 12%

Grupo IMSA 5%

Pemex 7%

Bimbo 7%

GMAC Insurances Holdings 7%

Telmex 10%

Cemex 16%

América Movil 13%

Ford 12%

Coca-Cola FEMSA 11%

Sources: Bolsa Mexicana de Valores; JPMorgan; Zervos (2004).

short-term securities. Most of the trading of government debt is carried out through the repo market, with the volume traded in this market being about two and a half times the volume traded in the spot market for government debt. The private sector bond market remains illiquid and is characterized by high fragmentation, which, by spreading liquidity too thin, amplifies price volatility. Despite significant participation by foreign investors, trading in the local stock market remains low, reaching only 6.3 percent of GDP during 2004. Stock market illiquidity is exacerbated by high ownership concentration and fragmentation. Ownership of listed companies is highly concentrated, and there is a limited free float.[89] Listed firms issue many different types of nonfungible shares to avoid diluting corporate control, thus creating a high fragmentation of securities and increasing illiquidity.[90] As mentioned above, there has been a significant migration of issuers and trading abroad, which has also reduced domestic market activity. Transactions of Mexican-listed shares abroad, mostly through ADRs, represented more than two-thirds of total value traded during 2005.

Participation in International Capital Markets

As described in the section on global context, in this chapter, globalization has advanced over the past decades with increased cross-border capital flows, tighter links among financial markets, and greater commercial presence of foreign financial firms around the world. An important element of this globalization trend has been the internationalization of financial services, which has meant the use of international financial intermediaries by local issuers and investors. Many firms from emerging markets now cross-list their shares in global markets. As part of this globalization process, depositary receipts (DRs) have become increasingly popular instruments.[91] Trading in DRs in U.S. exchanges has expanded from US$75 billion in 1990 to US$1 trillion in 2005, and there are currently more than 1,900 sponsored ADR programs, issued by firms from 73 countries, compared to 352 programs in 1990. International bond markets have also grown significantly, from a total amount outstanding of US$1.6 trillion in 1990 to US$14 trillion in 2004. The participation of developing countries in these markets has increased exponentially in the past 15 years, from a total amount outstanding of US$100.3 billion in 1990 to US$801.9 billion in 2004.

Latin American firms and governments have actively participated in international equity and bond markets. This participation has been significant not only in terms of GDP, but also relative to domestic stock and bond markets activity. In fact, for many countries, share trading, equity capital raising, and bond issuance in international markets are higher than domestic securities market activity. Furthermore, the extent of internationalization of Latin American securities markets in most cases exceeds that of developed and East Asian countries.[92]

The participation of Latin American firms in international equity markets has usually taken the form of cross-listings in the U.S. market through ADRs. Compañía de Teléfonos de Chile (CTC), the national telecommunications company, was the first major Latin American firm to cross-list its shares on the New York Stock Exchange in July 1990. This cross-listing was followed by the successful privatization of Teléfonos de México (Telmex) through a public offering that included an ADR tranche in May 1991. The investor response to these offerings demonstrated the existence of a significant demand for Latin American equities in foreign markets, prompting most of the major firms in the region to look for a cross-listing in the U.S. market.[93] Latin American firms represented more than 20 percent of total value traded in the ADR market in 2005, and some regional firms, such as America Movil (Mexico), Petrobras (Brazil), and CVRD (Brazil), are among the most actively traded, with their value traded exceeding US$20 billion.

The activity of Latin American firms in international equity markets has grown exponentially since the early 1990s. The number of firms with international activity increased from only 11 firms in 1990 to 249 in 2000, representing 18.2 percent of total firms listed in domestic stock markets (see figure 2.25).[94] The market capitalization of firms with international activities increased from an average of 0.7 percent of GDP in 1990 to 12.9 percent in 2000 (see figure 2.26). Trading of Latin American firms in the international market has grown from less than 0.1 percent of GDP in 1990 to 5.4 percent in 1996 and 5.7 percent in 2000 (see figure 2.26). Capital raised abroad has also increased significantly although it has been less stable and foreign equity financing has usually dried up in crisis periods. In terms of GDP, capital raised in foreign markets increased from less than 0.1 percent in 1990 to 0.6 percent in 1996, declining to 0.2 percent in 2000 (see figure 2.26).

The participation of Latin American firms in international equity markets has been significant compared to that of firms from other regions. As figure 2.25 shows, the share of listed firms with international activities is significantly higher in Latin America than in developing countries and East Asia. However, the market capitalization of international firms as a percentage of GDP is lower in Latin America than in other regions (see figure 2.26). This is explained by the fact that overall stock market capitalization in terms of GDP is significantly lower in Latin America, as described in Section 4. Trading of Latin American firms' shares in international markets is significantly higher in terms of GDP than that of firms from other regions, standing at 5.7 percent in 2000, compared to 2.5 percent for developing countries and 2.1 percent for East Asia (see figure 2.26).

For many countries in the region, international trading and capital raising are significantly higher than domestic market activity. Figure 2.27 shows international activity relative to domestic activity. The market capitalization of international firms as a percentage of total domestic stock market capitalization in Latin America has increased from 3.5 percent in 1990 to 43.1 percent in 2000 and is higher than that of East Asian countries. Trading in international stock markets in 2000 exceeded domestic trading by more than 20 percent. This high degree of trading abroad in Latin America stands in contrast to developing and East Asian countries, where trading in international markets is almost negligible relative to domestic activity, standing at 3.4 percent of domestic trading in developed countries and 4.0 percent in East Asia in 2000. Equity capital raised

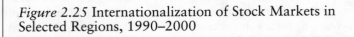

Figure 2.25 Internationalization of Stock Markets in
Selected Regions, 1990–2000

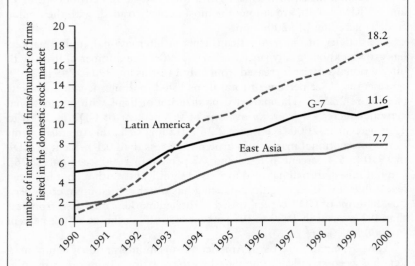

Sources: Bank of New York; Euromoney; LSE; NASDAQ; NYSE; S&P
Emerging Markets Database; World Federation of Exchanges.

Note: G-7 is the average of Canada, France, Germany, Italy, and Japan.
The United Kingdom and the United States are not included because they are
considered international financial centers. East Asia is the average of Hong
Kong (China), Indonesia, Republic of Korea, Malaysia, the Philippines, Taiwan
(China), and Thailand. Latin America is the average of Argentina, Brazil,
Chile, Colombia, Mexico, Peru, and República Bolivariana de Venezuela.
International firms are those identified as having at least one active depositary
receipt program at any time in the year, or having raised capital in international
markets in the current or previous years, or trading on the LSE, NYSE, or
NASDAQ.

abroad has also become very significant in Latin American countries,
reaching 91.9 percent of domestic capital raised in 2000, compared to
32.5 and 17.1 percent in developed and East Asian countries, respectively.
However, it is necessary to consider that capital-raising abroad is highly
dependent on international market conditions and has almost disappeared
during crisis periods, standing at only 6 percent of domestic capital raised
in 1995 and less than 2 percent in 1998.

As mentioned above, the increasing internationalization of Latin
American equity markets has been associated with a reduction in the

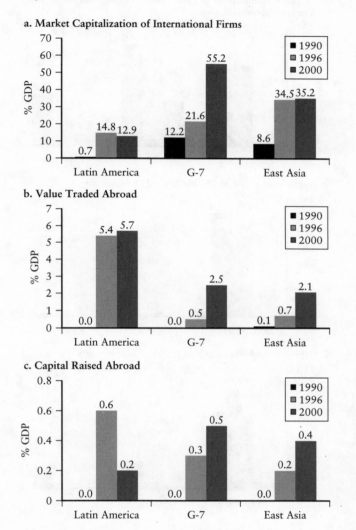

Figure 2.26 Internationalization of Stock Markets Relative to GDP, Selected Years

a. Market Capitalization of International Firms

b. Value Traded Abroad

c. Capital Raised Abroad

Sources: Bank of New York; Bloomberg; Euromoney; LSE; NASDAQ; NYSE; Worldscope; World Bank.

Note: G-7 is the average of Canada, France, Germany, Italy, and Japan. The United Kingdom and the United States are not included because they are considered international financial centers. East Asia is the average of Hong Kong (China), Indonesia, Republic of Korea, Malaysia, the Philippines, Taiwan (China), and Thailand. Latin America is the average of Argentina, Brazil, Chile, Colombia, Mexico, Peru, and República Bolivariana de Venezuela. International firms are those identified as having at least one active depositary receipt program at any time in the year, or having raised capital in international markets in the current or previous years, or trading on the LSE, NYSE, or NASDAQ.

Figure 2.27 Internationalization of Stock Markets Relative to Domestic Activity, Selected Years

a. Market Capitalization of International Firms/Total Market Capitalization

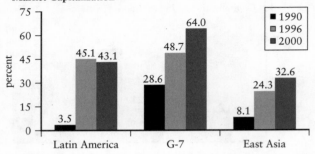

b. Value Traded Abroad/Value Traded Domestically

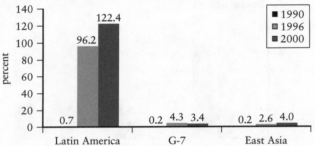

c. Capital Raised Abroad/Capital Raised Domestically

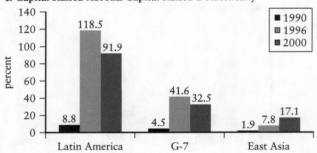

Sources: Bank of New York; Bloomberg; Euromoney; LSE; NASDAQ; NYSE; World Federation of Exchanges; Worldscope; World Bank.

Note: G-7 is the average of Canada, France, Germany, Italy, and Japan. The United Kingdom and the United States are not included because they are considered international financial centers. East Asia is the average of Hong Kong (China), Indonesia, Republic of Korea, Malaysia, the Philippines, Taiwan (China), and Thailand. Latin America is the average of Argentina, Brazil, Chile, Colombia, Mexico, Peru, and República Bolivariana de Venezuela. International firms are those identified as having at least one active depositary receipt program at any time in the year, or having raised capital in international markets in the current or previous years, or trading on the LSE, NYSE, or NASDAQ.

number of domestic stock market listings and activity, raising significant questions regarding the sustainability of local markets.[95] Internationalization may affect domestic stock market development adversely as a major share of market capitalization and trading migrates abroad, reducing the remaining companies' liquidity and ability to raise new funds.[96] Large scale internationalization may thus make it more difficult to sustain fully-fledged local stock markets. This might increase segmentation, since larger and well-known firms may be able to access international markets, but medium-sized firms might not be able to go abroad.[97] If internationalization adversely affects domestic stock markets, these firms might see their access to capital reduced as domestic markets shrink.

Latin American governments and firms have also participated very actively in international bond markets, with the total amount outstanding of international bonds from the region increasing from US$61.5 billion in 1990 to almost US$359.1 billion in 2004. Around 71 percent of this amount outstanding corresponds to government bonds. In terms of GDP, the average amount outstanding of public sector bonds from Latin American countries in international markets has increased significantly, from 10 percent in 1994 to 18.1 percent in 2004 (see figure 2.28). Private sector bonds in international markets have also grown over this period, but their increase has been lower than that of government bonds.

The amount outstanding of international government bonds in Latin America is significantly higher in terms of GDP than in other regions, standing at 18.1 percent in 2004, compared to 5.8 percent in G-7 and East Asian countries (see figure 2.28). The tendency of Latin American governments to borrow in foreign markets might be explained by the fact that in many cases foreign lending can be less expensive than domestic lending (or at least appear to be so) and that foreign markets offer longer maturities (see figure 2.17). However, foreign issued bonds are usually denominated in foreign currency, exposing governments to exchange rate risk, as government revenues typically relate to domestic currency values. The high level of government debt securities in international markets stands in contrast to the relatively low amount outstanding of private sector bonds. International private sector bonds in Latin America represented 4.8 percent of GDP in 2004, compared to 36.2 and 9.7 percent in developed and East Asian countries, respectively (see figure 2.28).

Figure 2.29 shows the amounts outstanding of public and private sector bonds in international markets relative to the domestic market. The top panel shows that there has been a significant decrease in the ratio of international to domestic public sector bonds in Latin America. This result is driven mostly by Mexico (and Brazil to a much lesser extent), where the domestic government bond market has grown significantly in recent years, while there has also been a reduction in foreign indebtedness. Despite this decrease, Latin American countries still have a higher amount of international government bonds relative to domestic ones than other regions,

Figure 2.28 Internationalization of Bond Markets Relative to GDP, Selected Years

a. Amount Outstanding of Public Sector International Bonds/GDP

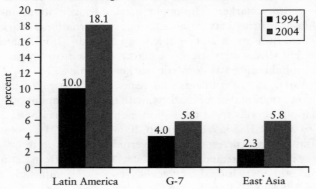

b. Amount Outstanding of Private Sector International Bonds/GDP

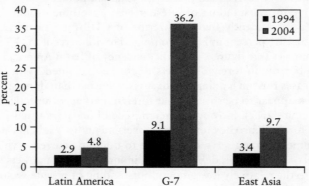

Sources: BIS; World Bank.

Note: G-7 is the average of Canada, France, Germany, Italy, and Japan. The United Kingdom and the United States are not included because they are considered international financial centers. East Asia is the average of Indonesia, Republic of Korea, Malaysia, the Philippines, and Thailand. Latin America is the average of Argentina, Brazil, Chile, Colombia, Mexico, and República Bolivariana de Venezuela.

Figure 2.29 Internationalization of Bond Markets Relative to Domestic Activity, Selected Years

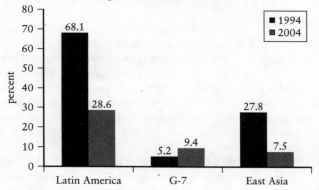

a. Amount Outstanding of Public Sector International Bonds/ Amount Outstanding of Public Sector Domestic Bonds

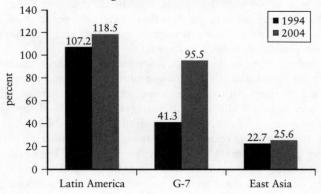

b. Amount Outstanding of Private Sector International Bonds/ Amount Outstanding of Private Sector Domestic Bonds

Sources: BIS; World Bank.

Note: G-7 is an average of Canada, France, Germany, Italy, and Japan. The United Kingdom and the United States are not included because they are considered international financial centers. East Asia is an average of Republic of Korea, Malaysia, and Thailand. Latin America is an average of Argentina, Brazil, Chile, and Mexico. Data for government domestic bonds excludes Argentina because of measurement problems after currency devaluation and default.

with this ratio reaching 28.6 percent in 2004, compared to 9.4 percent in developed countries and 7.5 percent in East Asia. Similarly, for the case of private bonds, Latin America shows a higher degree of internationalization than East Asia and G-7 countries.

Conclusions

Global financial markets underwent significant changes during the past decades. The global financial system expanded substantially since the early 1970s and boomed in particular during the 1990s. Financial intermediation through both financial institutions and securities markets expanded at a remarkable rate, and the spectrum of financial services and instruments reached new dimensions. Latin America was not immune to these global developments, and what happened in domestic capital markets was to a large extent a reaction to global forces linked to financial globalization and innovation.

This chapter has tried to provide a better understanding of the current state of development of Latin American domestic capital markets in light of the recent wave of financial globalization. After documenting the developments in international financial markets and the increasing globalization process, we describe how developing countries, and in particular Latin America, responded to these worldwide changes. Policy makers throughout the region pursued an extensive reform agenda in an effort to attract capital flows and emulate the role that capital markets have played in industrialized countries for economic development.

An analysis of the evolution of capital markets in Latin America in the last decades shows that the high expectations generated by the reforms have not been met. Although domestic securities markets in the region have grown substantially since the early 1990s, regional developments have been dwarfed by outcomes in both industrial and East Asian countries. A closer look reveals an even more disheartening picture. Latin American capital markets continue to be dominated by banks and are characterized by short-termism and illiquidity and, in several countries, by a high degree of dollarization. Although bond markets have achieved a significant increase in volume, most of it is accounted for by government paper. Private sector bond markets and stock markets show a high degree of concentration in both supply and demand and lack adequate liquidity.

Because the performance of capital markets cannot be fully understood without taking into account the recent trends in financial globalization, we also analyze the participation of Latin American countries (sovereign and corporate) in international securities markets. We find that Latin American firms and governments have actively joined the international equity and bond markets and that their participation has been very significant, both relative to GDP and to domestic securities market activity. Furthermore, the extent of internationalization of Latin American capital markets in most cases exceeds that of developed and East Asian countries.

The poor state of development of capital markets in Latin America and their high degree of internationalization raise several questions that are relevant for the reform agenda going forward. Is the development of securities markets in Latin American countries what it should be, given their economic fundamentals? Is the poor state of development of securities markets in the region the consequence of lack of reforms relative to other regions? Have reforms had the expected impact on domestic capital markets? Is the high degree of internationalization a result of the economic fundamentals of Latin American countries? How has internationalization affected domestic securities markets? All these questions will be explored in detail in the next chapter.

Annex: When "Marking to Market" Becomes "Marking to Model"

Illiquidity in securities markets is a major handicap because it undermines what is considered to be a distinctive contribution of capital markets to financial development: continuous price revelation. In highly illiquid markets, the important practices of "marking to market" and "fair value accounting" become inherently difficult.

It is in fact widely recognized that the book value is too crude a measure of economic value. The purchase price of an asset becomes a historical detail of little importance given inflation and continued asset repricing in light of changes in asset values. Thus, the best measure of value of an asset is given by the market price, provided that that market meets minimum standards of liquidity and transparency.

Therefore the idea of marking to market, that is, using secondary market prices as a measure of value, has become common practice. However, for marking to market to be the best estimator of value, liquid and transparent markets are essential. If markets are illiquid, or if market prices are not accurately observed, the observed market prices may be poor estimators of value. Marking to market of illiquid assets presents a real challenge for authorities in emerging markets, where illiquidity is widespread. To recover a "fair value" in the absence of frequently traded prices, authorities in emerging markets are forced to rely on "price vendors" who produce prices using different methods and models. "Mark to model" techniques, depending on the instrument, are based on matrix pricing, valuation models, formula-based pricing, as well as analogy to reliable quotations of similar instruments. Model-based valuation is not without shortcomings. Depending on the availability of reliable, relevant data, the significance of assumptions made, and the complexity and sub-jectivity of the overall valuation process, illiquid investments can be sub-ject to varying degrees of risk of material misstatement of value.

The Mexican experience in developing a methodology for the valuation of securities is instructive (Glaessner 2003). At first the authorities pro-mulgated regulations prescribing how valuation and marking to market were to be carried, but they failed to specify a well-defined framework. This resulted in confusion and uncertainty. As a remedy, authorities estab-lished a high-level technical committee that included specialists from the markets, regulatory agencies, the central bank, and other government agencies. In addition, special subcommittees were established to inves-tigate specific issues, such as the sources of information that would be used and how to assess the integrity of transaction prices. As a control instance, Mexico's banking and financial regulatory authority (the CNBV) was empowered to exclude certain transaction data to correct for price manipulation.[98] At first, model-based valuation was applied to the more liquid securities and then extended to less liquid securities. Over time, this approach has led to a widely accepted valuation convention and the gradual establishment of private independent price vendors, which are bound by strict standards.

3

Factors behind the Development and Internationalization of Capital Markets

THE PREVIOUS CHAPTER SHOWED THAT capital markets have grown considerably in developed and developing economies over the past two decades, though with high heterogeneity across regions and countries. This growth took place in a context of growing financial globalization—increased cross-border capital flows, substantial foreign direct investment in the financial sector, and securities issuance and trading that was increasingly taking place abroad. In this chapter, we analyze the factors behind the processes of domestic capital market development and internationalization of securities activity. Although the focus in this book is the experience of the Latin American region, the analyses in this chapter encompass the whole available sample of countries. This helps to understand more comprehensively the effects of fundamentals and reforms on capital markets.

We start by focusing on local capital markets and study two types of factors driving their development. First, we analyze the role of macroeconomic and institutional factors, such as monetary stability, fiscal policies, income, and the legal environment. How are economic fundamentals related to capital market development? We address this question by analyzing cross-country evidence on stock and bond markets over a long period. In the case of bond markets, we study not only their size but also their currency and maturity structure, as these issues have elicited significant interest among policy makers and academics alike, given their relevance to recent financial crises. We analyze how institutional factors relate to the currency composition of government bond markets and also discuss why emerging markets tend to borrow short term, even though this type of debt increases their exposure to liquidity crises.

Second, we study the specific role of reforms. Chapter 2 showed that over the past two decades many developing countries undertook extensive reforms to foster capital market development. This chapter investigates empirically how these reforms are related to domestic stock market development. The motivation for this analysis comes from the idea that reforms promote domestic capital market development and that markets in some countries have not developed because of the lack of reforms. This type of study is complementary to the analysis of economic fundamentals. Cross-country evidence might not be very helpful for policy makers interested in capital market development, as some variables are completely exogenous and/or beyond their control. Even panel data analysis may be of limited assistance for policy makers, as there may be little time variation in the macroeconomic and institutional environment, and panel results might thus be driven by cross-country differences. By shifting the attention away from estimating the cross-sectional relation between fundamentals and capital market development and focusing instead on the within-country changes in stock market development around capital market reforms, we tackle these problems.

Next, we analyze the internationalization of stock market activities (listing, capital raising, and trading abroad). Similar to the analysis of capital market development described above, our study assesses how economic fundamentals and reforms are related to the extent of internationalization in a country. Our main interest is to understand whether the factors that drive domestic capital market development also affect the internationalization process and, if so, in what direction. The outcome is not straightforward in principle. On the one hand, a good domestic environment could encourage firms to develop stock market activities in the local market relative to markets abroad, thus debilitating the process of internationalization. On the other hand, a transparent and well-functioning domestic market could induce international investors to offer better financing terms for local firms, thus deepening the internationalization process. Furthermore, we analyze how the stock market internationalization process affects the trading activity and liquidity of local markets. If the internationalization encourages the migration of trading activities toward markets abroad or produces a downfall in aggregate trading that reduces economies of scale, then it could hamper domestic market activity. If, on the other hand, internationalization promotes market integration and enhances market transparency, domestic market activity could experience a rise.

Finally, using the evidence on economic fundamentals and reforms, we further study the state of capital markets in Latin America. Why have Latin American capital markets grown less than expected? Is there a shortfall between the extent of reform in Latin American countries and the actual outcomes? Or is the state of securities markets in Latin America what it should be, given economic fundamentals and the extent of reforms? These questions have important implications for the policy debate and the reform agenda. To shed light on these issues, we study how fundamentals and reforms are related to the development of capital markets in Latin America in relation to other countries.

Although we believe that the type of analysis presented in this chapter is very informative, it also has several limitations, as mentioned in chapter 1. First, we look at one particular aspect of internationalization—the use of international capital markets by local securities issuers and investors. Second, we concentrate only on capital markets and on certain indicators to capture their development. Third, we omit studying how other parts of the financial system (importantly banks) and how aggregate savings are affected as the mentioned capital market indicators change. Fourth, to ascertain the determinants behind indicators of capital markets' development, we only estimate reduced form equations, without making explicit the underlying structural relationships and transmission channels. Fifth, although the empirical work presented here has tried to control for issues related to reverse causality and omitted variables, more research in this direction would be welcome to understand better the direction of causality and the role of other factors. Thus, the relations presented in this chapter should be taken more as associations among variables of interest, not necessarily as causal links. Despite these limitations, this book comprehensively describes and addresses key aspects of capital market development, including the local and international activity in emerging country bonds and stocks. This kind of approach has been mostly absent from previous studies.

The rest of the chapter is organized as follows. In the next section we discuss how the development of local capital markets is affected by economic fundamentals and reforms. Next we analyze the effect of these factors on stock market internationalization and discuss how the internationalization process affects local markets. In the last two sections we evaluate the state of capital markets in Latin America and conclude.

Factors behind Capital Market Development

Many factors are associated with the development of capital markets. In this section, we analyze the relation between economic and institutional fundamentals and capital markets. We also analyze how reforms are related to capital markets.

The Role of Economic and Institutional Fundamentals

In recent years, with the accumulation of evidence that financial development is not just correlated with a healthy economy but actually tends to cause growth, there has been increasing interest in understanding the determinants of financial market development. The literature has highlighted the role of several factors, including fiscal and monetary policies, income levels, and the institutional and legal environment.[99] Though most of these factors are associated with both stock and bond markets, a differentiation between the two types of instruments is worth making in order to analyze the distinct variables that may affect each of them.[100] For instance, the intrinsic characteristics of bonds make this class of instruments dependent on factors such as bankruptcy laws and currency regimes, which do not exert as large an effect on the development of stock markets. Stocks, on the other hand, do not generate balance sheet mismatches, neither from a maturity or a currency perspective, owing to the fact that this type of instrument does not expose the issuer to mandatory payments independent of its particular economic performance.

In what follows we discuss the relevance of four groups of variables that may affect both bond and stock markets. They are income level, macroeconomic policies, institutions, and size. Then we analyze specific issues of bond markets, such as currency composition and maturity structure.

First, the evidence suggests that more developed countries tend to have, systematically, larger financial markets. Figure 3.1 illustrates the relation between domestic stock market development and GDP per capita. Specifically, the top panel shows a bivariate scatter-plot of GDP per capita and value traded domestically as a percentage of GDP, and the bottom panel presents the same data using market capitalization as a measure of stock market development.[101] In both cases there is a statistically significant and positive relation between income level and stock market development. Figure 3.2 presents similar data for the case of bond markets. The top panel shows the relation between domestic government bond market capitalization and GDP per capita, and the bottom panel presents similar data for private bonds.[102] As in the case of stock markets, a strong positive relation exists between the development of domestic bond markets (both for government and private sector bonds) and income. These relations may be explained in several ways. Richer countries tend to have higher-quality institutions, including better property rights and rule of law, which could affect financial development (as discussed below). Also, less developed countries tend to have more volatile investment environments and a larger government involvement in the economy, which could affect financial markets.[103] The findings shown have been extensively documented in the literature (see, for example, Beck, Demirgüç-Kunt, and Levine 2001a). Moreover, there is evidence that economic development is associated not only with financial deepening but also with a shift toward more market-based financial systems (see, for example, Demirgüç-Kunt and Levine 2001).

Second, monetary and fiscal polices, as well as overall macroeconomic stability, are also positively related to capital market development. The reason is that financial contracting becomes more difficult in high-inflation environments. Firms and individuals find it more difficult to plan when future real values are uncertain, and therefore they are less likely to engage in financial contracting when inflation is imperfectly predicted. In addition, high inflation rates (even if predicted) can exacerbate credit market frictions, leading to credit rationing and lower investment. High inflation rates also distort relative prices and create incentives in favor of short-term

Figure 3.1 Relation between Domestic Stock Market
Development and Income Level

a. Domestic Market Capitalization and GDP per Capita

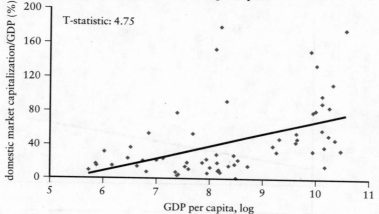

b. Value Traded Domestically and GDP per Capita

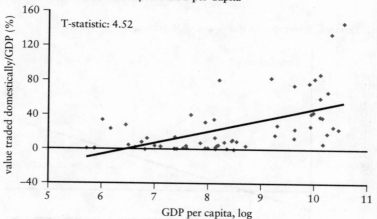

Sources: S&P Stock Market Factbook; World Bank.
Note: A value of 8 is equivalent to a GDP per capita of US$2,981. Data
are averages for 1990–2004. See annex table 1 for the sample of countries
included in the analysis.

Figure 3.2 Relation between Domestic Bond Market
Development and Income Level

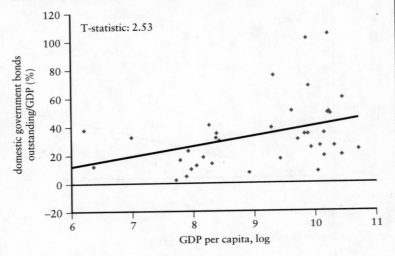

a. Domestic Government Bonds and GDP per Capita

T-statistic: 2.53

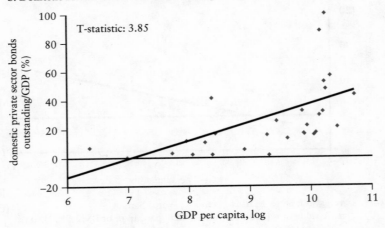

b. Domestic Private Sector Bonds and GDP per Capita

T-statistic: 3.85

Sources: BIS; World Bank.

Note: A value of 8 is equivalent to a GDP per capita of US$2,981. Data
are averages for 1994–2004. See annex table 1 for the sample of countries
included in the analysis.

projects, discouraging long-run investments. In the case of bond markets, this may result in short-term, variable-rate debt structures, or dollarized debt, as means to reduce exposure to unexpected changes in inflation rates. Fiscal policies may also affect capital market development. A large fiscal deficit may contribute to macroeconomic volatility, reducing incentives to engage in financial contracting. Furthermore, the need to avoid monetary financing of the deficit may lead the government to tap financial markets, crowding out private financing activities. On the other hand, if the government has modest financing needs, it may have little incentive to develop an active government bond market. This may negatively affect corporate bond market development, since well-functioning sovereign bond markets are key for providing benchmarks—including the yield curve for the presumably risk-free asset—without which corporate bonds cannot be adequately priced. In addition to the mentioned factors, the extent of price, trade, and exchange rate distortions in the economy may also affect the willingness of agents to engage in financial contracting.

The literature has highlighted the role of all the factors described above and empirical analyses find supportive evidence.[104] Most studies report a negative, albeit nonlinear, relation between inflation and financial development.[105] There is also evidence of a negative impact of price distortions and fiscal deficit on financial markets. Figure 3.3 illustrates the relation between fiscal deficit and stock market development. The top panel shows a significant and negative relation between value traded and fiscal deficit, and the bottom panel shows a similar relation between market capitalization and the deficit.[106]

Third, the legal and broader institutional environment plays an important role in the development of financial markets. Laws and enforcement mechanisms that protect investors, clearly define property rights, and support private contractual arrangements are crucial for the adequate functioning of financial markets. A large and growing literature on law and finance emphasizes the role of legal institutions in explaining differences in financial development across countries.[107] The empirical evidence shows that regulations that protect creditors and minority investors are associated with deeper and more active financial markets, increased valuations, lower concentration of ownership and control, and greater dividend payouts.[108] Figure 3.4 illustrates the relation between securities laws and regulations and stock market development. The top panel shows that countries with laws that better protect investors against expropriation by controlling shareholders have more developed stock markets, as measured by market capitalization over GDP. The bottom panel shows that countries where securities regulations require more extensive disclosure also have larger stock markets.

At a more basic level, some papers analyze factors driving the laws and regulations that underlie financial development. Some authors emphasize the role of the different legal traditions in explaining cross-country differences in

Figure 3.3 Relation between Domestic Stock Market
Development and Fiscal Deficit

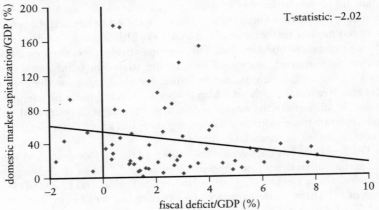

a. Domestic Market Capitalization and Fiscal Deficit

T-statistic: −2.02

b. Value Traded Domestically and Fiscal Deficit

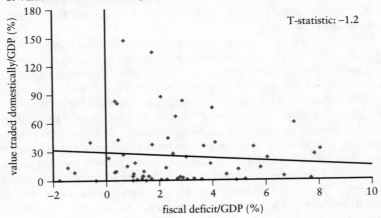

T-statistic: −1.2

Sources: S&P Stock Market Factbook, World Bank.
Note: Data are averages for 1990–2004. See annex table 1 for the sample
of countries included in the analysis.

Figure 3.4 Relation between Domestic Stock Market Development and Securities Market Regulations

a. Domestic Market Capitalization and Investor Protection, quintiles

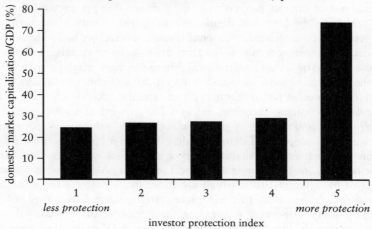

b. Domestic Market Capitalization and Disclosure Requirements, quintiles

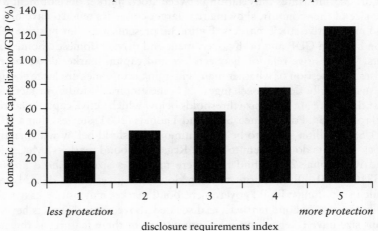

Sources: World Bank (2006); La Porta, Lopez-de-Silanes, and Shleifer (2006); S&P Stock Markets Factbook.

Note: Countries in 3.4a are grouped in five categories based on their protection of investors against expropriation by insiders as measured by World Bank (2006) index of investor protection. Countries in 3.4b are grouped in five categories based on their mandatory disclosure requirements, as measured by the disclosure index from La Porta, Lopez-de-Silanes, and Shleifer (2006). Higher values of the indexes imply better protection of shareholders and more disclosure. Data are averages for 1990–2004. See annex table 1 for the sample of countries included in the analysis.

investor and creditor protection and the contracting environment.[109] Others question whether the legal heritage is a crucial factor in explaining legal institutions, stressing instead that politics determine the extent to which legal systems protect property rights.[110] From this perspective, those in power shape the laws and regulations that affect financial development to protect their interests. Additionally, some researchers highlight the role of cultural differences in shaping attitudes toward financial development, while others stress that geographical differences have played a critical role in shaping institutions, including those related to financial markets.[111]

Finally, another factor that may affect capital market development is the size of the economy. Securities markets can gain efficiency by expanding their volume and number of participants through both supply- (economies of scale and scope) and demand-side effects (network externalities).[112] More information is available in larger economies, which reduces information costs for both foreign and local investors. Also, larger economies tend to have larger firms, which are more likely to meet the minimum size threshold necessary to achieve adequate liquidity. Economies of scale might also be important in creating the infrastructure for capital markets, because the costs of establishing clearing and settlement systems and developing the legal framework for issuing and trading are mostly fixed. Figure 3.5 illustrates the relation between stock market development and the size of the economy, showing that larger countries tend to have bigger and more active stock markets. Figure 3.6 presents a similar positive relation between GDP and both government and private domestic bond markets. The positive relation between size and capital market development raises the question of whether many emerging economies are large enough to sustain fully fledged exchanges.[113] Some empirical studies in fact suggest that there are some size thresholds below which active capital markets fail to develop. For instance, Shah and Thomas (2001) suggest that a GDP of US$20 billion seems to be the minimum threshold below which active stock markets do not seem to occur. Regarding bond markets, McCauley and Remolona (2000) find that there may be a size threshold around US$100–200 billion of outstanding domestic government debt, below which sustaining a liquid government bond market may not be easy.

In the case of bond markets, as discussed above, several aspects beyond their size have received much attention. One of these features is the currency composition of bonds. For some countries, particularly emerging markets, foreign currency debt can be less expensive than domestic currency debt (or at least appear to be so), prompting governments and firms to borrow in foreign currency. But foreign currency debt exposes issuers to exchange rate risk, as their revenues typically relate to domestic currency values. This mismatch increases the likelihood of financial crises and makes self-fulfilling runs possible.[114]

A separate literature has emerged that analyzes specifically the currency choice of debt and highlights the phenomenon of the "original sin,"

Figure 3.5 Relation between Domestic Stock Market Development and Size of the Economy

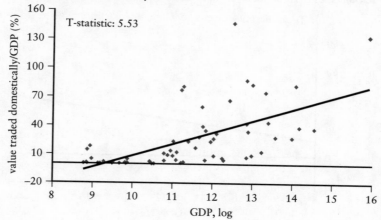

a. Domestic Market Capitalization and GDP

T-statistic: 4.06

b. Value Traded Domestically and GDP

T-statistic: 5.53

Sources: S&P Stock Market Factbook; World Bank.

Note: As a point of reference, a value of 12 is equivalent to a GDP of US$163 billion. Data are averages for 1990–2004. See annex table 1 for the sample of countries included in the analysis.

Figure 3.6 Relation between Domestic Bond Market
Development and Size of the Economy

a. Domestic Government Bonds and GDP

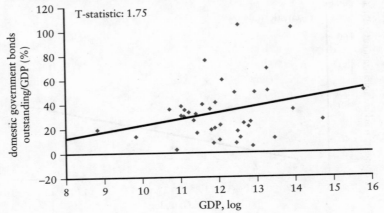

b. Domestic Private Sector Bonds and GDP

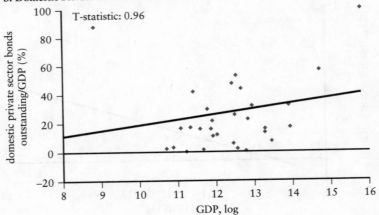

Sources: BIS; World Bank.

Note: A value of 12 is equivalent to a GDP of US$163 billion. Data
are averages for 1994–2004. See annex table 1 for the sample of countries
included in the analysis.

defined as the inability of emerging markets' governments and firms to borrow abroad in their domestic currency and to borrow long term at fixed rates in domestic currency in the local market.[115] This literature generally finds that only a small number of institutional and macroeconomic factors explain the ability of countries to issue domestic denominated instruments in foreign markets ("international original sin") and long-term domestic currency debt in domestic markets ("domestic original sin"). For instance, Eichengreen, Hausmann, and Panizza (2003) and Hausmann and Panizza (2003) find that only country size matters for explaining their measures of "international original sin."

While the original sin literature downplays the importance of specific macroeconomic and institutional factors and argues that it is difficult to pinpoint the exact causes behind the inability of governments to issue domestic currency bonds, it highlights the role of international factors and path dependence in foreign exchange borrowing. In the presence of international transaction costs, investors have limited incentives to hold currencies issued by small countries, since these countries offer limited diversification benefits relative to transaction costs. This implies that larger countries have an advantage when issuing debt in local currency, consistent with the results mentioned above. Additionally, this literature argues that historical factors have played a significant role in helping countries overcome the original sin and that network externalities have given rise to path dependence, since once a currency is used in some international transactions it becomes more advantageous for additional traders and investors to use it. This path dependence and the evidence from the original sin literature imply that there are few policy options available to emerging countries needing to raise long-term local-currency financing, as policy makers cannot alter initial conditions and improvements in policies and institutions may not affect their ability to issue domestic currency debt.

To better understand the determinants of bond market development we reconsider the hypotheses presented by the original sin literature and discuss empirical evidence on the role of size and currency composition. We depart from the original sin literature by focusing on the currency denomination of government bonds without distinguishing the place of issuance. In a world of increasing financial integration, investors are not restricted to the domestic market and can purchase bonds in foreign international markets. So, aside from the legal and regulatory considerations discussed elsewhere, the distinction between domestic and international markets is increasingly blurred.

The evidence suggests that there are several institutional and economic factors that do relate to the currency composition of government debt and the size of both domestic and foreign currency bond markets, which contrasts with the original sin literature. These factors are related to both domestic and foreign currency government bond markets in a similar fashion. In particular, countries with lower inflation rates, larger government expenditures, and more democratic institutions tend to have more developed government bond markets in both domestic and foreign currency. As high inflation is typically associated with macroeconomic instability and occasionally with government defaults, it can lower investor demand for bonds denominated in any currency. Larger government expenditures imply a larger demand for financing. The significance of government expenditure could also reflect an underlying desire of citizens for a larger distributive role of the government, both within a given period, through larger expenditures, and between generations and over time, through larger deficits and higher debt stocks. The finding that countries with more democratic institutions have larger domestic and foreign currency bond markets relative to their GDP suggests that these institutions are relevant for investors, arguably because they are associated with a greater credibility of the state, better quality of decision making, easier acceptance of government policies by the public, and more legitimate contracts.[116] Strong democratic institutions imply better systems of checks and balances which can reduce the (perceived) risks of default on government debt, including "default" through inflation spikes.[117] The results also indicate that foreign investor demand is associated with larger government bond markets in both domestic and foreign currency. These results are presented in formal econometric analysis in Claessens, Klingebiel, and Schmukler (forthcoming).[118]

As regards economic size, it is found to have a significant but asymmetric impact on domestic and foreign currency government bond markets, in accordance with the tenets of the original sin literature. The top panel of figure 3.7 shows that larger economies have more domestic currency–denominated government bonds as a share of GDP, and the bottom panel shows a negative relation between the size of the economy and foreign currency bond issuance. The results also indicate that countries with relatively larger banking systems have bigger domestic currency government bond markets and smaller foreign currency markets. Figure 3.8 illustrates these latter relations. The significance of the banking deposit variable might reflect the fact that deposit-taking banks directly invest in government paper as well as that a more developed banking system is associated with a larger investor base. A more developed banking system may also create demand for government securities among the general public through better-developed distribution channels. Those channels possibly include the presence of a primary dealers network, which may indirectly increase investors' interest in buying bonds, and more liquid secondary markets. These factors may reduce the need to issue foreign currency debt. In all, the results regarding the size of the economy and the banking sector suggest the existence of scale effects, implying that smaller domestic economies may find it relatively more attractive to issue bonds in foreign currency.

Figure 3.7 Relation between Government Bonds
Outstanding, by Currency, and Size of the Economy

a. Domestic Currency Government Bonds and GDP

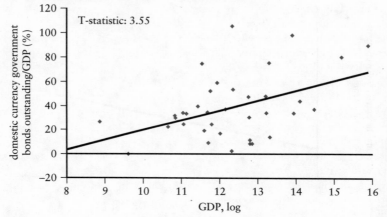

b. Foreign Currency Government Bonds and GDP

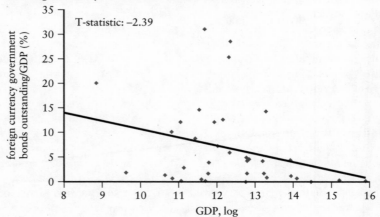

Sources: BIS; World Bank.
  Note: A value of 12 is equivalent to a GDP of US$163 billion. Data
are averages for 1994–2000. See annex table 1 for the sample of countries
included in the analysis.

Figure 3.8 Relation between Government Bonds Outstanding, by Currency, and Size of the Domestic Financial Sector

a. Domestic Currency Government Bonds and Total Deposits

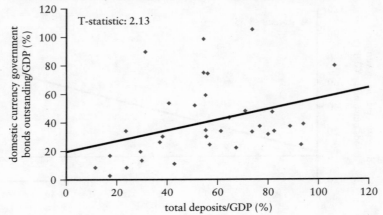

b. Foreign Currency Government Bonds and Total Deposits

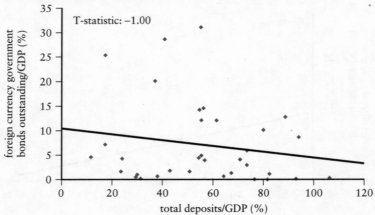

Sources: BIS; IMF; World Bank.

Note: Data are averages for 1994–2000. See annex table 1 for the sample of countries included in the analysis.

An important institutional factor that relates to the currency denomination of debt is the exchange rate regime. Some claim that a fixed exchange rate increases the incentives for both the government and the private sector to issue more foreign currency debt in the short run, feeding the process of "liability dollarization." Fixed exchange rates can, for example, generate moral hazard in the presence of (implicit) guarantees provided by international reserves or bailout guarantees offered by other governments and/or international organizations.[119] Also, governments with fixed regimes might want to signal the credibility of their regime by issuing relatively more foreign currency debt. As foreign currency debt tends to be cheaper (at least in nominal terms) where the exchange rate is pegged, it is difficult for governments to justify politically the issuance of domestic currency debt instead of less expensive foreign currency debt and, at the same time, claim that the supposedly rigid regime will persist over time.[120] In Claessens, Klingebiel, and Schmukler (forthcoming) the econometric evidence is consistent with these arguments—that is, that countries with a more fixed exchange rate regime tend to have smaller domestic currency bond markets and larger foreign currency markets.

The results presented above focus on analyzing the overall size of both domestic and foreign currency government bond markets. But what happens when one studies the currency structure of government bonds, that is, foreign currency bonds as a share of total? To answer this question, it is necessary to analyze the effect of the institutional and macroeconomic factors discussed so far on the ratio of foreign currency bonds to total bonds, that is, the share of foreign exchange–denominated government borrowing.[121]

The evidence indicates that the size of the economy and the ratio of deposits to GDP have a negative effect on the share of foreign currency government bonds; that is, countries with larger economies and relatively more developed financial systems have a higher share of domestic currency debt. Figure 3.9 illustrates these relations. The top panel shows the negative correlation between the size of the economy and the ratio of foreign currency bonds over total bonds, and the bottom panel presents the relation between the deposit base and the share of foreign currency bonds. Moreover, countries that follow a more fixed exchange rate regime and those with more foreign investor demand tend to have a higher share of foreign currency bonds.[122] Figure 3.10 illustrates these positive relations. Interestingly, the relation between foreign investor demand and the currency composition of debt is opposite to the one displayed by the domestic financial system variable (banking system deposits), suggesting that domestic investors tend to purchase bonds in domestic currency and international investors demand more bonds in foreign currency, which implies that the investor base matters. The results also indicate that capital account openness is associated with a higher share of foreign currency bonds. This is consistent with domestic investors being less restricted in

Figure 3.9 Currency Composition of Government Bonds:
Relation with GDP and Total Deposits

a. Share of Foreign Currency Government Bonds and GDP

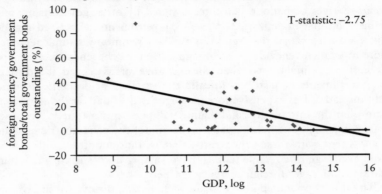

b. Foreign over Domestic Currency Government Bonds and Total Deposits

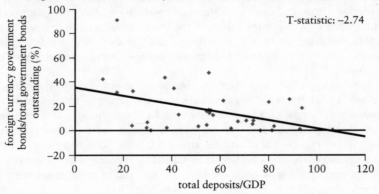

Sources: BIS; IMF; World Bank.

Note: A value of 12 is equivalent to a GDP of US$163 billion. Data
are averages for 1994–2000. See annex table 1 for the sample of countries
included in the analysis.

Figure 3.10 Currency Composition of Government Bonds: Relation with Exchange Rate Regime and Government Notes and Bonds

a. Share of Foreign Currency Government Bonds and Exchange Rate Regime

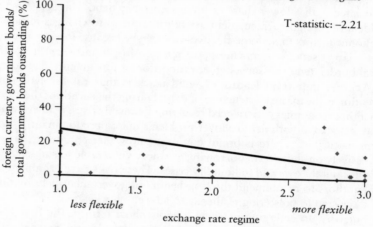

b. Share of Foreign Currency Government Bonds and Foreign Investor Demand

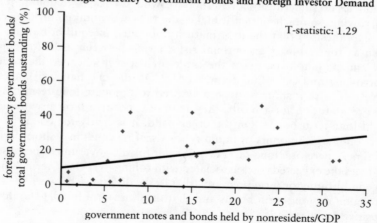

Sources: BIS; IMF; Levy, Yeyati, and Sturzenegger (2003); World Bank.
    Note: The exchange rate regime is measured by the index of the de facto exchange rate regime from Levy, Yeyati, and Sturzenegger (2003). Higher values indicate more flexible regimes. Foreign investor demand is measured by the government bonds and notes held by nonresidents over GDP. Data are averages for the 1994–2000 period. See annex table 1 for the sample of countries included in the analysis.

their asset allocation under an open capital account, leading them to demand less domestic currency debt. Similarly, foreign investors are more likely to invest in a country's bonds when its financial market is open, but they tend to do so by purchasing foreign currency bonds, as discussed above.

With respect to the impact of other macroeconomic and institutional variables on the currency composition of government bonds, Claessens, Klingebiel, and Schmukler (forthcoming) find that higher inflation rates are associated with a lower share of foreign currency debt. This suggests that holders of foreign currency debt are more sensitive to changes in macroeconomic factors than domestic investors, maybe because foreign investors face a larger set of investment opportunities. Also, countries with a higher fiscal burden tend to issue a higher proportion of foreign currency debt.

Another important feature of bond markets that has received much attention is the maturity structure of debt. During the decade of the 1990s, emerging economies experienced recurring financial crises, many of which were associated with debt rollover problems due to predominantly short-term maturities. There is broad consensus now that countries that rely excessively on short-term borrowing are more vulnerable to sudden reversals in capital flows and to liquidity crises. These risks have prompted several authors to recommend the lengthening of government debt maturity as a key step to bolstering resiliency to adverse shocks.[123]

But why do emerging markets borrow short term in the first place, in spite of the well-known associated risks? An obvious reason is that countries do so because short-term borrowing is cheaper than long-term borrowing, so much so that it makes the risks worth taking. It thus can be hypothesized that the debt maturity obtained in equilibrium can be seen as the result of an optimal risk-sharing between a debtor country and bondholders, given the trade-off between cheaper short-term borrowing and safer long-term debt.[124] On the one hand, risk-averse investors with a short horizon may need to liquidate long-term bonds before maturity. As a result, they require a positive term premium to hold long-term bonds. On the other hand, it is costly for countries to generate large amounts of liquidity (or fiscal revenue) in a short period of time. Therefore, long-term debt is safer for the government because it reduces the expected costs associated with rolling over short-term bonds. In equilibrium, the term premium (that is, the difference between the risk premium on long-term bonds and that on short-term bonds) should be positive on average.[125]

To empirically evaluate these theoretical predictions, Broner, Lorenzoni, and Schmukler (2004) use weekly data from 1990 to 2003 for eight emerging economies and compare it with data on sovereign bonds for Germany and the United States (considered default-free) to calculate yield spreads.[126] As predicted, the evidence shows that the cost of issuing long term is, on average, higher than the cost of issuing short term. When considering all the countries in the sample, excess returns are positive for all coupon sizes and maturities. More important, excess returns increase with maturity in all cases, so the term premium is also positive.[127] What do these results tell us about how much emerging market bonds pay relative to comparable default-free bonds? On average, investors receive an annualized return 3 percent higher when investing in a three-year emerging market bond than when investing in a U.S. or German three-year bond, and an annualized return 7 percent higher when investing in a 12-year emerging market bond than when investing in a U.S. or German 12-year bond. In other words, emerging market bonds pay a positive risk premium and a positive term premium. In all, the data show a negative relation between the relative cost of long- versus short-term borrowing and the maturity of new debt issued. In other words, when long-term debt becomes expensive, countries rely more on short-term debt. The evidence also shows that countries are less likely to issue bonds during crisis times and, more generally, when spreads are high.

The above results have important policy implications for the discussion on how to deal with financial crises. If moral hazard were the main problem behind government actions, efforts to avoid or reduce the cost of crises through loans from the International Monetary Fund or other liquidity provision mechanisms would exacerbate the moral hazard problem, thereby debilitating policy discipline and even reducing welfare. However, the evidence does not support the view that, where moral hazard is a problem, countries borrow short term in order to pre-commit to the right policies. If, on the other hand (and as the evidence discussed suggests), countries borrowed short term simply because long-term debt is too expensive, the same crisis-prevention mechanisms would improve welfare. The benefits would come not only from fewer and less severe crises, but also from cheaper long-term borrowing as a result of the reduction in the price risk of long-term debt.

The Impact of Reforms

As discussed in chapter 2, over the past 20 years, many countries fostered domestic capital market development by implementing significant reforms, including financial liberalization, improved systems for securities clearance and settlement, and development of regulatory and supervisory frameworks. However, capital markets in many emerging markets failed to develop as expected. The large number of policy initiatives and reforms and the disappointing performance of capital markets raise several questions. Is it possible that capital markets do not significantly respond to reforms and that policy prescriptions and expectations were based just on cross-country evidence, similar to the one reported above? Are other factors affecting domestic capital markets and driving out the impact of reforms? Is more time needed to see the full fruits of reforms? Were initial expectations too optimistic?

Answering these questions requires econometric analysis of the impact of reforms on domestic capital market development. As discussed above, this type of analysis complements the cross-sectional evidence on the role of fundamentals, as it concentrates on the within-country impact of reforms abstracting from cross-country differences. It also may be more informative to policy makers since it focuses on variables that are within their control.

In this section, we thus examine the evidence on the effects of capital market–related reforms on the development of domestic stock markets. We focus on six types of reforms: stock market liberalization, enforcement of insider trading laws, introduction of fully automated electronic trading systems, privatization programs, structural pension reform (i.e., shifting from a public, defined–benefit, pay-as-you-go system to a privately managed, funded, defined-contribution system), and institutional reform.[128] We also discuss the evidence from de la Torre, Gozzi, and Schmukler (2006b). Before presenting the findings, we briefly describe the reforms under analysis and the ways in which they were expected to foster domestic capital market development.

Stock market liberalization is the decision by a government to allow foreign investors to purchase shares in the local stock market and domestic investors to purchase shares abroad. International asset pricing models predict that the integration with world financial markets should lead to a reduction in the cost of capital.[129] A number of papers have empirically assessed the impact of stock market liberalization on the cost of equity capital, finding evidence of an increase in share prices around the liberalization date and a reduction in the cost of capital afterwards.[130] Other papers analyze the impact of stock market liberalization on real variables, reporting significant increases in investment and economic growth following liberalization.[131] Regarding stock market development, liberalization increases the pool of capital available to local firms and broadens the investor base. This is likely to lead to increased liquidity and larger amounts of research, improving the quantity and quality of information available to market participants. Furthermore, the scrutiny of foreign investors and analysts may increase transparency and promote the adoption of better corporate governance practices, reducing agency problems. Therefore, liberalization was expected to result in deeper and more efficient stock markets.

As described in chapter 2, over the past decades governments approved new laws and regulations aimed at creating the proper legal and regulatory framework for capital markets to flourish. Many countries tried to improve corporate governance practices by introducing new standards in a number of different areas, including voting rights, tender procedures, and the structure of the board of directors. Some countries also enacted new insider trading regulations and improved accounting and disclosure standards. As discussed above, the recent literature has emphasized the role of the protection of minority investors for the development of stock markets. Most of the cross-country data available for this variable are time invariant and therefore cannot be used to analyze the impact of reforms. An alternative to account for improvements in the legal framework for investors is to focus on the enforcement of insider trading regulations.[132]

Policy makers also made important strides toward establishing and improving the basic environment for market operations, including new policies related to centralized exchanges, securities clearance and settlement systems, trading platforms, and custody arrangements. These reforms were expected to improve market performance by increasing liquidity, enhancing efficiency, and reducing trading costs. Available evidence seems to confirm this expectation. For example, the introduction of automated electronic trading systems has been found to increase liquidity and improve efficiency by reducing transaction costs and increasing information availability; these trading systems also help in attracting new pools of liquidity by providing affordable remote access to investors.[133]

As described in chapter 2, in the last 20 years, governments all over the world have undertaken significant privatization programs. Worldwide revenues from privatization soared during the 1990s, peaking in 1998 at over US$100 billion. The privatization process was motivated by the desire to increase government revenues, promote economic efficiency, and reduce government interference in the economy. Domestic capital market development was also an explicit objective of privatization programs in many countries. Privatizations had a direct impact on domestic stock market capitalization, as many governments carried out privatization sales through share offerings on local exchanges.[134] Because of the positive externalities generated by listing decisions, these share issues were expected to foster stock market development by increasing the diversification opportunities available to investors and therefore encouraging trading activity and new listings by private firms. Share issue privatizations could also increase the participation of uninformed retail investors in local stock exchanges, reducing adverse selection in the market and increasing liquidity.[135] Privatization programs, even without share offerings on local exchanges, may also foster stock market development by reducing political risk and signaling commitment to market-oriented policies.

Another significant reform in many countries, especially in Latin America and Eastern Europe, was the shift from publicly administered pay-as-you-go pension systems to privately managed funded systems of individual pension accounts.[136] Among other benefits, structural pension reforms were expected to improve macroeconomic stability, by reducing the demographic pressures of pay-as-you-go systems and inducing fiscal reform to absorb the costs of the transition, reduce labor market distortions, increase aggregate savings, and reduce political interference in the system.[137] Pension reform was also seen as conducive to domestic capital market development through three main channels (Walker and

Lefort 2002): by inducing authorities to improve the regulatory framework (accumulating "institutional capital"), increasing specialization in
the investment decision-making process, and improving incentives for
financial innovation.[138]

As noted, cross-country evidence on the potential drivers of stock market development shows that countries with better institutional environments tend to have more active stock markets. However, for many developing countries it may be very difficult, if not impossible, to replicate the
institutional environment existing in developed countries, which is the
environment found to be crucially associated with capital market development. Therefore, it is important to analyze the impact of improvements
over time in the institutional environment (that is, the impact of reforms)
on stock market development, rather than the level of institutional quality
across countries.

Analysis of average capitalization, trading, and capital raisings before
and after the reform processes for all local markets that implemented a
specific reform suggests that these did have a positive impact on domestic
stock market development, contrary to the claim that they were not effective. Indeed, in some countries the observed increases in stock market
activity following the reforms are quite large. In the case of privatization, for example, the average stock market capitalization over GDP for
those countries that implemented the reform was 22 percent in the five
years before the reform, and the within-country difference between the
pre-reform (five years before) and post-reform (five years after) periods is
nearly 16 percentage points. Figure 3.11 illustrates these results. The top
panel shows the average domestic stock market capitalization over GDP
for those countries that carried out privatization programs for each year
around the initiation of these programs (five years before and five years
after). We observe a large increase in the average market capitalization
after the reform. The bottom panel also shows a large increase in value
traded over GDP following the initiation of privatization programs. Figures 3.12 and 3.13 present similar results for the introduction of electronic
trading platforms and improvements in institutions. In all cases, there is
a large increase in domestic market capitalization and trading following
the reforms.

To confirm these findings in a formal analysis framework, we refer
to the results in de la Torre, Gozzi, and Schmukler (2006b), who find
that all the reforms were followed by significant increases in capitalization, trading, and capital raising in the local market. Moreover, most
of these results are robust to controlling for domestic and international
macroeconomic variables. These controls are important because capital
market reforms can be contemporaneous to other policy changes (such as
macroeconomic stabilization programs, trade liberalization, and the eas-
ing of exchange rate controls) or may occur at high points in the domestic
and/or international business cycle, and therefore the observed increases

Figure 3.11 Relation between Domestic Stock Market Development and Privatization

a. Domestic Market Capitalization and Privatization

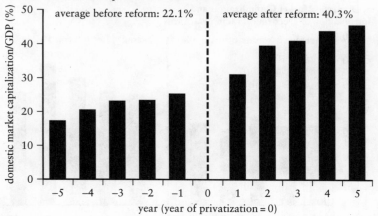

b. Value Traded Domestically and Privatization

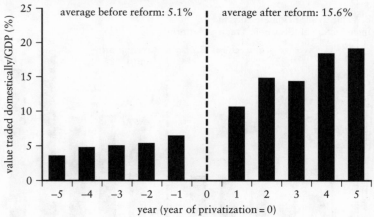

Sources: de la Torre, Gozzi, and Schmukler (2006b); S&P Stock Markets Factbook; World Bank.

Note: Data are averages for countries implementing the reform, with at least two annual observations before and after the reform. See annex table 2 for the sample of countries included in the analysis and the dates of the reforms.

Figure 3.12 Relation between Domestic Stock Market
Development and Introduction of Electronic Trading
Platforms

**a. Domestic Market Capitalization and
Introduction of Electronic Trading Platforms**

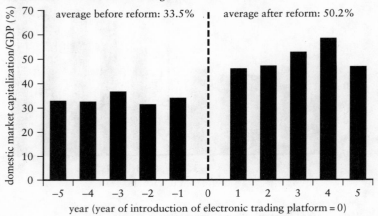

**b. Value Traded Domestically and
Introduction of Electronic Trading Platforms**

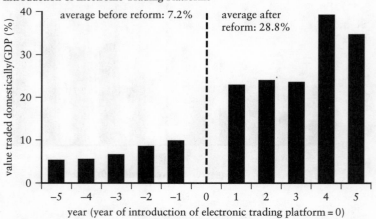

Sources: de la Torre, Gozzi, and Schmukler (2006b); S&P Stock Markets
Factbook; World Bank.

Note: Data are averages for countries implementing the reform, with at least
two annual observations before and after the reform. See annex table 2 for the
sample of countries included in the analysis and the dates of the reforms.

Figure 3.13 Relation between Domestic Stock Market Development and Institutional Reform

a. Domestic Market Capitalization and Institutional Reform

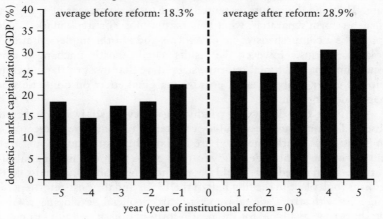

average before reform: 18.3%   average after reform: 28.9%

b. Value Traded Domestically and Institutional Reform

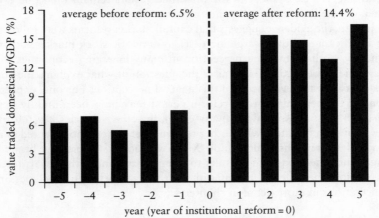

average before reform: 6.5%   average after reform: 14.4%

Sources: de la Torre, Gozzi, and Schmukler (2006b); S&P Stock Markets Factbook; World Bank.

Note: Data are averages for countries implementing the reform and with at least two annual observations before and after the reform. See annex table 2 for the sample of countries included in the analysis and the dates of the reforms.

in stock market activity could be explained by these factors and not by the reforms. Another concern when analyzing the impact of reforms is that most countries implemented several capital market reforms in a relatively short period. Thus, the observed changes in stock market activity around a reform may not have been caused by the specific reform under analysis, but rather by other capital market reforms implemented around the same date. Although the results presented above focus on measuring the impact of each reform separately, what may matter most for stock market development is a comprehensive set of reforms and not the implementation of isolated reforms. However, the results remain mostly unchanged when controlling for additional reforms, suggesting that most of the individual reforms under analysis had a positive marginal effect on domestic stock market development.

A difficult question when conducting an event study is whether the observed changes in the variables of interest (in our case, indicators of domestic stock market activity) are explained by some underlying trend and not by the event under study (capital market reforms in our analysis). In the case analyzed, this could be a significant problem, as most of the reforms took place in the first half of the 1990s and the post-reform period coincides with strong global trends toward financial development. Given the short time available for the post-reform period, it is quite difficult to statistically separate the impact of reforms from that of an underlying time trend. Nevertheless, most of the presented results remain the same even when controlling for possible time effects.

In sum, the evidence suggests that capital market reforms were followed by significant and quite large increases in domestic stock market activity, contrary to the prevailing perception in many emerging economies that they were not effective. This raises the question of what explains the contrast between the evidence and this general perception. For one, expectations at the beginning of the reform period may have been unduly optimistic.[139] Also, despite what many claim, in some countries key reforms were not even initiated, while other reforms were often implemented in an incomplete or inconsistent fashion. Moreover, policy makers have been too impatient, often expecting results to materialize sooner than warranted. We explore the different explanations for the gap between outcomes and expectations in more detail in chapter 4.

Stock Market Internationalization

As discussed in chapter 2, financial globalization advanced substantially over the past decades, with increased cross-border capital flows, tighter links among financial markets, and greater commercial presence of foreign financial firms around the world. An important element of this globalization trend has been the increase in the stock exchange activities that take place abroad, most notably for emerging markets but also for developed countries. Many firms now cross-list in international exchanges, with depositary receipts being a particularly popular instrument to access international markets. For several countries, activity abroad now exceeds domestic market activity.

This section analyzes the factors behind the internationalization of stock market activity and its effects on local markets. An important point to consider is that it is not straightforward to determine ex ante how different factors are related to the internationalization process, and therefore empirical tests are required to assess the validity of different explanations.

Factors behind Internationalization

We first focus on the relation between economic and institutional fundamentals and the extent of stock market internationalization. Then, we analyze the relation between reforms and the internationalization process.

The Role of Economic and Institutional Fundamentals A central question about the internationalization of exchange activities is how economic fundamentals relate to this process and, in particular, how internationalization is affected by those factors that were shown in the preceding section to drive the development of local capital markets. The answers to these questions are not obvious, and there are, in principle, at least two possible views on the relation between fundamentals and internationalization.

One view is that better institutional and macroeconomic environments spur the development of domestic stock markets, reducing the need and desire to use international markets. The first part of this view is uncontroversial, as the evidence and literature discussed in the preceding section illustrate. The second part is behind a number of recent papers on internationalization and is more debatable. According to this view, poor domestic environments prompt firms and investors to use international markets more intensively. An unfavorable domestic environment has long been considered one of the main reasons for capital flight and greater use by domestic residents of all types of financial services offered internationally.[140] Such an environment may also affect the services offered by stock markets, in which firms may want to escape a poor domestic system with weak institutions. Karolyi (2004), for instance, argues that the growth of ADR programs in emerging economies is the consequence of badly functioning stock markets, resulting from economic, legal, or other institutional forces that create incentives for firms to leave. Furthermore, some authors argue that international markets are more attractive to firms from poor institutional environments since they offer them the ability to "bond" themselves to a system that offers better protection to minority investors.[141] As a consequence, according to this view, poor domestic environments are associated with less domestic market development but greater use of international markets. It follows in this view that improvements in fundamentals that help develop domestic markets would reduce the use of international markets.

A second view considers that, rather, better domestic environments increase the attractiveness of assets to investors, raising the role of international markets. Markets in general will offer larger amounts of external financing, higher liquidity, and lower cost of capital when a firm's host country's fundamentals improve. Under this view, macroeconomic and institutional factors determine the relative willingness of domestic and international investors to supply financing to firms. Investors in international markets may, with the ability to invest globally, reward a better environment more than investors in domestic markets. Thus, better domestic fundamentals will, under this view, lead to more (not less) use of international capital markets.

Note that under the first view, any firm, regardless of its domestic institutional environment, can choose to go abroad and in so doing can escape a poor domestic environment. Under the second view, however, only firms from good institutional environments are able to go abroad, as the suppliers of capital grant them access to international markets at attractive enough terms.

In sum, though theoretical arguments are made for both a positive and a negative impact on internationalization of improved domestic fundamentals, empirical tests are needed to ascertain which view is best supported by the data. In this respect, figures 3.14 and 3.15 provide some initial support for the second view. The top panel in figure 3.14 shows that a positive association between GDP per capita and the market capitalization of international firms as a percentage of GDP. The bottom panel shows the positive correlation between the size of the economy and the level of internationalization. In figure 3.15, the top panel shows a positive relation between financial openness—measured by total equity flows over GDP—and the capitalization of international firms, and the bottom panel illustrates the negative relation between fiscal deficits and internationalization.

More formal econometric analysis shows that these results are robust. Claessens, Klingebiel, and Schmukler (2006) analyze the impact of fundamentals on stock market internationalization (listing, trading, and capital raising abroad) for a large sample of countries over the period 1984–2000, specifically the effect of fundamentals on three measures of stock market internationalization: market capitalization of "internationalized" local firms, value traded abroad, and capital raised abroad.

The results of the Claessens, Klingebiel, and Schmukler study indicate that stock market internationalization is influenced by some of the same factors that influence local stock market development. In particular, countries with higher income levels, a better enforcement of laws, greater financial openness, and better growth opportunities tend to see more activity

Figure 3.14 Stock Market Internationalization Relative to GDP: Relation with GDP per Capita and GDP

a. Market Capitalization of International Firms and GDP per Capita

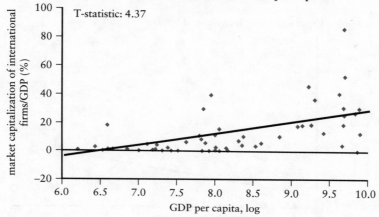

b. Market Capitalization of International Firms and GDP

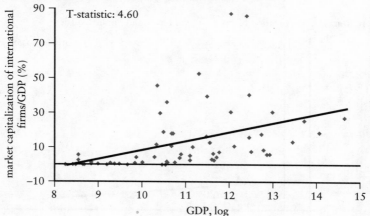

Sources: Bank of New York; Bloomberg; Euromoney; LSE; NASDAQ; NYSE; Worldscope; World Bank.

Note: In the top panel a value of 8 is equivalent to a GDP per capita of US$2,981, and in the bottom panel a value of 12 is equivalent to a GDP of US$163 billion. International firms are those identified as having at least one active depositary receipt program at any time of the year, or having raised capital in international equity markets, or trading on the LSE, NYSE, or NASDAQ. Data are averages for 1990–2000. See annex table 1 for the sample of countries included in the analysis.

Figure 3.15 Stock Market Internationalization: Relation
with Equity Flows and Fiscal Deficit

a. Market Capitalization of International Firms and Equity Flows

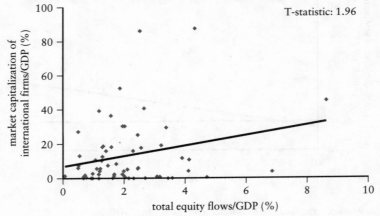

T-statistic: 1.96

b. Market Capitalization of International Firms and Public Deficit

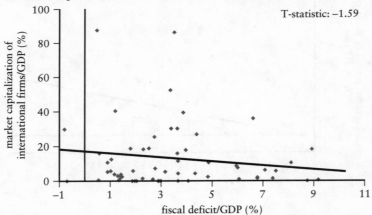

T-statistic: −1.59

Sources: Bank of New York; Bloomberg; Euromoney; LSE; NASDAQ;
NYSE; Worldscope; World Bank.

Note: International firms are those identified as having at least one active
depositary receipt program at any time of the year, or having raised capital in
international equity markets, or trading on the LSE, NYSE, or NASDAQ. Data
are averages for 1990–2000. See annex table 1 for the sample of countries
included in the analysis.

in international markets. Also, consistent with the results presented for domestic stock market development, larger economies tend to have a higher level of internationalization. On the other hand, higher inflation and government deficits tend to have a negative impact on internationalization. In other words, better economic fundamentals help to develop local markets *and* increase the internationalization of stock issuance and trading. These findings are at odds with the hypothesis that countries with worse fundamentals are the ones that see more stock exchange activities in international markets. Rather, these findings support the view that firms tap foreign investor bases more as their countries become more attractive.[142]

The results discussed above do not reveal whether the processes of local stock market development and internationalization are similarly sensitive to changes in macroeconomic and institutional fundamentals. A way to measure the differences in sensitivity is to study how fundamentals are related to the ratio of foreign to domestic activity. If foreign and domestic activities are affected in a similar fashion by fundamentals, then the mentioned ratio should not change significantly. Figures 3.16 and 3.17 illustrate some of these relations and suggest that improvements in fundamentals may actually boost internationalization more than local stock market activity. In particular, the top panel of figure 3.16 shows that countries with higher GDP per capita tend to have a higher market capitalization of international firms as a share of total market capitalization, while the bottom panel documents a similar positive relation between economic size and internationalization. In figure 3.17, the top panel shows the positive correlation between financial openness and internationalization. The bottom panel shows the positive relation between growth opportunities and internationalization, which suggests that firms with better opportunities tend to go abroad.

Again a more formal empirical analysis is needed to assess the foregoing bivariate illustrations. Claessens, Klingebiel, and Schmukler (2006) performed this analysis with the results indicating that the degree of internationalization relative to local market activity is in fact enhanced by better fundamentals. In other words, while stock market development and the level of internationalization are driven by the same factors, improvements in these fundamentals tend to accelerate internationalization. Specifically, increases in GDP per capita, reductions in inflation, improvements in legal institutions, more openness (both in terms of rules and actual integration), and better growth opportunities lead to an increase in the share of stock market activities (listing, trading, and capital raising) that take place abroad.

To further examine whether firms internationalize to escape poor domestic environments, it is useful to investigate the relation between internationalization and (past) stock market development. If local market development is positively associated with the share of activity in international markets

Figure 3.16 Stock Market Internationalization: Relation with GDP per Capita and GDP

a. Market Capitalization of International Firms/Total Market Capitalization and GDP per Capita

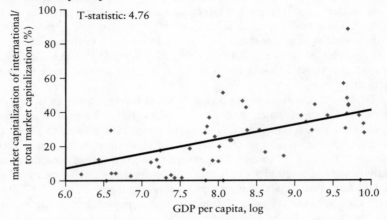

T-statistic: 4.76

GDP per capita, log

market capitalization of international/total market capitalization (%)

b. Market Capitalization of International Firms/Total Market Capitalization and GDP

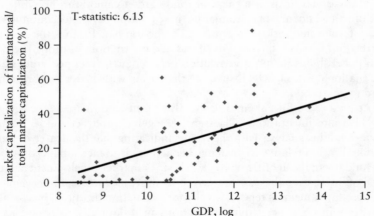

T-statistic: 6.15

GDP, log

market capitalization of international/total market capitalization (%)

Sources: Bank of New York; Bloomberg; Euromoney; LSE; NASDAQ; NYSE; Worldscope; World Bank.

Note: In the top panel a value of 8 is equivalent to a GDP per capita of US$2,981, and in the bottom panel a value of 12 is equivalent to a GDP of US$163 billion. International firms are those identified as having at least one active depositary receipt program at any time of the year, or having raised capital in international equity markets, or trading on the LSE, NYSE, or NASDAQ. Data are averages for 1990–2000. See annex table 1 for the sample of countries included in the analysis.

Figure 3.17 Stock Market Internationalization: Relation
with Equity Flows and Growth Opportunities

**a. Market Capitalization of International Firms/Total Market Capitalization
and Equity Flows**

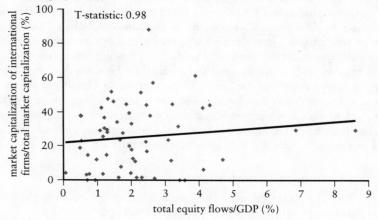

**b. Market Capitalization of International Firms/Total Market Capitalization
and Growth Opportunities**

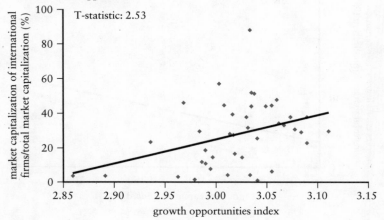

Sources: Bank of New York; Bloomberg; Euromoney; LSE; NASDAQ;
NYSE; Worldscope; World Bank; Bekaert et al. (forthcoming).

Note: International firms are those identified as having at least one active
depositary receipt program at any time of the year, or having raised capital
in international equity markets, or trading on the LSE, NYSE, or NASDAQ.
Data are averages for 1990–2000. The index of country growth opportunities
is from Bekaert et al. (forthcoming). See annex table 1 for the sample of
countries included in the analysis.

in subsequent years, then there would be further support for the hypothesis that countries with good domestic environments also experience more internationalization. A negative relation would support, on the contrary, the idea that firms internationalize in order to leave less-developed local markets. Figure 3.18 shows that domestic stock market development, as measured by market capitalization over GDP, is correlated with the degree of internationalization. Moreover, Claessens, Klingebiel, and Schmukler (2006) find that domestic market development is positively and significantly associated with subsequent internationalization. However, testing this relation is not straightforward, because the true underlying link between domestic stock market development and the degree of internationalization is not obvious, as countries with more developed markets may see more migration abroad, but stock market development may then be hampered by this internationalization. It is difficult to know whether one has the right econometric model, and therefore the results should be interpreted with care.

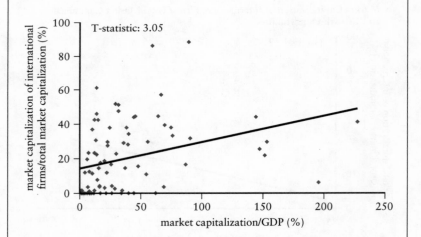

Figure 3.18 Relation between Stock Market Internationalization and Domestic Stock Market Development

Sources: Bank of New York; Bloomberg; Euromoney; LSE; NASDAQ; NYSE; Worldscope; World Bank.

Note: International firms are those identified as having at least one active depositary receipt program at any time of the year, or having raised capital in international equity markets, or trading on the LSE, NYSE, or NASDAQ. Data are averages for 1990–2000. See annex table 1 for the sample of countries included in the analysis.

In sum, the evidence is not consistent with the view that countries with bad fundamentals should see relatively more stock market international-ization (and less local market development). Rather, it supports the view that access to international markets depends in part on investors' assess-ment of the home country environment, and that better fundamentals make firms more attractive to investors in international markets. These results suggest that, while countries may worry about internationalization, the process of integration with the international financial system may be a natural part of their overall economic and institutional development.

The Impact of Reforms To complement the preceding analysis of the im-pact of fundamentals on stock market internationalization, it is also use-ful to study the within-country impact of capital market reforms on this internationalization process. As noted, this type of analysis may be more informative for policy makers, as it shows the impact of variables that are within their control. Furthermore, when reforms start to be implemented, there is the expectation that they will contribute to domestic capital mar-ket development, not only through their direct impact on local markets, but also by reducing incentives for firms to internationalize. By analyzing the within-country impact of reforms on internationalization we can test whether these expectations have been met.

We analyze evidence on the impact of capital market–related reforms on the activity in international markets (listing, trading, and capital rais-ing), focusing on the six reforms we've mentioned: stock market liberaliza-tion, enforcement of insider trading laws, introduction of fully automated electronic trading systems, privatization programs, structural pensions, and broader institutional reforms. Figures 3.19 and 3.20 illustrate the evidence. The top panel in figure 3.19 shows the average stock market capitalization of international firms five years before and five years after stock market liber-alization, and the bottom panel shows the average value traded abroad over GDP for the same period. In both cases, it is possible to see a large increase in internationalization following liberalization. Figure 3.20 shows that the introduction of electronic trading platforms and privatizations are both fol-lowed by large increases in the market capitalization of international firms over GDP. These relations are analyzed econometrically in de la Torre, Gozzi, and Schmukler (2006b), who find evidence consistent with these plots. The estimates show that these reforms tend to be followed not only by increases in domestic stock market activity, but also by a higher activity abroad. The results presented suggest that reforms may make local firms more attractive to foreign investors, who then grant them access to international markets at attractive terms. This is consistent with the results on the role of fundamen-tals reported above. Some of the results may also reflect the direct impact of reforms. In the case of privatization, for example, some firms were privatized through public offerings in international markets, which should have a direct effect on the internationalization measures analyzed.

Figure 3.19 Relation between Stock Market
Internationalization and Stock Market Liberalization

**a. Market Capitalization of International Firms
and Stock Market Liberalization**

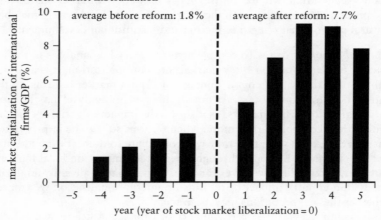

b. Value Traded Abroad and Stock Market Liberalization

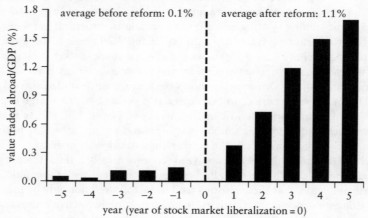

Sources: de la Torre, Gozzi, and Schmukler (2006b); Bank of New York;
Bloomberg; Euromoney; LSE; NASDAQ; NYSE; Worldscope; World Bank.
Note: Data are averages for countries implementing the reform, with at
least two annual observations before and after the reform. International firms
are those identified as having at least one active depositary receipt program at
any time of the year, or having raised capital in international equity markets,
or trading on the LSE, NYSE, or NASDAQ. See annex table 2 for the sample
of countries included in the analysis and the dates of the reforms.

Figure 3.20 Relation between Stock Market
Internationalization and Reforms

**a. Market Capitalization of International Firms and
Introduction of Electronic Trading Platforms**

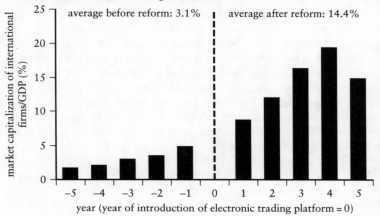

average before reform: 3.1%   average after reform: 14.4%

year (year of introduction of electronic trading platform = 0)

b. Market Capitalization of International Firms and Privatization

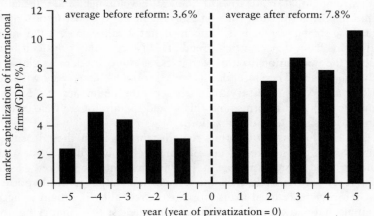

average before reform: 3.6%   average after reform: 7.8%

year (year of privatization = 0)

Sources: de la Torre, Gozzi, and Schmukler (2006b); Bank of New York;
Bloomberg; Euromoney; LSE; NASDAQ; NYSE; Worldscope; World Bank.
Note: Data are averages for countries implementing the reform, with at
least two annual observations before and after the reform. International firms
are those identified as having at least one active depositary receipt program at
any time of the year, or having raised capital in international equity markets,
or trading on the LSE, NYSE, or NASDAQ. See annex table 2 for the sample
of countries included in the analysis and the dates of the reforms.

A relevant question is whether the reforms are followed by similar increases in both domestic and international activity. To answer this question, we analyze the impact of reforms on the ratio of international to domestic activity. Figure 3.21 shows that stock market liberalizations tend to be followed by large increases in the market capitalization of international firms relative to total market capitalization and in the ratio of value traded abroad to value traded domestically. Although stock market liberalization is a necessary condition for internationalization to take place, this positive association is not obvious, as most countries opened their stock markets with the intention of attracting foreign investment and developing their own local financial markets, not to see their firms migrate to international financial markets. Figure 3.22 shows that the introduction of electronic trading platforms and the enforcement of insider trading regulations are both followed by increases in the degree of internationalization. These results can be confirmed using de la Torre, Gozzi, and Schmukler (2006b), who, in effect, find that most of the reforms under analysis are followed by large and significant increases in the share of activity that takes place in international equity markets.

As discussed in the section "The Impact of Reforms" in this chapter, a difficult question we encounter when analyzing the impact of reforms is whether the observed increases in stock market activity are caused by some underlying trend and not by the reforms themselves. Most of the reforms took place in the first half of the 1990s; the post-reform period coincides with strong global trends toward financial development and internationalization. Given the short time series available for the post-reform period and these strong trends, it is difficult to statistically separate the impact of reforms from that of a time trend. This is particularly difficult in the case of the internationalization variables, as there are data available for only one decade. Therefore, the evidence should be interpreted with care. Further analysis is necessary to clearly separate the impact of a common trend from that of reforms, and this would require longer time series of our measures of internationalization.

Our conclusions should thus remain tentative. But they do suggest that reforms did not result in a lower level of activity abroad and a concentration of stock market activity in the domestic market, as some arguments predicted. Rather, our conclusions support the hypothesis that reforms make local firms more attractive, allowing them to access international markets. These findings also suggest that financial globalization could pose a significant challenge to policy makers if, as some arguments suggest, the migration of trading to international markets adversely affects the liquidity of those firms that remain in the local market and their ability to raise new equity capital. We now turn to analyzing those arguments.

Figure 3.21 Relation between Stock Market
Internationalization and Stock Market Liberalization

**a. Market Capitalization of International Firms/Total Market
Capitalization and Stock Market Liberalization**

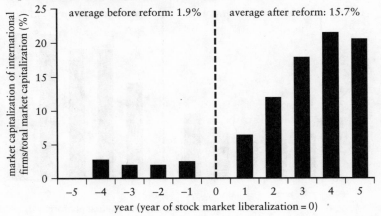

**b. Value Traded Abroad/Value Traded
Domestically and Stock Market Liberalization**

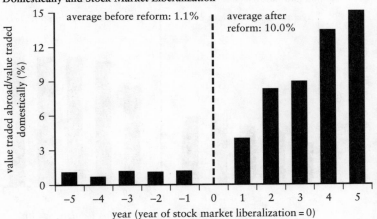

Sources: de la Torre, Gozzi, and Schmukler (2006b); Bank of New York;
Bloomberg; Euromoney; LSE; NASDAQ; NYSE; Worldscope; World Bank.

Note: Data are averages for countries implementing the reform, with at
least two annual observations before and after the reform. International firms
are those identified as having at least one active depositary receipt program at
any time of the year, or having raised capital in international equity markets,
or trading on the LSE, NYSE, or NASDAQ. See annex table 2 for the sample
of countries included in the analysis and the dates of the reforms.

Figure 3.22 Relation between Stock Market
Internationalization and Reforms

**a. Market Capitalization of International Firms/Total Market
Capitalization and Introduction of Electronic Trading Platforms**

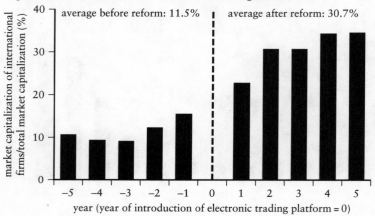

average before reform: 11.5%   average after reform: 30.7%

year (year of introduction of electronic trading platform = 0)

**b. Market Capitalization of International Firms/Total Market
Capitalization and Enforcement of Insider Trading Regulations**

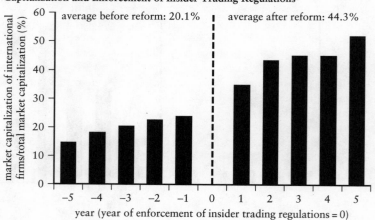

average before reform: 20.1%   average after reform: 44.3%

year (year of enforcement of insider trading regulations = 0)

Sources: de la Torre, Gozzi, and Schmukler (2006b); Bank of New York;
Bloomberg; Euromoney; LSE; NASDAQ; NYSE; Worldscope; World Bank.

Note: Data are averages for countries implementing the reform, with at
least two annual observations before and after the reform. International firms
are those identified as having at least one active depositary receipt program at
any time of the year, or having raised capital in international equity markets,
or trading on the LSE, NYSE, or NASDAQ. See annex table 2 for the sample
of countries included in the analysis and the dates of the reforms.

The Impact of Internationalization on Local Stock Markets

An extensive literature analyzes the effects of stock market internationalization on firms that actually access international financial markets, finding that internationalization tends to have a positive impact.[143] However, emerging market policy makers increasingly express concerns that even if internationalization is good for the individual firms involved, it appears to be hurting their domestic stock markets taken as a whole. Against this background, it is surprising that little research has examined the impact of internationalization on domestic stock markets and on the domestic firms that do not access international markets.[144]

The literature provides conflicting predictions regarding the impact of internationalization on local stock market trading and liquidity. Consider first the two-part "migration and spillover" mechanism. "Migration" means that internationalization induces a shift in the trading of international firms out of the domestic market and into international financial centers. This may occur because international markets have lower information and transaction costs (Chowdhry and Nanda 1991; Lang, Lins, and Miller 2003), lower settlement risk (Velli 1994), or more efficient risk pricing (Patro 2000). "Spillover" means that the aggregate trading in a market is related to the liquidity of individual equities. Using data from the United States, Chordia, Roll, and Subrahmanyam (2000), Hasbrouck and Seppi (2001), and Coughenour and Saad (2004) find that liquidity is not simply an asset-specific attribute; rather, an individual asset's liquidity correlates with market liquidity. Beyond the possibility that common factors influence the liquidity of all firms in a market, spillovers also might occur, whereby aggregate market activity influences the liquidity of individual firms. Spillovers could occur because of fixed costs associated with operating a market, such as running brokerage firms and clearing and settling transactions. With spillovers, therefore, the migration of trading of international firms could increase the per-trade cost of domestic stock transactions and reduce the liquidity of domestic firms. Combined, migration and spillovers imply that cross-listing or issuing depositary receipts in public international stock markets hurts the liquidity of domestic firms.

The internationalization process might also affect domestic markets beyond the migration-spillover channel. First, internationalization may induce a compositional shift in domestic market trading. Firms that internationalize may become more attractive to traders in the domestic market if internationalization induces improvements in reputation, disclosure standards, analyst coverage, and the shareholder base.[145] Thus, traders in the domestic market may shift their trading out of domestic firms that do not internationalize and toward domestic firms that do internationalize. All else being equal, this trade diversion implies less trading of domestic firms and more trading of international firms in the domestic market. Second, if it is more desirable to trade securities in major international financial centers, and if investors are concerned about country-specific risk, then as some firms from a country internationalize, investors will shift their trading of that country's risk (as embodied in both internationalized and domestic firms) toward the firms that migrate to the international market. Indeed, there is evidence that U.S. investors prefer ADR over non-ADR stocks of a given local firm.[146] The resultant shift in investor interest from trading of domestic firms in local markets to trading of internationalized firms abroad could hurt the liquidity of domestic firms beyond any effect of the direct reduction in domestic trading of internationalized firms.

Despite these predictions, some authors question the negative effects of internationalization on domestic stock markets. Hargis (2000) argues that cross-listings can transform a segmented equity market with low liquidity into an integrated market with high trading activity and liquidity. Alexander, Eun, and Janakiramanan (1987) and Domowitz, Glen, and Madhavan (1998) hold that internationalization stimulates domestic trading of international firms by increasing market integration. Moreover, Halling et al. (2005) find that foreign trading of European firms declines after an initial increase, with liquidity returning to the domestic market (the "flowback" effect). Also, if internationalization improves transparency, this could increase the domestic trading of internationalized firms with positive spillover effects for the rest of the domestic stock market. Moreover, integration may lead to trade creation at home—that is, it would induce a compositional shift in domestic trading toward domestic firms that do not internationalize—as the trading of internationalized firms migrates abroad. It is also legitimate to question whether the finding of spillovers in the U.S. market generalizes to emerging stock exchanges and whether investors indeed prefer international to domestic firms. Thus, the links between internationalization and domestic market liquidity remain open empirical questions.

To shed light on the effects of internationalization on domestic stock markets, we summarize our analysis of Levine and Schmukler (forthcoming),which assembles annual, firm-level data on trading activity for over 3,000 firms across 55 emerging market countries for the period 1989–2000. Trading activity is proxied by turnover, which equals the value of a firm's stock transactions divided by the firm's market capitalization.[147] The results support the view that internationalization is negatively associated with the turnover of domestic firms.[148] In particular, the turnover of domestic firms (those firms that never internationalize during the sample period) decreases as the share of international firms in the domestic market increases, after controlling for other firm and country characteristics that may affect trading activity, such as size, GDP per capita, and the institutional environment.[149] The results also indicate that there is a strong positive link between the trading of internationalized firms in international markets and the turnover of domestic stocks.

Some caution is needed in interpreting these results, however. Some may argue that they simply reflect the possibility that firms that internationalize are good firms and firms that do not internationalize are comparatively poor. Though potentially true, this would not fully negate the value of the results. First, some theories discussed above suggest that internationalization would boost domestic turnover by making markets more integrated. The results reported above provide no support for those arguments. Second, when controlling for firm quality, the same results are obtained. Third, the argument that bad firms will remain in the domestic market does not necessarily predict that trading in those firms will diminish as more firms in the country become international, which is what the results show. Fourth, the turnover of internationalized firms in the domestic stock market is found to decline with internationalization (see below), which is inconsistent with the simple story that the turnover of firms that internationalize increases while turnover of firms that do not internationalize falls.[150]

Although the results so far provide evidence of the adverse direct impact of internationalization on the turnover of domestic firms, they do not provide information on the mechanisms through which this impact works. To assess this, we further examine the channels through which internationalization affects the turnover of domestic firms by following again the analysis in Levine and Schmukler (forthcoming).

Two possible channels are migration and spillovers, as discussed earlier. To assess whether these channels are at work, we need to ascertain whether the trading of internationalized firms actually migrates from domestic to international markets and test whether this migration has adverse spillover effects on the turnover of the remaining domestic firms (that is, the firms that do not internationalize). The evidence is consistent with the migration channel: as the fraction of internationalized firms in a country increases, the trading of these firms shifts from domestic to international markets; that is, the domestic turnover of internationalized firms falls. Furthermore, there is evidence that adverse spillover effects are at work too. Specifically, the domestic trading of internationalized shares is strongly and positively related to the turnover of domestic firms. Thus, the data are consistent with the migration and spillover channels: as the turnover of internationalized firms in the domestic market dries up because of migration, the turnover of domestic firms diminishes because of spillovers.

Consistent with the migration channel, when a firm cross-lists or issues depositary receipts in a public international exchange (for example, the New York Stock Exchange, the London Stock Exchange, or NASDAQ), the domestic trading of its shares does not rise; rather, trading tends to migrate out of the domestic market and into international markets. However, firms that raise capital abroad *without* providing an easy vehicle for having their shares traded internationally tend to experience an increase, not a decrease, in domestic trading activity.[151] The migration channel is quantitatively important. Levine and Schmukler (forthcoming) find that, on average, the share of trading in the domestic market falls to less than 60 percent after internationalization, with no significant flow-back effect in the sample of emerging economies. Furthermore, the evidence using direct measures of liquidity constructed from daily data suggests that an individual stock's liquidity is closely related to aggregate trading activity in the market, which is consistent with spillovers.[152]

Migration and spillovers are not the only channels through which internationalization may adversely affect the trading and liquidity of domestic firms. In effect, Levine and Schmukler (forthcoming) show that the share of international firms in the market is negatively associated with the turnover of domestic firms even after controlling for the migration and spillover channels. This negative association points to a third channel: the trade diversion channel. The evidence in effect suggests that as firms internationalize, the domestic market intensifies its trading of the internationalized shares, while trading of firms that do not internationalize wanes. This does not offset the result mentioned above: internationalization leads to a net reduction in the domestic turnover of internationalized firms. The findings are consistent with arguments that emphasize that when a firm internationalizes, this enhances its reputation, transparency, and shareholder base in ways that make it more attractive relative to domestic firms. In sum, domestic trade diversion is another mechanism through which internationalization reduces the turnover of firms that do not internationalize.

Finally, there is another channel through which internationalization may affect domestic market trading and liquidity. Levine and Schmukler (2006) find that the fraction of total trading of a country's stocks occurring in international markets is strongly and negatively related to the liquidity of non-internationalized firms. For example, the results indicate that as New York becomes a more important trading place for Mexican stocks (relative to the total trading of Mexican stocks), the turnover of domestic Mexican stocks declines. Internationalization is thus associated with a drop in the trading of domestic firms, even after controlling for local market conditions. Although it is impossible to have only one interpretation of these results, the findings are consistent with arguments that investors seeking to hold country-specific risk shift their trading of a country's stocks to the lower-cost, lower-risk international markets when firms from that country internationalize. This shift reduces the trading of domestic firms in the local market, with negative repercussions on the liquidity of these firms beyond the effects of trading migration on domestic trading.

The results presented above have important implications. First, international financial integration could have distributional implications. Firms that internationalize win: internationalization boosts their total trading, reduces their cost of capital, and helps them to expand. But non-internationalized (domestic) firms lose. The liquidity of their shares falls as other firms internationalize. Thus, different firms are likely to have very different views about public policies related to internationalization. For instance, if there are high fixed costs of internationalizing and a country lowers its legal barrier to internationalization, then its largest firms will tend to benefit relative to smaller firms, for which the fixed costs represent a comparatively large barrier. It would be valuable for future research to explore more fully the country, industry, and firm characteristics that drive corporate internationalization decisions and to investigate whether domestic firms receive countervailing benefits from the internationalization process. Second, there is evidence of spillovers in stock markets around the world. This has potentially important implications for markets in an era of globalization. The prevalence of spillovers represents a powerful force encouraging liquidity to concentrate in a few major financial centers, domestically or abroad.

Though the discussion above has described some negative effects of internationalization, it does not imply that the overall effects of financial globalization are welfare reducing. In effect, we are not deriving welfare implications from this analysis, and the counterfactual is difficult to assess. We are only focusing on particular interactions between internationalization and domestic (especially stock) market development. In other words, the net effects of internationalization could be positive even if some firms stand to lose (as regards equity markets) from the process. In fact, the literature has highlighted many benefits from integrating with the international financial system. For example, internationalization might allow firms to access funds at lower cost and longer maturities, as well as help supply funds to savings-scarce countries, where the marginal product of capital is relatively high. Moreover, the internationalization process could enhance transparency and monitoring in domestic capital markets and reduce information costs. Because of these contradictory effects, the jury is still out on the overall welfare effects of internationalization.[153] We now know better some of the specific channels through which internationalization affects the financial system, but the pros and cons of the internationalization process need to be better understood and analyzed in a more comprehensive manner.

Domestic Capital Market Development in Latin America

As illustrated in chapter 2, the state of securities markets in Latin America is rather disheartening given the intensity of the reform effort. In particular, Latin American capital markets remain underdeveloped when compared with markets in industrial and East Asian countries. In this section, we discuss formal evidence to further understand how the state of stock markets in Latin America differs from that in other regions. The section "Factors behind Capital Market Development" shows that improvements in macroeconomic and institutional fundamentals lead to more domestic stock market activity and that the implementation of capital market reforms spurs domestic stock market development. Using these findings, this section evaluates the state of Latin American stock markets. In particular, we are interested in assessing whether there is a gap between fundamentals and policies, on the one hand, and actual stock market development, on the other. This issue is highly relevant for the policy debate, as we discuss in more detail in chapter 4.

One possibility is that there is not such gap—that is, that the observed lag in capital market development in Latin America relative to other regions is consistent with poorer macroeconomic and institutional fundamentals in Latin America. If that were the case, there would be an unambiguous argument in favor of forging ahead with the reform effort, as conventionally defined, in order to improve economic and institutional fundamentals, which in turn should result in more developed capital markets. What if, alternatively, there is such a gap—that is, that the actual development of local capital markets in Latin America is significantly below what would be predicted by its economic and institutional fundamentals? If that were the case, it would follow that reforms and improvements in fundamentals have so far not had the expected results in Latin America. This result would instead suggest the need to revisit and revise the reform agenda and related expectations to take into account certain characteristics of these countries that may limit the scope for developing deep domestic securities markets.

The way to unveil whether the mentioned gap exists is through formal empirical analysis, taking into account the effect of observable differences in fundamentals across the relevant regions and, subsequently, comparing their relative performance. To do this, we extend the methodology used in de la Torre, Gozzi, and Schmukler (2006b), which analyzed the impact of economic and institutional fundamentals on domestic stock market activity (measured using three different variables: market capitalization, value traded, and capital raised, all as a percentage of GDP) for 117 countries for the 1975–2004 period. The methodological extension focuses on gauging the performance of Latin American markets relative to other regions and to the rest of the sample.

Our results indicate that, after controlling for many relevant factors, including per capita income, macroeconomic policies, and measures of the legal and institutional environment, capital markets in Latin America exhibit a systematically lower-than-expected level of development. In other words, Latin American countries have smaller and less active stock markets than countries with similar fundamentals and policies in other regions.[154] Moreover, the differences are quite large. For instance, market capitalization over GDP in Latin American countries is, on average, 16 percentage points below the level predicted by their institutional fundamentals and macroeconomic policies. The quantitative significance of this estimate is clearer when one considers that the average market capitalization over GDP for Latin American countries included in the analysis is 18 percent. Figure 3.23 illustrates these results. It compares each country's actual stock market development with the level predicted on the basis of its economic and institutional fundamentals for a sample of Latin American countries.[155] The top panel shows the results for market capitalization over GDP, and the bottom panel presents the results for value traded abroad over GDP. In virtually all cases, there is a gap, in the sense that the predicted level of stock market development (especially when measured by the ratio of value traded to GDP) is higher than the one actually observed. In other words, local stock markets in Latin American countries should be higher if the quality of their macro policies and institutions are all that matter.

A significant concern with this type of analysis is whether some variables that may affect capital market development are not included—that is, that omitted variables would account for what appears to be a lag in the development of Latin American local stock markets. To address this concern, we tested several additional control variables suggested by the literature. First, we controlled for macroeconomic volatility, including measures of inflation and interest rate volatility at different time horizons. Second, we also tried alternative measures of the quality of the institutional environment, including indicators of corruption, bureaucratic quality, political risk, government stability, expropriation risk, accounting standards, the functioning of the judicial system, and legal tradition. Third, we also controlled for the size of the economy. Finally, measures of a country's savings rate were included, to gauge the resources available for investment in the domestic financial system. In all cases the results proved to be robust and, hence, the puzzle remained: Latin American countries have smaller and less active domestic stock markets, after controlling for a host of variables that may affect stock market development. This suggests that certain intrinsic yet not fully understood features of the Latin American countries, beyond those usually highlighted by the capital market development literature, are limiting local stock market development in the region. Some potential candidates to help deal with this puzzle could be the different histories of default experiences and disparities in aggregate saving rates across countries and regions. Nevertheless, this is a much broader topic that needs to be carefully addressed within a formal framework, which we leave for future research.

Conclusions

This chapter has summarized formal empirical evidence on the factors behind the development of capital markets and their internationalization. First, the study of macroeconomic and institutional factors shows that size

Figure 3.23 Actual and Predicted Domestic Stock Market Development, Selected Latin American Countries

a. Domestic Market Capitalization

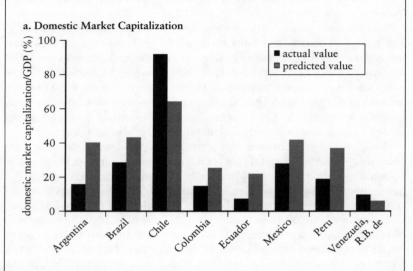

b. Value Traded Domestically

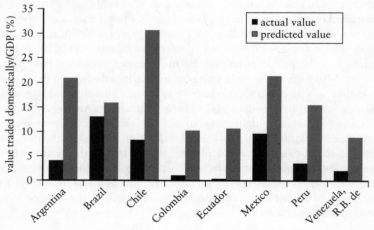

Sources: de la Torre, Gozzi, and Schmukler (2006b); S&P Stock Market Factbook; World Bank.

Note: Predicted values are estimated from a regression of the variables of interest on GDP per capita, fiscal deficit over GDP, and total equity flows over GDP, and shareholder rights for a sample of 63 countries over 1975–2004. The data displayed are averages for 1990–2004.

matters for capital market development. The size of the economy is a key determinant of both domestic stock and bond market development. Also, countries with a higher GDP and larger banking systems tend to have a higher share of local currency government bonds, which makes them less exposed to currency risk.

Second, the evidence suggests that the processes of domestic stock market development and internationalization are driven by the same factors. Improvements in economic fundamentals and the introduction of reforms lead to more domestic stock market activity but are also associated with a higher internationalization of stock issuance and trading. Moreover, reforms and improvements in fundamentals appear to have a pro-internationalization bias—they are associated with an increase in the ratio of stock market activities taking place abroad over local stock market activity.

Third, the evidence shows that the financial globalization process may have adverse implications for domestic stock market development. In particular, stock market internationalization reduces the domestic trading activity and liquidity of those firms that do not internationalize. This could have significant implications, as lower liquidity has been found to be associated with higher cost of capital, poorer firm performance, and lower economic growth. On the other hand, internationalization has been found to help those firms that access international markets. All of these results can create tensions for policy and raise critical questions for future research. Do domestic firms receive countervailing benefits from the internationalization process? What is the net effect for the domestic economy of stock market internationalization? What is the future for domestic markets and companies that are unable to internationalize? And, in the case of bond markets, does internationalization have negative consequences on the maturity structure of government bonds to the extent that international investors may require a higher term premium than domestic investors?

Finally, the results indicate that the level of local stock market development in Latin America is below what can be expected, given the region's economic and institutional fundamentals. In particular, our results show a shortfall in domestic stock market activity (market capitalization, trading, and capital raising) in the region after controlling for many relevant factors, including per capita income, macroeconomic policies, and measures of the legal and institutional environment. This suggests that certain intrinsic features of these countries, that are beyond those usually highlighted by the capital market development literature but that are still not well understood, may limit the scope for developing deep stock markets in the region. Further research is needed to explain this puzzling fact unearthed by the empirical analysis.

Annex—Table 1 Economies Included in the Analyses

Domestic Market Capitalization	Argentina, Armenia, Australia, Austria, Azerbaijan, Bahrain, Bangladesh, Barbados, Belgium, Bermuda, Bhutan, Bolivia, Botswana, Brazil, Bulgaria, Canada, Cayman Islands, Chile, China, Colombia, Costa Rica, Côte d'Ivoire, Croatia, Cyprus, Czech Republic, Denmark, Dominican Republic, Ecuador, Egypt, El Salvador, Estonia, Fiji, Finland, France, Georgia, Germany, Ghana, Greece, Guatemala, Guyana, Honduras, Hong Kong (China), Hungary, Iceland, India, Indonesia, Islamic Republic of Iran, Ireland, Israel, Italy, Jamaica, Japan, Jordan, Kazakhstan, Kenya, Republic of Korea, Kuwait, Kyrgyz Republic, Latvia, Lebanon, Lithuania, Luxembourg, Macao (China), FYR Macedonia, Malawi, Malaysia, Malta, Mauritania, Mauritius, Mexico, Moldova, Mongolia, Morocco, Namibia, Nepal, the Netherlands, Netherlands Antilles, New Zealand, Nigeria, Norway, Oman, Pakistan, Panama, Papua New Guinea, Paraguay, Peru, the Philippines, Poland, Portugal, Qatar, Romania, Russia, Saudi Arabia, Serbia and Montenegro, Singapore, Slovak Republic, Slovenia, South Africa, Spain, Sri Lanka, Swaziland, Sweden, Switzerland, Taiwan (China), Tanzania, Thailand, Trinidad and Tobago, Tunisia, Turkey, Uganda, Ukraine, the United Arab Emirates, the United Kingdom, the United States, Uruguay, Uzbekistan, República Bolivariana de Venezuela, West Bank and Gaza, Zambia, and Zimbabwe.
International Market Capitalization	Argentina, Australia, Austria, Bangladesh, Belgium, Botswana, Brazil, Bulgaria, Canada, Chile, China, Colombia, Côte d'Ivoire, Croatia, Czech Republic, Denmark, Ecuador, Egypt, Estonia, Finland, France, Germany, Ghana, Greece, Hong Kong (China), Hungary, India, Indonesia, Ireland, Israel, Italy, Jamaica, Japan, Jordan, Kazakhstan, Kenya, Republic of Korea, Latvia, Lithuania, Luxembourg, Malaysia, Malta, Mauritius, Mexico, Morocco, the Netherlands, New Zealand, Nigeria, Norway, Pakistan, Peru, the Philippines, Poland, Portugal, Romania, Russia, Saudi Arabia, Singapore, Slovak Republic, Slovenia, South Africa, Spain, Sri Lanka, Sweden, Switzerland, Taiwan (China), Thailand, Trinidad and Tobago, Tunisia, Turkey, Ukraine, República Bolivariana de Venezuela, and Zimbabwe.

Annex—Table 1 Economies Included in the Analyses *(continued)*

Value Traded Domestically	Argentina, Armenia, Australia, Austria, Bahrain, Bangladesh, Barbados, Belgium, Bermuda, Bolivia, Botswana, Brazil, Bulgaria, Canada, Chile, China, Colombia, Costa Rica, Côte d'Ivoire, Croatia, Cyprus, Czech Republic, Denmark, Ecuador, Egypt, El Salvador, Estonia, Fiji, Finland, France, Georgia, Germany, Ghana, Greece, Guatemala, Guyana, Hong Kong (China), Hungary, Iceland, India, Indonesia, Islamic Republic of Iran, Ireland, Israel, Italy, Jamaica, Japan, Jordan, Kazakhstan, Kenya, Republic of Korea, Kuwait, Kyrgyz Republic, Latvia, Lebanon, Lithuania, Luxembourg, Macao (China), FYR Macedonia, Malawi, Malaysia, Malta, Mauritius, Mexico, Moldova, Mongolia, Morocco, Namibia, Nepal, the Netherlands, New Zealand, Nigeria, Norway, Oman, Pakistan, Panama, Papua New Guinea, Paraguay, Peru, the Philippines, Poland, Portugal, Qatar, Romania, Russia, Saudi Arabia, Serbia and Montenegro, Singapore, Slovak Republic, Slovenia, South Africa, Spain, Sri Lanka, Swaziland, Sweden, Switzerland, Taiwan (China), Tanzania, Thailand, Trinidad and Tobago, Tunisia, Turkey, Uganda, Ukraine, the United Arab Emirates, the United Kingdom, the United States, Uruguay, Uzbekistan, República Bolivariana de Venezuela, West Bank and Gaza, Zambia, and Zimbabwe.
Value Traded Abroad	Argentina, Australia, Austria, Bangladesh, Belgium, Botswana, Brazil, Bulgaria, Canada, Chile, China, Colombia, Côte d'Ivoire, Croatia, Czech Republic, Denmark, Ecuador, Egypt, Estonia, Finland, France, Germany, Ghana, Greece, Hong Kong (China), Hungary, India, Indonesia, Ireland, Israel, Italy, Jamaica, Japan, Jordan, Kazakhstan, Kenya, Republic of Korea, Latvia, Lithuania, Luxembourg, Malaysia, Malta, Mauritius, Mexico, Morocco, the Netherlands, New Zealand, Nigeria, Norway, Pakistan, Peru, the Philippines, Poland, Portugal, Romania, Russia, Saudi Arabia, Singapore, Slovak Republic, Slovenia, South Africa, Spain, Sri Lanka, Sweden, Switzerland, Taiwan (China), Thailand, Trinidad and Tobago, Tunisia, Turkey, Ukraine, República Bolivariana de Venezuela, and Zimbabwe.

Annex—Table 2 Economies That Implemented Reforms, and Year Implemented

Introduction of Electronic Trading Platforms	Armenia (1996), Australia (1987), Austria (1996), Azerbaijan (1997), The Bahamas (2000), Bahrain (1999), Bangladesh (1998), Barbados (2000), Belgium (1996), Bermuda (1998), Brunei (2002), Bulgaria (1997), Canada (1977), Cayman Islands (1997), Channel Islands (1998), China (1990), Colombia (1996), Costa Rica (1991), Côte d'Ivoire (1999), Croatia (1999), Cyprus (1999), Czech Republic (1998), Denmark (1988), El Salvador (1994), Estonia (1996), Finland (1988), France (1986), Georgia (2000), Greece (1992), Honduras (1993), Hong Kong (China) (1986), Hungary (1998), Iceland (1989), India (1995), Indonesia (1995), Islamic Republic of Iran (1994), Ireland (2000), Israel (1997), Italy (1994), Jamaica (2000), Japan (1982), Jordan (2000), Kazakhstan (1997), Republic of Korea (1988), Kuwait (1995), Kyrgyz Republic (1999), Latvia (1997), Lithuania (1993), Luxembourg (1991), FYR Macedonia (2001), Malaysia (1992), Malta (1996), Mauritius (2001), Mexico (1996), Moldova (1998), Mongolia (1999), Morocco (1997), Mozambique (1999), Namibia (1998), the Netherlands (1994), New Zealand (1991), Nigeria (1999), Norway (1988), Oman (1998), Pakistan (1997), Panama (1999), Papua New Guinea (1999), the Philippines (1993), Poland (1996), Portugal (1991), Romania (1995), Russia (1994), Saudi Arabia (1990), Singapore (1989), Slovak Republic (1994), Slovenia (1993), South Africa (1996), Spain (1989), Sri Lanka (1997), Sweden (1989), Switzerland (1996), Taiwan (China) (1985), Thailand (1991), Tunisia (1996), Turkey (1993), Ukraine (1996), the United Arab Emirates (2000), Uruguay (1994), Uzbekistan (1996), and República Bolivariana de Venezuela (1992).
Enforcement of Insider Trading Regulations	Argentina (1995), Australia (1996), Bangladesh (1998), Belgium (1994), Brazil (1978), Canada (1976), Chile (1996), Czech Republic (1993), Denmark (1996), Finland (1993), France (1975), Germany (1995), Greece (1996), Hong Kong (China) (1994), Hungary (1995), India (1998), Indonesia (1996), Israel (1989), Italy (1996), Japan (1990), Republic of Korea (1988), Malaysia (1996), the Netherlands (1994), Norway (1990), Oman (1999), Peru (1994), Poland (1993), Singapore (1978), Slovenia (1998), Spain (1998), Sri Lanka (1996), Sweden (1990), Switzerland (1995), Taiwan (China) (1989), Thailand (1993), Turkey (1996), the United Kingdom (1981), and the United States (1961).

(continued)

Annex—Table 2 Economies That Implemented Reforms, and Year Implemented *(continued)*

Stock Market Liberalization	Argentina (1989), Bangladesh (1991), Botswana (1990), Brazil (1991), Bulgaria (1992), Canada (1973), Chile (1992), Colombia (1991), Côte d'Ivoire (1995), Czech Republic (1993), Denmark (1973), Ecuador (1994), Egypt (1992), Estonia (1996), Finland (1990), France (1973), Germany (1973), Ghana (1993), Greece (1987), Hong Kong (China) (1973), Hungary (2000), Iceland (1991), India (1992), Indonesia (1989), Ireland (1992), Israel (1993), Italy (1973), Jamaica (1991), Japan (1983), Jordan (1995), Kenya (1995), Republic of Korea (1992), Latvia (1993), Lithuania (1993), Malaysia (1988), Malta (1992), Mauritius (1994), Mexico (1989), Morocco (1988), New Zealand (1987), Nigeria (1995), Norway (1989), Oman (1999), Pakistan (1991), Peru (1992), the Philippines (1991), Poland (1991), Portugal (1986), Saudi Arabia (1999), Slovenia (2001), South Africa (1996), Spain (1985), Sri Lanka (1991), Sweden (1980), Taiwan (China) (1991), Thailand (1987), Trinidad and Tobago (1997), Tunisia (1995), Turkey (1989), the United Kingdom (1973), the United States (1973), República Bolivariana de Venezuela (1990), and Zimbabwe (1993).
Pension System Reform	Argentina (1994), Australia (1993), Bolivia (1997), Bulgaria (2002), Chile (1981), Colombia (1994, Costa Rica (2000), Croatia (2002), Denmark (1993), Dominican Republic (2003), El Salvador (1998), Estonia (2002), Hong Kong (China) (2000), Hungary (1998), Kazakhstan (1998), Latvia (2001), Lithuania (2001), FYR Macedonia (2003), Mexico (1997), the Netherlands (1985), Nicaragua (2000), Peru (1993), Poland (1999), Russia (2004), Slovak Republic (2003), Sweden (2001), Switzerland (1985), the United Kingdom (1988), and Uruguay (1995).

(continued)

Annex—Table 2 Economies That Implemented Reforms, and Year Implemented *(continued)*

Privatization	Argentina (1990), Armenia (1996), Australia (1991), Austria (1988), Azerbaijan (1997), Belgium (1990), Benin (1988), Bolivia (1992), Brazil (1991), Bulgaria (1991), Cameroon (1998), Chile (1985), China (1992), Colombia (1991), Côte d'Ivoire (1991), Croatia (1992), Czech Republic (1991), Egypt (1993), Estonia (1993), Finland (1988), France (1986), Germany (1988), Ghana (1989), Greece (1997), Honduras (1988), Hungary (1989), India (1991), Indonesia (1991), Ireland (2001), Italy (1985), Jamaica (1989), Jordan (2000), Kazakhstan (1994), Kenya (1992), Lao PDR (1991), Latvia (1995), Lithuania (1992), FYR Macedonia (1994), Malaysia (1989), Mexico (1985), Morocco (1993), Mozambique (1989), the Netherlands (1993), New Zealand (1987), Nicaragua (1991), Nigeria (1989), Pakistan (1991), Panama (1992), Peru (1991), the Philippines (1991), Poland (1990), Portugal (1989), Romania (1992), Russia (1991), Senegal (1997), Slovak Republic (1992), Slovenia (1992), South Africa (1997), Spain (1988), Sri Lanka (1990), Sweden (1992), Tanzania (1992), Thailand (1993), Togo (1990), Tunisia (1988), Turkey (1988), Uganda (1992), Ukraine (1992), the United Kingdom (1981), República Bolivariana de Venezuela (1991), Zambia (1993), and Zimbabwe (1994).
Institutional Reform	Albania (1993), Argentina (1991), Bangladesh (1987), Benin (1992), Bolivia (1985), Botswana (1998), Brazil (1999), Bulgaria (1997), Cambodia (1999), Chile (1976), China (1978), Costa Rica (1990), Croatia (2000), Czech Republic (1991), Djibouti (1996), Dominican Republic (1996), Ecuador (2000), El Salvador (1994), Estonia (1995), Georgia (1995), Ghana (1985), Guatemala (1994), Guinea-Bissau (1994), Guyana (1991), Honduras (2003), Hungary (1995), Indonesia (1985), Islamic Republic of Iran (1999), Jamaica (1993), Jordan (1998), Korea (1998), Kuwait (1986), Latvia (1999), Lithuania (2000), FYR Macedonia (1994), Malta (2004), Mauritius (1985), Mexico (1991), Namibia (1995), Nicaragua (1994), Nigeria (2003), Panama (2000), Paraguay (2004), Peru (1993), the Philippines (1994), Poland (1990), Romania (2000), Russia (2000), Senegal (1994), Sierra Leone (2002), Slovak Republic (2000), Slovenia (2000), South Africa (1996), Sri Lanka (1990), Syrian Arab Republic (1987), Taiwan (China) (1980), Tanzania (1997), Togo (1985), Trinidad and Tobago (1993), Turkey (2001), Uganda (1996), Ukraine (2000), the United Arab Emirates (1988), and Zambia (1997).

4

Whither the Reform Agenda?

THIS STUDY WAS MOTIVATED BY the observation that the state of development of domestic securities markets in many emerging economies, and especially in Latin America, is perceived as disheartening and puzzling. Disheartening because of the low level of development of local capital markets relative to the expectations of the early 1990s. Disheartening also because of what seems to be too meager a payoff for the intense reform efforts of the past two decades. Puzzling because of the lack of clarity and consensus as to how to modify the capital market reform agenda going forward.

In previous chapters, we described the sense in which the state of domestic capital markets in many emerging economies is in fact disheartening. Although some developing countries experienced growth of their domestic markets since the early 1990s, this growth in most cases has not been as significant as the one witnessed by industrialized nations. Other countries experienced an actual deterioration of their capital markets. Stock markets in many developing countries have seen listings and liquidity decrease, as a growing number of firms have cross-listed and raised capital in international financial centers, such as New York and London. In many emerging economies, stock markets remain highly illiquid and segmented, with trading and capitalization concentrated on few stocks. Also, bonds tend to be concentrated at the short end of the maturity spectrum and denominated in foreign currency, exposing governments and firms to maturity and currency risks.

In the case of Latin America, the results appear even more discouraging given the intensity of reform efforts in the region over the past decades plus the better evolution of capital markets in East Asia and their rapid growth in developed economies. Furthermore, the evidence shows that capital markets in Latin America are below what can be expected (in terms of commonly used measures of size and liquidity), even after controlling for per capita income, economic size, macroeconomic policies, and legal and institutional development. The evidence thus suggests that certain characteristics of these countries, beyond those usually highlighted in the literature on capital market development, limit the scope for developing deep domestic securities markets.

The evidence from the previous chapters also shows that the relation between globalization and domestic market development is complex and differs from what was expected at the beginning of the reform process. In particular, the results presented in chapter 3 indicate that improvements in fundamentals and capital market reforms lead to a higher share of activity in international financial markets. This may pose a significant challenge to policy makers, as their efforts to develop local markets seem to translate into more migration to international markets, which in turn may adversely affect the liquidity of domestic markets. In all, disenchantment is warranted by the evidence, especially to the extent that the initial expectations were concerned with domestic capital market development.

In this chapter, we turn to the puzzling and more normative side of the motivating observation—that is, to the question of what to do with the capital market reform agenda going forward. To this end, we discuss how different lines of thought would assess the evidence presented in previous chapters. This exercise will help us gain a better understanding of the possible reasons for the divergence between actual and expected outcomes and sharpen the criteria to guide an appropriate reformulation of future reform recommendations. Our main objective is to put on the table of the reform debate some basic issues with far-reaching implications that—we argue—have not been adequately factored in yet. All along, we keep the discussion at the level of the "big picture"—sacrificing technical detail for a better view of the landscape—and try to derive broad directions and criteria to reassess capital market reforms. We do not take the additional important step of weaving the general threads that emerge from our discussion into specific reform recommendations. Neither do we restrict the policy analysis to the conclusions that can be obtained from the previous chapters. Instead, we discuss the policy implications more loosely, based both on the evidence presented in this book and on other evidence that is often featured in the ongoing debates.

Our approach leaves us open to at least two sorts of criticism. For one, securities markets experts—for example, professional market practitioners, experts in regulation and supervision, specialists in securities clearance and settlement, and experts in trading platforms—may complain that our analysis fails to provide sufficient operational guidance as to what they should do differently. For another, reform-minded policy makers might throw their hands up, noting that our analysis pokes holes in the reform agenda without charting a well-defined, specific alternative. We stand guilty as charged on both counts. In our defense, we submit that a fresh look at basic issues is a necessary first step, without which a discussion of specific technical recommendations is likely to be hasty or presumptuous. Hasty if recommendations emerge in an unduly fragmented or ad hoc manner, without the benefit of an integrating rationale, or worse yet, if they simply replay the same recommendations of the past (recall the lapidary dictum, attributed to Einstein, according to which the beginning of madness is to do more of the same and expect different results). Presumptuous if a view is already formed but remains implicit, risking becoming an unquestioned prior with faulty premises that are not corrected for lack of an open discussion. Crafting more specific recommendations is no doubt an essential task for future work, and one that should, in any case, be carried forward mainly by those with specialized expertise in the micro dimensions of securities markets.

The rest of this chapter is organized into three sections. The second section discusses three typological views on why the state of capital markets is different from that previously expected given the reform efforts. These views also shed light on what to do next. The first two views are general characterizations of two different diagnoses that have emerged repeatedly in the debate. The third view is essentially our reevaluation of the first two views, based on how we interpret the evidence presented in the previous chapters. Though each of the three views emphasizes distinct aspects of the evidence, reaching different diagnoses and drawing different lessons, they are not necessarily incompatible.

The first view, encapsulated in the message "be patient and redouble the effort," contends that past reforms were right, despite their teething pains, that the reforms needed in the future are essentially known, and that reforms—especially second-generation ones—have long gestation periods before producing visible dividends.[156] The first view thus recommends letting market discipline work, while forging ahead patiently with further reform implementation efforts. The second view, encapsulated in the message "get the sequence right," draws attention to problems that arise when some reforms are implemented ahead of others. Its central prescription is that key preconditions should be met—including the achievement of a minimum institutional strength—before fully liberalizing domestic financial markets and allowing free international capital mobility.

Despite their important contributions and insights, we argue that these two views do not properly address some relevant aspects of the evidence. We thus introduce a third view, which arises from the identification of some of the shortcomings of the previous two views. This third view can be encapsulated in the message "revisit basic issues and reshape expectations." It contends that there are important deficiencies with respect to the expectations and design of past reforms, related to the failure to take appropriately into account the implications of certain basic issues. This third view is, therefore, less prescriptive. Rather, it emphasizes the need to step back and reconsider basic issues with a fresh look. This analysis will hopefully help articulate a better-grounded reform agenda in the years to come.

Though the three views differ in their diagnoses, their prescriptions are in many respects complementary. Indeed, each of the three views has many important things to say about the question of why the development of capital markets after the reform process has not met the ex ante expectations and about what to do next. In no way do we claim that any one view trumps the others. The only claim we make is that the third view points in directions that, in our opinion, have not been adequately explored in the debate so far. In all, we believe that a sensible reformer would not be an ardent partisan of any individual view. He or she would instead combine different elements from the three views in ways suited to specific country circumstances.

Following the presentation of the different views, the third section turns to a discussion of the basic issues raised by the third view. For presentation purposes, the discussion is organized around three main themes (whose importance is suggested by the evidence presented in previous chapters): financial globalization, liquidity, and risk diversification. We are highly selective in the choice of issues to revisit and do not claim to have identified all of the important ones. In fact, we consciously leave out issues that are arguably as important as the chosen ones—such as systemic risk, information asymmetry, risk aversion, and moral hazard.[157] In addition, we do not pretend to cover all the important angles of each of the chosen issues or to analyze them in the depth that they deserve. All of this we do by design, however, as we aim to illustrate the usefulness of going back to basics in a broad sense, rather than to provide an exhaustive discussion.

As regards globalization, we argue that taking financial globalization seriously calls for a redefinition of success, one that emphasizes less the outcomes in local capital markets and more the depth and breadth of access by residents to capital market services, regardless of whether these are provided at home or abroad. We stress that, although financial globalization augments, through competition, the pressures in favor of structural reforms, it also complicates the reform agenda with respect to fixed income markets, to the extent that it magnifies the problems associated with weak currencies—that is, currencies that are not accepted even at home (let alone abroad) as a reliable store of value for savings. We thus see a major need to bring the discussion on the links between money and financial market development more explicitly into the reform debate.

As regards domestic market liquidity and risk diversification, our view is that securities markets in many emerging economies perform poorly in both respects for reasons that are much more difficult to overcome than commonly believed. We note that illiquidity begets illiquidity—by limiting the capacity of investors to unwind their positions without affecting prices, illiquidity discourages the entry of new players, which in turn further limits liquidity—and that illiquidity fundamentally hinders "price revelation" (one of the most distinctive functions of securities markets relative to banking markets). Similarly, in most emerging economies, domestic securities markets do not seem to add much directly to risk diversification, beyond the risk diversification function already performed at home by banks, and risk diversification by international portfolio investors tends to marginalize small countries and small corporate issuers.

We argue that illiquidity and insufficiently diversified portfolios are intrinsically related to two other characteristics of many emerging economies, namely, small size—of countries and corporations—and a highly segmented participation of issuers. Small size is a key structural feature of many emerging markets and one that matters for liquidity, as liquidity is a positive function of scale economies and agglomeration effects. This fact points to the flaws in taking the large developed financial markets as the model to imitate and the benchmark to measure progress. To the extent that liquidity is structurally undermined by the small size of the domestic economy, the basic question is whether a suitable type of domestic securities market exists for small open economies and what would be the expected role of such market. We also argue that size matters for risk diversification through securities markets in various ways. Diversification within small economies is limited by asset scarcity. Moreover, to the extent that there is a fixed cost of gathering information on issuers, investors would require investments of a minimum size, which would tend to segment the market, excluding small issuers and issues, and limit the scope of risk diversification. This may explain why the few companies and governments that participate in international capital markets tend to be relatively large. Furthermore, this may also be related to the problem of lack of access to domestic capital markets for small firms and to international capital markets for issuers from small economies.

The fourth section concludes with some final remarks. It calls for eclecticism and for a more varied reform agenda, because a one-size-fits-all approach is destined to fail. It emphasizes that a key step in designing country-specific reforms going forward should be a determination of whether the emerging economy in question can realistically meet the size thresholds to sustain a liquid domestic market for private sector securities. It argues that much more thought is needed to sketch a suitable "light" version of a domestic capital market for small countries, one that is not overengineered and is complementary to international financial integration. It argues that, ultimately, any reform agenda for capital markets needs to be couched within a broader vision of financial development for emerging markets. Such a broader vision would emphasize access to high-quality and diverse financial services by securities markets or other financial intermediaries, regardless of whether such services are provided at home or abroad. Rather than emphasizing domestic securities markets per se, a broader vision would emphasize links between financial markets and, in particular, the ways in which capital markets' services can enhance the workings of the financial system. Examples of such links can be found in housing financing and structured finance operations, where local and international securities markets can help bring institutional investors to the scene and enable the emergence of financial products and services that would not be possible otherwise. Finally, a broader vision would seek the diversification of vehicles and instruments to mobilize investable funds from the widest possible base of savers and allocate them to the broadest possible range of efficient newcomers, including those that do not participate in the international or domestic securities markets proper.

What Went Wrong and What to Do Next?

Assessing the evidence to draw implications for the reform agenda is a process that, by nature, involves significant resorting to judgment calls. The same evidence examined from different perspectives can and does lead to different diagnoses and policy recommendations. Thus, there is ample scope for differing yet reasonable arguments regarding the question of what went wrong with the past capital market reform agenda and what to do next. This section aims at providing a flavor of the range of perspectives on such questions by identifying three typological views. The main message of each view can be summarized as follows: (a) "be patient and redouble the effort," (b) "get the sequence right," and (c) "revisit basic issues and revise expectations." To be sure, the categorization of perspectives into three views is arbitrary, for things are not as clear-cut in real life. The typology is used mainly for presentation purposes, to help depict the nature of the debate and highlight the policy issues under discussion. We now turn to the characterization of the three views.

Be Patient and Redouble the Effort

According to this view—which is commonly held among experts trying to build capital markets—the salient elements of the capital market reform package are well known. Although actions are required on various fronts and the application of reforms to specific country circumstances is not easy, little disagreement exists about what those actions should be in general terms. Thus, this view points to broad agreement on the following propositions. (a) Reforms are needed to improve the enabling environment for capital markets—by strengthening macroeconomic stability and contract-related institutions, including the rights of minority shareholders and creditors. (b) These reforms should be accompanied by measures to enhance efficiency and market discipline through greater competition—including opening the capital account of the balance of payments. (c) Reforms in other areas can play a particularly important complementary role—including pension reforms to create privately administered pension funds, which can increase the demand for private sector securities and exert pressure to improve governance and transparency, and the privatization of public enterprises, which can boost the supply of securities and help democratize ownership. (d) There is a need for more technical and specialized reforms to enhance capital market transparency and integrity by fortifying their micro underpinnings. These include the upgrading of capital market–specific legislation and regulation, the improvement of supervisory enforcement, the strengthening of the legal framework for (and practices of) corporate governance, and the modernization of key dimensions of securities markets' "plumbing," such as securities valuation, accounting and disclosure standards, securities trading, custody, clearing, and settlement systems.

This view further notes that many of the objectives, principles, and best practices that are germane to the adequate functioning of domestic capital markets are increasingly being captured in the relevant international standards and codes.[158] Assessments of country practices in light of these standards would help identify weaknesses and development needs, thus guiding the formulation of the reform agenda. To be sure, such assessments run the risk of degenerating into mechanical checks of compliance with items in a template. In practice, however, this risk is not very large, since assessors tend to be experts in the field, often with considerable international experience and enough good sense to stay away from a simplistic, formulaic approach. They tend to be careful to take into account the particular stage of financial development of the country in question, tailoring their assessments to individual country circumstances. Moreover, compliance with international standards is typically evaluated in the context of broader reviews of a country's financial system, which further limits the risks of a "template approach."[159] This said, the main point still stands—that the key benchmarks of what domestic capital markets should strive toward are relatively well known and that reforms should foster convergence toward such benchmarks.

This view thus argues that past reforms were essentially right regarding their objectives, content, and even design. Moreover, this point of view is consistent with the evidence presented in chapter 3, which shows that reforms were part of the solution, not the problem. In effect, the evidence suggests that economies with sounder macro policies, more efficient legal systems, and greater openness tend to have more developed capital markets and that capital market reforms—including the controversial liberalization—tend to be followed by significant increases in domestic market capitalization, trading, and capital raising.

This view also recognizes that past reforms provided visible gains, though not without costs, which, in the case of financial crises, were extremely high. However, this is more or less as it should be, since teething pains and even crises are part and parcel of the financial development process, as confirmed by observation and increasingly suggested by theory.[160] In effect, the opening and competition that result from liberalization may increase instability in the short run but also help expose weaknesses and foster a cleansing process that ultimately strengthens defenses and stimulates further reform.[161] Over time, through both pain and success, learning takes place and incentives are eventually set right, yielding durable results. If some doubt remains, just look at the successful case of Chile's financial development, which owes today's strengths in no small part to a constructive reaction to the painful crisis of the late 1970s and early 1980s.

What went wrong? Why have many capital markets not developed as expected? According to this view, the failures are mostly related to a combination of insufficiently implemented reforms and impatience. In effect, despite what many claim, key reforms were in some cases not even initiated, while those reforms that were initiated were often implemented in an incomplete or inconsistent fashion. In many cases, laws were passed, but they were not duly implemented through regulatory changes, institutional adaptations, and capacity building, nor were they adequately enforced. Although the measures of the institutional and economic environment reported in previous chapters may have increased as a result of the reforms, they might fail to adequately capture the quality of those reforms, which—most would agree—varied widely across countries. Moreover, reformers have been too impatient, often expecting results to materialize sooner than warranted. Though the expectation of a rapid payoff may be justified with respect to some types of first-generation reforms, it is the wrong expectation to have when it comes to the more complex second-generation reforms. It would be difficult to disagree that these later reforms typically require long implementation and gestation periods before producing visible dividends.

The above considerations lead naturally to the prescription encapsulated in the title of this subsection: "be patient and redouble the effort."[162] The emphasis should therefore be on forging ahead persistently (and patiently) with the hard work of overcoming resistance to the implementation of reforms—especially second- and third-generation reforms—that, albeit difficult, are already well understood for the most part. Moreover, along the path to financial development a premium should be placed on letting market discipline work, recognizing that such discipline sets in motion a process that involves short-term pain and long-term gain—a process that is essentially one of creative destruction.

Finally, among the many important contributions to the reform debate, one that is worth noting is this view's implicit recommendation that much more attention should be directed toward understanding the political economy of reform implementation. This is an essential complement to the technical soundness of reform design, and one that is necessary to consider in order to more effectively dislodge the resistance to reform.

Get the Sequence Right

This second view reflects what is arguably the most well-known line of criticism of the first view, as it contends that reforms were—to one degree or another—part of the problem rather than the solution. This second view draws attention to the problems that arise from misguided reform sequencing, that is, the unwise adoption of certain reforms before others are in place. The most familiar rendition of this view focuses on the pitfalls of premature financial market liberalization as it is broadly understood, including the deregulation of the domestic financial system as well as its integration into international capital markets. However, this view also concerns sequencing arguments that are not related to liberalization proper but to other aspects of the "building block" nature of capital market development, whereby links across markets make certain reforms preconditions for, or necessary complements to, the success of others.

Proceeding without due regard to sequencing is, this view argues, like venturing into the sea in stormy weather without an appropriately built vessel—a brash decision. This is not to deny that some costs are unavoidable on the path to financial development. But trying to advance along that path with the wrong sequencing can turn the normal pains of growing up into gains that do not endure (because preconditions for capital market development were not properly in place) or unnecessary suffering (because financial crises can rapidly wipe out the gains achieved over decades).[163]

The sequencing arguments to consider first relate to financial liberalization. A prominent strand in connection with this step has focused on the instability and unsoundness that result from a too-rapid opening of the capital account. These negative effects tend to occur when liberalization is implemented before the market achieves a minimum threshold of institutional strength, in terms of the legal framework, the regulatory system, the supervisory capacity, the accounting and disclosure standards, and so forth.[164] The earlier versions of this argument applied mainly to the domestic banking system. Weak banking systems were found to be, time and again, ill prepared to prudently intermediate the surges in capital inflows, which led to credit bubbles (characterized by excessive risk taking and even looting) followed by credit busts.[165] During the 1990s, this type of sequencing argument was extended to the problems of excessive currency and maturity mismatches in the balance sheets of corporations that borrowed in banking and securities markets in the midst of a liberalized market environment. Such mismatches were a salient factor behind the Asian crisis of 1997 and the Argentine crisis of 2001. The basic policy prescription of this analysis is that reforms that focused on enhancing prudential oversight, corporate governance, and transparency should precede financial market liberalization and international opening.[166]

The implications of the prescription in favor of consolidating regulatory and institutional reforms before liberalizing vary, depending on the initial conditions (for example, how open the country is). Proponents of this argument do not normally disagree in the case of countries that are still closed—they concur that these countries should not open too soon or too fast. Disagreements arise, however, with respect to countries whose financial system is already liberalized. Proponents of a strong version of the prescription would counsel emerging economies to roll back capital market opening and "throw sand in the wheels," including through the use of Chilean-style capital controls on short-term inflows. Some would even suggest that financial integration should be managed on a permanent basis, as full integration might never be desirable.[167] Proponents of a softer and perhaps more widely accepted version would advocate only delaying any further liberalization while attention is reoriented toward reprioritizing reforms, in favor of strengthening in earnest the regulatory and institutional preconditions.

Also associated with liberalization, a second class of sequencing arguments can be derived from views that emphasize the need for a minimum presence of domestic securities markets to help absorb shocks and sustain intermediation when the banking system is in crisis.[168] These views can be extended to a sequencing prescription: that a greater development of the local markets for debt and equity securities should be achieved before fully opening the external capital account. In effect, in purely bank-dominated systems, capital flow volatility tends to propagate rapidly through deposit withdrawals (at face value), while governments tend to feel compelled to bail out depositors for fear that a contagious run could bring the banking and payment systems to their knees. By contrast, in a more balanced domestic financial system, where securities markets have a significant presence, much of the losses need not be propagated throughout the system; they would presumably be absorbed directly by capital market investors and thus not shifted to the government.

A more specific rendition of this latter type of sequencing argument arises from the "original sin" literature. This literature draws attention to the major vulnerabilities that result from the inability of emerging-economy sovereigns and corporates to issue long-term domestic currency–denominated debt. In its earlier stages, this literature tended to recommend the adoption of formal dollarization as the preferred route to overcome the original sin and develop domestic financial markets more safely within a financially globalized context.[169] In light of the disastrous collapse of the Argentine currency board or "convertibility" system, however, the same original sin problem has led to a contrasting prescription that emphasizes the need for sequencing. That is, that the road to redemption requires that priority be given to the development of the market for domestic currency–denominated debt, and that this preferably would be achieved before completely opening the capital account (Eichengreen, Hausmann, and Panizza 2005). Proponents of this view point to Australia as an example of a country that got this sequence right, a sequence that is arguably being adopted also by the two largest emerging economies—India and China (Lane and Schmukler forthcoming).

A third type of sequencing argument associated with liberalization focuses on various dimensions of domestic market deregulation. One example concerns the deregulation of pension fund investments. An oft-repeated recommendation is that the limits imposed on pension fund investments at home should be relaxed, in order to enhance their capacity to diversify risk. If sequencing issues are ignored, however, this recommendation could backfire. In effect, the liberalization of pension funds' domestic investment regime, to yield durable benefits, would need to be preceded by a strengthening of risk-focused supervision and risk management capacity of pension funds, as well as by improvements in liquidity, disclosure, and price integrity in the local securities market.

As noted at the beginning of this section, not all sequencing arguments are related to liberalization. Some emphasize the building block nature of capital markets development. This leads to the recommendation that reforms should be ordered so as to ensure that preconditions are put in place to enhance the likelihood of success of subsequent reforms.[170] For example, well-functioning money markets are arguably a precondition for the sound development of bond markets, and deep sovereign bond markets are a precondition for the healthy development of corporate bond markets (Schinasi and Smith 1998). In effect, money markets link capital markets to the banking system (the ultimate provider of liquidity) and help anchor the short-term end of the yield curve, which is essential to the pricing of debt securities. A well-organized sovereign bond market, for its part, provides the safe asset class to which investors can switch in times of uncertainty and turmoil. It also provides needed benchmarks—including the yield curve for the presumably risk-free asset—without which corporate bonds cannot be adequately priced. Similarly, a case can be made that the combination of a deep money market and a liquid secondary market for securities is a precondition for safe and sound development of the derivatives markets—if the cash market for the underlying asset is illiquid, the unwinding of derivatives transactions would greatly magnify asset price volatility, increasing systemic risk.

Sequencing arguments based on the building block approach also apply to the case of reforms aimed at reducing the excessive exposure of domestic government debt to rollover, interest rate, and exchange rate risks. Other things being equal, as the government succeeds in reducing such exposure, it transfers the associated risks to private investors (for example, bank money desks, securities brokers, and mutual funds). In the absence of adequate oversight, including appropriate valuation (and related disclosure) of the securities held in their portfolios, brokers and asset managers may be ill prepared to manage the attendant risks, which would amplify distress in times of jittery markets.[171] It follows that a strengthening of the regulatory environment and the risk management capacity of, say, the domestic mutual fund industry is generally required to achieve a durable reduction in the risk exposure of government's debt.

In all, the "get the sequence right" view spans a wide range of capital market–related reforms. Though the international standards and codes mentioned in the previous section are no doubt helpful in identifying the needed reforms, they offer little or no guidance with respect to the question of how to sequence the reforms. The task of appropriately recasting the reform agenda going forward hinges, according to this view, on the success of efforts devoted to systematically clarifying sequencing issues.

Revisit Basic Issues and Reshape Expectations

This third view arises from the identification of shortcomings in the previous two views. In effect, even as their internal logic is accepted, these views appear subject to important qualifiers.

The first view—"be patient and redouble the effort"—has a crucial shortcoming in that it ignores a key finding reported in chapter 3. That is, it ignores the fact that improvements in institutional and macroeconomic fundamentals, and the introduction of reforms, spur not only the development of domestic securities markets but also (and even to a greater extent) the internationalization of securities issuance and trading. This finding, of course, does not invalidate the importance of undertaking reforms, but it clearly calls for a profound change in expectations, beyond simply learning to be patient. It also suggests that to reshape expectations appropriately, there is a need to revisit the issues associated with the process of financial globalization.

To be sure, the reformers of the 1990s—as noted in chapter 2—were not dismissive of the globalization process. On the contrary, they strongly supported it. But they tended to expect that the effect of reforms would be to attract foreign investors and global liquidity to their growing domestic markets, where risk-adjusted returns would presumably be systematically higher given the relative scarcity of capital in emerging economies. Reformers did not anticipate that the fruit of their efforts would be an increased tendency for the best securities issuers and issues to move to international markets and, in the process, adversely affect the liquidity of the domestic market.

The Achilles' heel of the second view—"get the sequence right"—is its questionable expectation that sequencing, even if technically correct, is consistent with sufficient pro-reform incentives. There is nothing wrong in principle with the prescription that unrestrained competition and full capital account opening should be postponed until a threshold of institutional maturity and risk management capacity is achieved. But the political economy's reality is that institutional reform does not happen simply because of good logic. Good logic is in most cases insufficient to dislodge the resistance coming from the incumbents—that is, from those who benefit from the status quo and, as a result, tend to use their economic power and political influence to shape reforms. In effect, the losses from reform are felt upfront, and incumbents, with much at stake, can organize vigorously to oppose those reforms that would eventually undermine their established positions. By contrast, the gains from reform accrue in the future and are spread among numerous winners who, as a result, face a collective action problem—with little incentive to act as a group, they tend to remain relatively voiceless and unorganized. Against these realities, nothing better serves the interests of incumbents than keeping them protected from the competition of local and international entrants.

Thus, the idea appears naive, that resistance to reform will yield without the pressures that come from domestic and foreign contestability. In fact, the historical experience with financial development around the world amply illustrates the special role played by competition, particularly by the openness to international competition, in reducing the power of incumbents and fostering reform. Competition from outsiders induces domestic insiders to become more efficient, and as a result it changes their incentives with regard to reform—efficient incumbents become supporters of the very reforms they had previously resisted.[172]

Another questionable aspect of the previous two views is their implicit premise that domestic capital market development in emerging economies should be measured against the benchmark of the developed capital markets. For those two views, the reform path may be long and difficult, and it may require a period of relative isolation before a full embrace of globalization, but the expected outcome, in most cases, is only one. The associated expectation is that, as reforms succeed, domestic capital markets in emerging markets will increasingly resemble those in developed countries. But it is difficult to accept the premise given the outcome—that is, the rather poor state of development of Latin American countries' capital markets in spite of the intense reform efforts of the 1990s, as documented in previous chapters. Furthermore, the evidence also shows that capital market development in Latin America is below the level predicted by the region's fundamentals and policies. These results suggest that certain intrinsic characteristics of Latin American countries, beyond those usually highlighted in the capital market reform literature, limit the scope for developing deep domestic markets. These limitations are difficult to overcome using the reform process. In other words, even if Latin American countries carry out all the necessary reforms, they might not achieve domestic capital market development comparable to that of industrialized countries.

In all, confronting the previous two views with relevant aspects of the evidence leads to the conclusion that important things are either left out or inadequately addressed by them. Thus, the third view focuses on the basic gaps in knowledge and is, as a result, much less prescriptive. Its main advice is to step back and revisit basic issues before moving forward. It anticipates that such a return to basics would provide a better ground to interpret the evidence, guide the reformulation of the reform agenda, and reshape expectations. In the next section, we attempt such an exercise, by briefly discussing a selected set of basic issues and seeking to draw, albeit tentatively, some general implications for the reform agenda going forward.

Back to Basics

In this section we illustrate the potential usefulness to the reform debate of revisiting basic issues from perspectives that are frequently underplayed. As mentioned early in this chapter, we are highly selective, choosing only a few issues to revisit, and we stay at a "big picture" level in our analysis. Our aim is to exemplify how a return to basics can unearth far-reaching implications for the reform agenda, rather than to provide an in-depth discussion of each issue. For presentation purposes, we organize the selected issues around three topics: financial globalization, liquidity, and risk diversification. Throughout the rest of the section, and the chapter, we illustrate the selected issues with the experience of Latin American countries, but we believe that these issues may be relevant for emerging economies in other regions as well. In the discussion, the issues of size and segmentation appear as recurring themes.

Financial Globalization

Financial globalization calls for a different measurement of capital market development, one that does not center only on the local dimension. However, the tendency in most studies and in policy discussions is to measure and compare financial development across countries mainly in terms of indicators of size and activity of the domestic financial system (for example, ratios to GDP of such variables as assets, liabilities, capital, income, and turnover). Essential as these measures are, they fail to reflect the simple fact that, in a globalized context, financial development has much to do with the extent and type of integration with international financial markets. Indeed, data to gauge such integration are often harder to obtain than data on the domestic financial system. But scarcity of data is itself no excuse for the failure to qualify the limitations of domestic-based measures and to adequately discuss financial market integration issues.

Financial globalization also invites a more general approach to understanding financial development—one that looks at the domestic and international sides of the process simultaneously. In this perspective, successful financial development is best characterized as the sustainable deepening and broadening of access to financial services, regardless of whether such services are provided at home or abroad, or by securities markets or other markets.[173] This more general approach requires an understanding of how reforms affect the development of the domestic market, the internationalization process, and the relation between these two. The evidence in chapter 3 shows that these links are complex and, in a sense, are unexpected. Reforms have led to a rising importance of internationalization (in securities issuance and trading) relative to the local securities markets, not least because the internationalization appears to have happened at the same time that local market development has stagnated or even deteriorated. Herein lies a major reason to reshape expectations and reconsider the meaning of reform success.

A greater attention to financial globalization does not imply, however, that the much wider scope for cross-border financial contracting that results from financial globalization renders domestic financial markets useless. It is difficult to imagine that international financial markets would, at least in the foreseeable future, become a perfect substitute for local markets in every respect, especially with regard to such financial services as local currency payments, local currency savings, small consumer loans, and loans to micro and small and medium enterprises. Indeed, rigorous empirical work suggests that, even where financial integration is very high, local financial development matters for the economic success of firms, especially the smaller ones (Guiso, Sapienza, and Zingales 2004). Thus, the point is not to deny the relevance of local financial markets but to stress that such relevance acquires meaning under globalization to the extent that domestic markets are a complement to, rather than a substitute for, the international market integration.

Emerging economies' integration into international financial markets facilitates the reform process in some respects. As noted earlier, through competition by outsiders, globalization dislodges the grip of domestic incumbents and augments the pressures in favor of institutional change. More often than not, and despite the likelihood of increased transitional instability, reforms get a boost as countries open up.

Financial globalization, however, complicates the reform agenda to the extent that it magnifies the problems in debt markets associated with weak currencies, as repeatedly noted by the international finance literature. The lessons that this literature yields are important for the capital market reform debate and highlight the need to build bridges between financial development experts and macro and international finance economists (Obstfeld and Taylor 2005). In effect, the current globalization wave—which in contrast with the gold-standard period is unfolding in a context of floating exchange rates—bestows benefits that rise depending on how well the local currency performs two functions simultaneously: the function of a shock absorber (with flexibility in facilitating, in particular, a nondeflationary adjustment in the real exchange rate toward a more depreciated equilibrium) and that of a reliable store of value for savings.[174] Performing these two functions well is already difficult in the case of currencies that are not in the small set of currencies used internationally as reserve assets. It is drastically more complicated if, in addition, the local currency is not well accepted, even at home, as a reliable receptacle for savings—the case of many emerging economies in which financial contracting is highly dollarized or dominated by short-termism. In such circumstances, policy is not only constrained, it is also liable to be torn between the goals of fostering the currency's role of shock absorption and promoting its role as a store of value for financial intermediation.

The problems arising at the interface of globalization and weak currencies are directly relevant only to debt markets. This is because in countries where the equilibrium real exchange rate is subject to significant fluctuations, borrowing in dollars (at home or abroad, it does not matter) systematically exposes debtors in the nontradable sector to real exchange rate risk and, as a result, exposes their creditors to the real exchange rate–induced default risk. This exposure goes unhedged if a reliable market for foreign exchange derivatives does not exist—the case, almost by definition, of countries where financial dollarization is high. Hence, globalization magnifies the weak currency problem because of adverse balance sheet effects stemming from the missing market for local currency–denominated debt or, to put it in technical terms that are more accurate and general, the missing market for debt contracts denominated in nontradable prices.[175]

In contrast, the weak currency problem is basically unrelated to equity contracts. This is because equity securities do not generate vulnerabilities in the balance sheet of issuers. These contracts are not subject to default risk because they do not commit the issuer to paying a flow that is independent of performance. As a result, the issuer of an equity security does not have any exposure to exchange rate risk, even if his or her income is derived from the emerging economy's nontradable sector. To be sure, the issuer's performance might be affected by real exchange rate fluctuations in various ways, but such effects are passed on to equity investors by changes in dividend payments. Therefore, the internationalization of equity markets carries, of itself, no systemic vulnerability implications, even if the integrating country has a weak currency.

It follows that as an emerging economy becomes more integrated into international financial markets, the incentives for issuers of equity securities rise in favor of issuing in international markets. If emerging economy corporations can break the cost and size thresholds to issue equity at a reasonable price in the deeper and immensely more liquid international financial centers, there is no advantage in issuing in the domestic stock markets. As noted, however, the migration of equity issuance and trading to international markets may entail adverse effects for the liquidity of the domestic stock market, and this—we insist—cannot be ignored when setting expectations and recasting reform recommendations.

In all, the reform agenda needs to pay much greater attention to the problems arising at the interface of financial globalization, weak currencies, and debt market development. At a minimum, this calls for an early determination, made on a country-by-country basis, of whether realistic prospects exist for reversing high financial dollarization. This determination should be followed by sensible recommendations to prevent or even roll back financial dollarization where feasible, and to live with financial dollarization while mitigating balance sheet vulnerabilities where appropriate. However, the development of practical recommendations in this area is at an early stage, particularly for the case in which financial dollarization might be too difficult to reverse.[176] Additional work is needed to set the future reform agenda with respect to these issues on a more solid empirical and analytical footing.

Finally, although our discussion in this chapter focuses on policy making by developing countries, one cannot forget that financial globalization raises the need to improve the international financial architecture. As this is an area outside the control of emerging markets, the onus is on the international financial community.[177] The salient gaps are in crucial areas such as contagion (i.e., the absence of an international liquidity facility to mitigate ripple effects unwarranted by fundamentals in the markets for sovereign bonds),[178] default (i.e., the lack of a functional framework for dealing efficiently with sovereign debt defaults),[179] and the mentioned "original sin" problem (i.e., the absence of an international market for local currency debt of emerging countries).[180] Improving the international financial architecture would disproportionately benefit emerging economies. Unfortunately, the economic and geopolitical power to address the flaws in the international financial architecture reside with the industrial countries, which are also the countries with the least incentive to worry about it, except in those rare occasions when their financial centers are threatened by contagion.

Liquidity

The focus here is on secondary market liquidity, as it is at the core of one of the unique contributions of capital markets to a sound and vibrant financial system. In effect, as noted in the annex to chapter 2, secondary market liquidity underpins "price revelation," a distinctive function of securities markets in relation to banking markets. In the absence of reasonable liquidity, concerns regarding price integrity cannot be completely dispelled. When the secondary market trading of a security is too sporadic, its valuation needs to be done using methods that, even where well designed and uniformly applied, are imperfect substitutes for the real thing—an observable and reliable market price. Even in the best of cases, those methods are quite blunt in their capacity to capture in real time the changes in the actual and perceived risks and prospects of the issuer.[181] By undermining price revelation—even where disclosure standards are high—secondary market illiquidity causes "marking to market" to lose much of its meaning and turns fair value accounting into an inherently tentative task.

In addition, secondary market liquidity is what enables investors to exit in a nondisruptive manner—that is, to unwind their positions without affecting asset prices. Illiquidity, therefore, constitutes a major hindrance to investor entry into the market (thereby undermining primary market liquidity) even in normal times, let alone in turbulent times, when illiquidity magnifies the effects of shocks on asset price fluctuations. In this sense, illiquidity begets illiquidity: new investors and issuers are discouraged from entering the market because of concerns about price integrity and exit, and in turn the lack of new entrants further undermines liquidity.

Liquidity in secondary markets constitutes, moreover, a building block for the safe and sound development of other key markets, such as the repo and derivatives markets. This largely explains why repo markets in most Latin American countries are typically circumscribed to using government debt paper (relatively more liquid, easier to price, and presumably the safest asset) as the underlying security. It also helps explain why the derivatives market that tends to develop first—in the few countries (Brazil, Chile, and Mexico) where it has developed at all—is the derivatives market for foreign exchange, given the relatively high liquidity of the underlying spot market. By contrast, the derivatives markets for interest rates, credit risk, and equity prices are, by and large, underdeveloped in the region.[182]

Against this background, a key issue to consider in the reform debate is that secondary market liquidity is a positive function of market size and of the related scale economies, network externalities, and agglomeration effects. This simple fact explains why global liquidity is increasingly clustering around few international financial centers. It also constitutes sobering news for the smaller economies. As evidenced by the results in chapter 3, market size is a major structural determinant of liquidity. Indeed, the experience in Latin America suggests that even the relatively small countries can sustain a not-too-illiquid market for government debt securities. However, beyond that—and, to an extent, because of that—most Latin American countries, except perhaps the largest ones, have been unable to generate reasonably liquid domestic markets for corporate debt and equity securities. Therefore, if local capital markets in Latin America, especially in the smaller countries, are unlikely to adequately perform their price revelation function, researchers and reformers alike need to address more frontally the question of what is expected to be the distinctive role played by these markets.

Furthermore, though not tested in chapter 3, a reasonable hypothesis is that the adverse effects on domestic liquidity of small market size are exacerbated by concentration, a feature of Latin American capital markets highlighted in chapter 2. In effect, the general pattern in the Latin American markets is that only a few firms are capable of issuing securities in amounts that meet minimum thresholds for liquidity, and these securities are mostly purchased by a few institutional investors—mainly pension funds—that dominate the scene.[183] These investors tend to follow buy and hold strategies, not least because of concerns of significantly affecting prices. The result is little trading. In the case of the equity market, low trading also reflects low "float" ratios—a low proportion of listed equities available for trading—in part due to concentrated property patterns and the associated reluctance to give up control.[184]

Given the constraints on liquidity arising from small size, and the possibly reinforcing effects of concentration, it is not surprising that many domestic securities markets—even those that, like Chile, are large in size (for example, assets relative to GDP) and thus have no shortage of investable funds—appear caught in a low-liquidity trap, especially with respect to private sector securities. Even the cases where liquidity is above average exemplify the small size constraint. An example is that of the relatively liquid government bond markets, to which we apply McCauley and Remolona's (2000) empirical analysis of bid-ask spreads for certain minimum transaction amounts. That study suggests that a highly liquid secondary market for government bonds would require a negotiable stock of such bonds in the range of US$100–200 billion. The problem with this conclusion is, of course, that only relatively few emerging economies have a GDP, let alone a government debt stock, that exceeds this range. Even what appear to be fairly liquid secondary markets for domestic government debt in several countries are really not that liquid, according to McCauley and Remolona's metric.

An additional complication is that in small countries with small investor bases there might not be enough room for liquid secondary markets for both sovereign and corporate bonds. As a result, smallness exacerbates the crowding out of corporate bond markets by government bond markets. At the same time, however, liquid government bond markets are arguably needed to generate a yield curve that is key to the development of corporate bond markets. Therefore, many small emerging countries appear caught between a rock and a hard place—with little or no room to ensure that domestic markets for government bonds play a salutary role in the development of corporate bond markets without crowding these markets out.

Views differ as to the threshold size for liquidity in corporate bond and equity markets. But market participants in most of the midsize and larger Latin American countries typically consider that bond issues below US$50 million would not whet the appetite of large institutional investors, in part because smaller issues would not generate sufficient secondary market liquidity to enable orderly exit.[185] However, US$50 million is quite an amount in relative terms for many Latin American countries. It is, for instance, a multiple of the capital of most of the corporations within these countries and, hence, it is a threshold that leaves only a handful of firms size-eligible to participate through securities issuance in the local market.

The structural constraints on liquidity posed by small market size do not eliminate the scope for enhancing liquidity in domestic markets. As documented in country-specific assessments of securities markets—including under the Financial Sector Assessment Program jointly conducted by the World Bank and the International Monetary Fund—there is nontrivial room for enhancing domestic market liquidity through suitable reforms focused on, for instance, reducing fragmentation in issuance and trading, enhancing securities clearance and settlement arrangements, organizing securities lending and borrowing facilities, improving valuation methods, promoting contract standardization, and upgrading financial reporting. But the same experts that recommend these reforms recognize that they would lead to modest improvements in liquidity rather than to qualitative jumps.

In sum, the reform agenda can no longer underestimate as blatantly as it has tended to do in the past the fundamental constraint to liquidity arising from smallness. An obvious and direct way to address the small-market constraint is, of course, to promote further international market integration. This is indeed a sure way to break free from the confines of local market illiquidity—for the few issuers that use the services of foreign capital market. But it brings back to the discussion table the two caveats that we have already emphasized: first, that the internationalization of securities issuance and trading can further reduce domestic market liquidity, and second, that with respect to bond markets, internationalization can magnify the vulnerabilities associated with the weak currency problem.

Risk Diversification

Do domestic capital markets in most emerging economies materially enhance risk diversification? This is such a basic question that one wonders why it has not been asked more frequently and more seriously. It is clear that the initial enthusiasm behind reforms to develop the local capital markets was full of hopes in this regard. Domestic capital markets were expected to significantly expand the risk diversification opportunities for local investors, freeing them from the traditional dependence on bank deposits and helping democratize firm ownership. In the process, local capital markets would broaden the range of financing options for corporations. The outcome, however, as documented in chapter 2, has been quite different on the whole. In the case of Latin America, with the exception of the contributors to mandatory pension funds, retail investors in the local securities markets continue to be a miniscule fraction of the population. Also, the portfolios of the domestic institutional investors in the majority of Latin countries are, by and large, quite undiversified and preponderantly invested in government debt securities. The investment that flows to private assets mainly takes the form of bank deposits. For most Latin American countries, therefore, it is difficult to avoid the conclusion that their local capital market has added little to the risk diversification function already performed by the banking system through its lending choices.

There are a handful of exceptions to this somber state of affairs for the regional average, as noted in chapter 2. First, in few countries—notably

Chile—the local institutional investors do allocate a significant share of their portfolios to domestic securities issued by nonbank corporate issuers. However, even in the case of Chile the set of issuers whose securities are held by institutional investors is rather narrow, with equity holdings concentrated in a small subset of the universe of listed companies, and bond holdings focused on very large companies rated A and above. Second, the local capital markets of few countries—notably Brazil, Chile, and Mexico—do feature fairly deep markets for derivatives, mainly foreign exchange hedges in the form of non–deliverable forwards. These important exceptions notwithstanding, the general conclusion stands that the role played by domestic securities markets in enhancing risk diversification is well below the initial expectations.

Although many conditions help explain this disappointing outcome—including crowding-out effects by governments thirsty for finance, and regulations that tightly restrict institutional investors' freedom—no doubt the small size of the domestic market is central to the story. Small domestic markets cannot sustain more than a limited number of issuers that could meet the size, quality, and liquidity thresholds required by local institutional investors. The result is compounded where concentration of ownership is high—as is the case of most Latin American countries—since few shares are traded. Moreover, even what appears to be a varied set of local securities would entail less "true" diversification if and when systemic risk is high. This is because systemic risk affects investments in local economy assets across the board and, as a consequence, cannot be diversified away by varying portfolio holdings within the domestic market.[186] The implications of small market size thus emerge as strongly for risk diversification as they do for liquidity.

The limited diversification opportunities in small domestic markets have prompted many analysts to argue for a relaxation of the regulatory regime to give local institutional investors greater latitude to invest in foreign assets. The argument is particularly compelling in the case of the fast-growing pension funds, whose primordial fiduciary function—to protect workers' savings so as to maximize retirement income for a given (relatively low) level of risk—is systematically thwarted if they live in a small domestic market and are not permitted to reduce risk through international diversification. While the argument has been transformed into action in a few Latin American countries—again, most notably Chile—that have raised the ceiling on pension fund investments abroad, in the majority of countries in the region the argument has run into a political wall. That is because allowing institutional investors to find assets in international markets smacks of an official blessing to capital flight. It is also because such action is dissonant with respect to the cherished expectation that pension funds can play a crucial role in stimulating the development of local financial markets, especially by supplying long-term financing to the private sector, without sacrifice to their primary fiduciary duty.[187]

Hence, others would argue that, rather than focusing on international diversification, the relaxation of regulatory limits should give priority to widening pension funds' ability to diversify their investments at home, a strategy that would be consistent with the objective of fostering pension funds' role in domestic financial development. There is clearly a point to this contention, considering that in many Latin American countries the regulatory regime is highly constraining and mandates pension funds to direct the lion's share of their funds to the purchase of government debt paper.[188] Would a more liberal domestic investment regime lead to a significant diversification of pension fund holdings? Again, the evidence suggests that expectations in this regard should be tamed. Consider, by way of illustration, the case of Chile, where efforts have been under way for some time to enhance risk diversification at home through a gradual relaxation of regulatory limits on domestic investment and the more recent introduction of a system of multiple funds with different risk-return profiles (among which contributing workers can choose). The results of these efforts, however, have been rather disappointing. In particular, the range of corporate issuers represented in the aggregate portfolio of pension funds has remained narrow despite the introduction of the multiple funds.[189] This suggests that, even under a more liberal investment regime, structural factors seem to be limiting the extent of diversification of institutional investor portfolios. This, together with illiquidity, leads to a strong segmentation of participation in the local capital markets in favor of the larger issuers.

Initial reform expectations regarding the participation of emerging market issuers in the risk diversification strategies of foreign investors were too modest in one sense but exaggerated in another. In effect, the evidence in chapter 2 shows that the degree of internationalization of the issuance and trading of Latin American securities is larger than in other regions. This might suggest larger holdings of Latin American assets by foreign investors. But even if that were the case, expectations turned out to be exaggerated with respect to the diversity of such holdings. Although the initial hope was that foreign investors' risk diversification strategies would be inclusive—that is, open equally to big and small countries and firms, selecting securities mainly in light of the quality of the issuer—the evidence proves that this hope was unrealistic.

That foreign portfolio diversification is not very inclusive is illustrated by the observation that the few and dominant investment managers actively investing in emerging markets display a highly selective strategy, heavily biased in favor of large-size issuers, both sovereign and corporate (see Ladekarl and Zervos 2004). These investors include only a few of the larger Latin American countries—ones with large locally and internationally listed companies and large quantities of international bond issues—in their set of "must invest" countries. These are typically the same countries that are included with relatively high weights in the benchmark indexes used by many investment funds to measure their performance.[190] Because such performance is also used to determine the asset manager's compensation, incentives are strong for managers not to deviate too much into off-index bets, which further accentuates the segmentation in favor of large issuers and issues.

The bias in favor of larger sizes in issuers and issues does not imply, however, that issuer quality does not matter. It does. As discussed in Ladekarl and Zervos (2004), international asset managers decide whether a country in the "must invest" list is under- or overweighted relative to the index, depending on perceptions regarding, importantly, the soundness of macroeconomic policies; the degree of political stability; the health and resiliency of the local financial system (including the size of the domestic investor base and reliability of the market infrastructures); the coverage, timeliness, and reliability of data disclosure; the quality of corporate governance; and the soundness of accounting and auditing practices. Moreover, these variables play a key role in determining which countries are included in investors' "may invest" list or in the "satellite" (as opposed to "core") list, regarding which asset managers are given greater discretion. Thus, there is room, albeit typically at the edges, for foreign investors to take positions in relatively marginal emerging economy assets. But even this is only to the extent that these assets can produce a risk diversification effect (significant enough to lower overall portfolio risk) or a return effect (high enough to raise total portfolio profitability). To achieve these effects, the investment requires a minimum threshold size. In sum, though caveats apply, the basic fact remains, namely, that risk diversification strategies of foreign investors—which are not restricted by limits imposed by regulation—are not as inclusive as originally envisaged. This leads to a greater than originally expected segmentation of participation in favor of large issuers and issues.[191]

The general observation of this section, that the portfolios of both foreign and local investors have less diversity in holdings than originally hoped for, suggests that the scope for diversification may be curbed by the economics of the risk diversification process itself. Our hypothesis is that the marginal risk reduction achieved by including one more issuer in the portfolio appears to be offset by the marginal cost of issuer screening and monitoring at a much earlier point than commonly believed. This would add yet another reason for why the direct participation in capital markets is segmented in favor of issuers and issues that meet a minimum size threshold. The evidence discussed in this section is consistent with this hypothesis, but research is needed to determine whether it passes more rigorous empirical and theoretical tests. Nonetheless, the implications can be significant, namely, that small issuers tend to systematically get short shrift in the process of risk diversification of securities portfolios—in domestic and international markets alike. Moreover, fiscal reforms (to stop force-feeding local institutional investors with government bonds) and regulatory reforms (to allow these investors greater freedom of choice regarding the composition of their portfolios) may have only modest effects in mitigating the segmented participation in the domestic capital market.

The observation that small and medium firms tend to be segmented out of direct access to securities markets does not imply, however, that such firms are, as a result, worse off in terms of access to financial services in general. Although biased in favor of the large firms, capital markets can enhance access for all through indirect effects. These markets may, for instance, lure away from banks the larger and blue chip corporate clients, thereby forcing banks to move down-market and seek new business by lending more to small and medium enterprises.

Final Remarks

This chapter has assessed alternative ways of interpreting the gap between expectations and outcomes in the development of capital markets in emerging economies, with an eye toward drawing lessons for the reform agenda going forward. We argued that two stylized views dominate the current reform debate in this regard. The first contends that the gap is due to the combination of impatience and imperfect and incomplete reform efforts. The second claims that the gap is due to faulty reform sequencing. We noted that, though differing in diagnoses and policy prescriptions, these views are not necessarily incompatible and both capture important aspects of the problems at hand, yielding considerable insights. Our main contention has been, however, that neither of the two views adequately addresses a number of salient questions posed by the evidence. We therefore proposed a third, complementary view that is much less prescriptive. It highlights the need to step back, revisit certain basic issues, and reshape expectations, as a prior step to ensure more solid grounds for a reformulation of the reform agenda. To illustrate the usefulness of revisiting basic issues from perspectives that are underplayed by the two main views, we selected and discussed three specific topics: financial globalization, liquidity, and risk diversification. The discussion showed that these topics are intertwined with problems of size and segmentation, that the issues involved have far-reaching implications for capital markets development, and that the associated complexities and challenges should not be underestimated in the reform debate.

The discussion of alternative views and the journey into basic issues invites eclecticism—a savvy reformer would combine elements from the three views, as appropriate to country circumstances. Our analysis clearly points to the flaws in using Wall Street as the ultimate benchmark for efforts to develop the domestic capital markets in emerging economies. It calls, instead, for a more varied reform agenda. The key to designing country-specific reforms would be a determination of whether the country in question can realistically meet the size thresholds to sustain a liquid domestic secondary market for private sector securities. For countries that do, the suitable reform package would be relatively easy to formulate, not least because the experience of developed capital markets would tend to be more relevant to such cases. Reform expectations, however, would still need to be significantly reshaped, particularly to better accommodate the implications of financial globalization. The elaboration of a suitable reform package for the smaller countries represents, in contrast, a more daunting challenge, not least because the thinking in this regard is at an early stage. Much more thought and analysis is needed to sketch a suitable "light" version of a domestic securities market for small countries, one that is not overengineered and is complementary to international financial integration. That sketch would have to be accompanied by a realistic definition of what can and cannot be expected from such a market. Related issues and challenges also arise regarding the participation of small firms in capital markets, irrespective of the country size.[192]

The journey into basic issues fortifies the already well-accepted thesis that any reform agenda for capital markets needs to be couched within a broader vision of financial development for emerging economies. Reforms should envisage improved integration into international financial markets with complementary financial development at home. Trying to avoid financial globalization is neither realistic nor desirable in the long run, not least because integration induces reform. A broader vision would emphasize links between financial markets and, in particular, the ways in which local capital markets can enhance the workings of the financial system as a whole, even if these markets fall short of expectations in terms of their price revelation function for private sector securities. Such links are crucial, for instance, in the development of markets for housing finance, infrastructure finance, and structured finance, where local and international securities markets can help engineer suitable products (such as asset-backed securities, hedges, and venture capital), spread risks among a greater number of players, and bring new institutional investors to the scene, all in ways that otherwise would not be possible. Ultimately, it will be through greater competition in financial markets, coupled with constant improvements in the contractual environment, that financial services provision will deepen and broaden, and will move down-market, resulting in new "bridging" vehicles and instruments that will fill any potential access gaps. Most likely, many such instruments and vehicles will be of a hybrid nature, flourishing at the interface of capital markets, banking markets, and other markets.

The analysis in this chapter suggests areas for future research that could be of special importance to the policy discussion. For example, further work is needed to understand the interactions between financial market internationalization and domestic capital market development. Our suggestion that globalization, liquidity, and risk diversification are linked with segmented participation in local and international capital markets needs deeper probing. Correlatively, a better grasp is required regarding the variety of ways in which financial development can fill eventual access gaps. Research is also needed to explain why, after controlling for economic fundamentals and reforms, Latin America has performed worse in terms of domestic capital market development. This puzzling fact was unearthed by our empirical research, but a full explanation is still pending.

Annex: Regional Capital Markets Integration— A Viable Alternative?

Over the past decade, there have been increasing attempts toward the regional integration of securities markets, with numerous cross-border agreements and alliances among exchanges and even some mergers. This process has been driven primarily by the intensified competition among national exchanges, as a result of the globalization of financial markets, deregulation and liberalization of domestic markets, and technological change.[193] The pressure from investors for improved liquidity, lower trading costs (both directly and indirectly, as narrower spreads), and access to international trading has led many exchanges to seek integration with other markets. Technological changes, such as electronic trading and automation, have also played a significant role in this process, by enabling the connection among geographically distant markets.

Regional integration could generate significant benefits, by allowing exchanges to capture economies of scale and increase trading and liquidity. Securities exchanges and settlement systems have a high ratio of fixed to variable costs, as high investments in information technology and communications systems are needed to operate them, but once all necessary infrastructure is in place, the cost of additional issuance or trading is small. The regional integration of domestic securities markets could help achieve a critical mass to exploit such scale economies, reducing the cost of financial services.[194] The consolidation of trading volume across regional markets would also lead to improvements in market liquidity, reducing asset price fluctuations. Given the network externalities that are intrinsic to securities trading, this increase in trading volume and liquidity would generate a positive feedback effect, attracting more participants to the market, who would bring additional trading opportunities and liquidity. A regional exchange could also improve the marketability of firms' securities, by allowing them to access a wider investor base, and could increase the opportunities for risk diversification available to domestic investors.[195]

Given all these potential benefits, there have been growing strides toward the regional integration of exchanges in recent years. This process has been particularly strong among European countries (see, for example, Licht 1998 and McAndrews and Stefanadis 2002).[196] Integration among

European domestic securities markets has taken different forms, ranging from establishing links among exchanges (in order to share some functions, such as marketing, listing, order routing, order execution, clearing, and settlements) to complete mergers or takeovers (see Claessens, Lee, and Zechner 2003).[197] One example of the linkage strategy is NOREX, which is a strategic alliance between four Scandinavian stock exchanges that allows cross-membership of firms across exchanges and uses a common trading system and regulatory standards, while exchanges remain independent. Euronext, created in 2002 as a result of the union between the Paris Bourse, the Amsterdam Exchange, and the Brussels Exchange, is an example of the merger strategy. In Latin America, by contrast, although the integration of national securities markets among themselves has been repeatedly proposed (see, for example, del Valle 2003; Dowers, Gomez-Acebo, and Masci 2003; IDB 2002), there has not been effective progress, beyond the emergence of agreements between exchanges that have yet to show an impact in terms of securities issuance and trading.[198]

Despite the potential benefits of securities market integration, few of the many attempts at cooperation between exchanges around the world have been implemented, and of those that have been realized, most have failed (Lee 1999). Euronext and NOREX are perhaps the most notable exceptions. There are many reasons for the failure of regional integration efforts. Legal and regulatory differences across countries can hinder the integration of domestic securities markets, as disparities in national rules require investors and firms to familiarize themselves with the regulatory regimes of several countries. Informational barriers across markets, such as differences in national accounting and disclosure standards, also limit the benefits of regional integration. The creation of regional securities markets, therefore, requires regulatory harmonization across countries, which might be very difficult to achieve. The integration of different market infrastructures or the development of new ones has usually proved to be more difficult and costly than initially anticipated. Conflicts of interest among participating exchanges, and also within each exchange, have also hampered market integration efforts. A more fundamental barrier to the regional integration of fixed income markets is the existence of national currencies, which exposes foreign investors to exchange rate variability, given the lack of deep markets for the required hedges.[199]

Given the mentioned difficulties, a relevant question is whether regional integration of securities markets would be superior to the alternative of global integration (that is, integration with financial centers in developed countries). More analysis and research is needed to ascertain whether there are specific roles for regional capital markets that cannot be played by the local or global markets. On first look, the answers are not simple. For example, though it is true that regional financial integration may reduce trading and issuance costs because of economies of scale, it seems doubtful that such cost reductions would be greater than those that could be achieved by global integration. Similarly, though it is true that neighboring investors may have informational advantages on regional assets and firms compared with more remote foreign investors, it is not clear that such advantages would be better exercised by trading in a regional market and not in a global one. Likewise, the conjecture that regional capital markets would facilitate access for small and medium enterprises (SMEs) needs to be reexamined. As noted in this chapter, SMEs are, in effect, segmented out of the local and international securities markets mainly because of the small size of their potential issues, and not because of the size of the markets. The solution, therefore, is not with bigger markets, regional or global, but with bigger issue sizes.[200] Finally, it is not clear why, in the absence of monetary unification, a regional debt market would have any advantage over a global market in overcoming the currency risk problem. In sum, it remains an open question whether and in what sense a regional integration agenda would provide more benefits than the alternative of seeking a better integration with the main international financial centers, which cannot be rivaled in terms of the depth of their liquidity pools and quality of their contractual environment.[201]

Endnotes

1. The literature on the finance-growth nexus is vast. Reviews of this literature can be found in a variety of forms that can suit different preferences. A comprehensive review is found in Levine (2005). Rajan and Zingales (2001, 2003b), by contrast, provide shorter reviews in less technical language. Caprio and Honohan (2001) offer an excellent rendition that emphasizes the World Bank contributions to the empirical literature. See the following section, "Why Does Financial Development Matter?" for further discussion.

2. For a detailed study on financial globalization see Obstfeld and Taylor (2005).

3. In fact, another aspect, which we analyze in chapter 3, is the share of foreign currency bonds, which some might view as an alternative indicator of internationalization.

4. An extensive literature analyzes the effects of internationalization on those firms that participate in international equity markets, focusing on the firms' trading and liquidity (see, for example, Noronha, Sarin, and Saudagaran 1996; Smith and Sofianos 1997; and Pulatkonak and Sofianos 1999); the impact of internationalization on stock prices and the cost of capital (see, for example, Alexander, Eun, and Janakiramanan 1988; Foerster and Karolyi 1999; Miller 1999; and Errunza and Miller 2000); and the effect of internationalization on firm size, growth, financing constraints, and financial structure (see, for example, Pagano, Roell, and Zechner 2002; Gozzi, Levine, and Schmukler 2006; Lins, Strickland, and Zenner 2005; and Schmukler and Vesperoni 2006). See Karolyi (2006) for a review.

5. See, for example, Coffee (1999, 2002), Stulz (1999), and Reese and Weisbach (2002).

6. Levine and Schmukler (2006, forthcoming) analyze the impact of migration to international markets on domestic stock market trading and liquidity. See also Moel (2001) and Karolyi (2004) for evidence on how the use of American depositary receipts (ADRs) can affect stock markets in emerging economies.

7. For a recent comprehensive study of banking in Latin America see IDB (2005).

8. A related limitation is that we estimate reduced-form equations and do not disentangle the structural links among the variables of interest.

9. See, for example, Robinson (1952), Lucas (1988), and Stern (1989).

10. See Levine (2005) for a detailed discussion.

11. Boyd and Prescott (1986), Allen (1990), and Greenwood and Jovanovic (1990) present theoretical models in which financial intermediaries arise to generate information on firms and sell it to investors.

12. See, for example, King and Levine (1993a), Blackburn and Hung (1998), Galetovic (1996), and Acemoglu, Aghion, and Zilibotti (2006).

13. See, for example, Saint-Paul (1992), Devereaux and Smith (1994), and Obstfeld (1994).

14. Levine (1991) develops a theoretical model that shows that, by facilitating trading, stock markets reduce liquidity risk. Bencivenga, Smith, and Starr (1995) show that reductions in trading costs affect investment decisions by making technologies with longer gestation periods more attractive to investors.

15. This literature was initiated by Goldsmith (1969). Also see King and Levine (1993b), Levine and Zervos (1998b), and Levine, Loayza, and Beck (2000).

16. See, for example, Levine, Loayza, and Beck (2000); Rousseau and Wachtel (2000); and Beck and Levine (2004).

17. See Rousseau and Wachtel (1998); Arestis, Demetriades, and Luintel (2001); and Xu (2000) for time series analyses. Wright (2002) presents a detailed study of how the financial system in the United States created conditions for economic growth after 1780. Haber (1991, 1997) compares industrial and capital market development in Brazil, Mexico, and the United States between 1830 and 1930. See also Cameron (1967) and McKinnon (1973) for historical case studies.

18. Also see Wurgler (2000), Claessens and Laeven (2003), Love (2003), Beck, Demirgüç-Kunt, and Martinez-Peria (forthcoming), and Beck, Demirgüç-Kunt, and Maksimovic (2005).

19. For instance, Beck, Demirgüç-Kunt, and Maksimovic (2005) find that the extent to which financial, legal, and corruption problems affect firm growth depends on firm size, with smaller firms being most affected by these factors. Similarly, Chong, Galindo, and Micco (2004) find not only that small and medium enterprises (SMEs) finance a significantly lower share of their investments with bank credit relative to large firms, but also that the difference in bank financing between SMEs and large firms is higher in countries with worse creditor protection and less efficient judicial systems.

20. See, for example, Banerjee and Newman (1993), Galor and Zeira (1993), and Rajan and Zingales (2003b).

21. See Beck and de la Torre (2006) and de la Torre, Gozzi, and Schmukler (2006a) for discussions of conceptual issues in access to finance.

22. Beck, Demirgüç-Kunt, and Martinez Peria (forthcoming) find that banking sector outreach is associated with lower firm-level financial constraints, even after controlling for financial sector depth.

23. See Merton and Bodie (1995, 2004) and Levine (1997), among others. Schmukler and Vesperoni (2001) find the degree of development of an economy much more important than its particular financial structure for explaining firms' financing choices.

24. See, for example, Beck and Levine (2002), Demirgüç-Kunt and Levine (2001), and Levine (2002).

25. French and Poterba (1991) and Tesar and Werner (1995) present evidence of home bias in international investment. Several papers have also found that investors exhibit a preference for larger, geographically and culturally closer firms, both within and across countries (see, for example, Coval and Moskovitz 1999; Grinblatt and Keloharju 2001; and Huberman 2001).

26. Eichengreen and Sussman (2000) offer a millennium perspective.

27. There are different ways to "list" domestic stocks in international financial markets. A traditional way is to cross-list the share in another exchange. European companies tend to use this method of internationalization most often. A very popular way to internationalize among emerging market firms has been through depositary receipts, called American Depositary Receipts (ADRs) or Global Depositary Receipts (GDRs). These are foreign currency–denominated derivative instru-

ments, issued by international banks such as the Bank of New York or Citibank, representing home securities held with a local custodian. Trading in ADRs and GDRs in U.S. exchanges has expanded from US$75 billion in 1990 to US$1 trillion in 2005, and there are currently more than 1,900 sponsored ADR programs, issued by firms from 73 countries. Depositary receipt programs grow or shrink depending on demand, since the issuance of ADRs and GDRs and the conversion back to the underlying shares involves only a small transaction cost. See Levy Yeyati, Schmukler, and van Horen (2006).

28. See, for example, Greenspan (1999), Herring and Chatusripitak (2000), IFC (2000), and Batten and Kim (2001).

29. The evidence from Chile suggests that pension reform can have a significant impact on capital market development and economic growth. See Corbo and Schmidt-Hebbel (2003).

30. Note that this heterogeneity also extends to developed countries.

31. Since 2003 several Latin American countries (Brazil, Colombia, and Uruguay) have issued domestic currency government bonds in international markets, and foreign investors have increased their participation in local bond markets. See IMF (2005), Tovar (2005), and UN-ECLAC (2005) for discussions of these trends.

32. Repo transactions involve the sale of an asset under an agreement to repurchase the asset from the same counterparty. Interest is paid by adjusting the sale and repurchase prices. Structured finance can be defined as a form of financial intermediation based on securitization technology. In its simplest form, it is a process whereby assets are pooled and transferred to a third party (commonly referred to as special purpose vehicle or SPV), which in turn issues securities backed by this asset pool. Typically, several classes of securities (called tranches) with distinct risk-return profiles are issued.

33. For a discussion on the similarities and differences between stock and bond markets see Herring and Chatusripitak (2001).

34. See Levine and Schmukler (2006, forthcoming) for a discussion and evidence on these channels.

35. The gold backing entailed the commitment to exchange dollars to gold at a rate of US$35 per ounce.

36. Some authors (see, for example, Alles 2001 and BIS 2005) differentiate between securitization (which only involves the pooling and transfer of assets to a third party and subsequent issuance of securities) and structured finance (which also involves the creation of different classes of securities). In keeping with common usage, we use the term *structured finance* to refer to both types of transactions. It is necessary to consider that accurately defining structured finance is quite difficult, as even among market participants there is no agreement on exactly what it encompasses. See Davis (2005) for a survey of alternative definitions.

37. While globalization at the beginning of the 20th century mainly entailed flows from rich countries (mostly the United Kingdom) to emerging economies, most of the action in the more recent globalization phase has taken place among developed economies. In this phase, capital flows among developed countries have increased sharply, and capital market activity has concentrated in only a few large international financial centers.

38. See IMF (2005). Nevertheless, international investors seem to be not yet taking full advantage of the risk diversification opportunities offered by cross-border securities investment. A certain preference for local securities persists. Information asymmetries and transaction costs could be possible explanations of this "home bias" phenomenon (French and Poterba 1991).

39. The strong growth of public sector bond markets is also partly explained by the need to sterilize capital inflows. Initially, central banks issued short-term bills to sterilize capital inflows. As global capital inflows strengthened and confidence

in public bond markets grew, most emerging-market governments began issuing long-term government bonds for this purpose.

40. In contrast, equity flows represented less than 13 percent of total capital flows during the 1976–82 period.

41. The top 10 countries in terms of private capital flows between 1990 and 2004 were (in decreasing order of magnitude): China, Brazil, Mexico, Argentina, Poland, India, Malaysia, Chile, Turkey, and Hungary.

42. Privatization may also promote stock market development through indirect channels. Perotti and Van Oijen (2001) and Perotti and Laeven (2002) show that privatization can lead to a reduction in political risk, which in turn helps build investor confidence. They argue that this effect was an important source behind the recent growth in stock markets in emerging economies. Bortolotti et al. (2003), in an analysis of OECD countries, find that privatization promotes stock market development by providing investors better diversification opportunities.

43. See chapter 1 for a discussion of literature on the finance-growth nexus.

44. See Herring and Chatusripitak (2000). Chatu Mongol Sonakul (2000), governor of the Bank of Thailand, remarked in reference to the Asian crisis: "If I [could] turn back the clock and [had] a wish, my list may be long. But high in its ranking would be a well functioning Thai baht bond market."

45. Past policies obstructive to capital market development included high budget deficits that were monetized and led to high inflation, volatile monetary policy that caused high and unpredictable monetary growth, poor credibility of macro policy makers, and financial repression that hindered financial intermediation (Roubini 2001).

46. Some Latin American countries (Argentina, Chile, and Uruguay) liberalized their financial systems in the 1970s, but these reforms were reversed in the aftermath of the 1982 debt crisis, and financial systems throughout the region remained repressed during most of the 1980s.

47. Brazil did not carry out a pension reform but pension funds account for a significant portion of Brazil's institutional investor base. At the end of 2004, pension fund assets represented about 19 percent of GDP.

48. A 1994 World Bank report on pension reform underlines the relevance of pension reform for capital market development. It argues that "a dominant pay-as-you-go public pillar . . . misses an opportunity for capital market development. When the first old generations get pensions that exceed their savings, national consumption may rise and savings may decline. The next few cohorts pay their social security tax instead of saving for their own old age (since they now expect to get a pension from the government), so this loss in savings may never be made up. In contrast, the alternative, a mandatory funded plan, could increase capital accumulation—an important advantage in capital-scarce countries. A mandatory saving plan that increases long-term saving beyond the voluntary point and requires it to flow through financial institutions stimulates a demand for (and eventually supply of) long-term financial instruments—a boon to development. These missed opportunities in a pay-as-you-go public pillar become lost income for future generations—and another source of intergenerational transfer" (p. 15).

49. Following the financial crises of the second half of the 1990s, initiatives to strengthen the international financial architecture resulted in an ambitious program to assess the degree of compliance of country practices with international standards. The International Monetary Fund and World Bank have been entrusted with a leading role in assessing the degree of observance of international standards and codes. These assessments are often conducted in connection with the Financial Sector Assessment Program (FSAP), a fairly thorough diagnosis of a country's financial system also led by these two institutions, and their results are summa-

rized in the so-called Reports on the Observance of Standards and Codes (ROSC). For details see http://www.worldbank.org/ifa/rosc.html. International standards that are relevant to the functioning of securities markets include the following: IOSCO Objectives and Principles of Securities Regulation, CPSS-IOSCO Recommendations for Securities Clearance and Settlement, Organisation for Economic Co-operation and Development (OECD) Principles of Corporate Governance, Accounting and Auditing Standards, and the World Bank Principles and Guidelines for Effective Insolvency and Creditor Rights Systems.

50. See Financial System Stability Assessment for Chile, which summarizes the 2004 FSAP and includes the ROSC on Securities Regulation at http://www.imf.org/external/pubs/cat/longres.cfm?sk=17665.0.

51. We also estimated the figures for East Asia, excluding Hong Kong (China), as it may serve as a regional financial center for corporations from mainland China and other Asian countries. Although this reduces the average values for East Asian countries, these countries still show significantly higher stock market capitalization and trading than Latin American countries. When excluding Hong Kong (China), the average capitalization for the remaining East Asian countries included in the figures stood at 82.6 percent of GDP in 2004, whereas their value traded in that year reached 77 percent of GDP.

52. Repo transactions involve the sale of an asset under an agreement to repurchase the asset at a future date. Interest is paid by adjusting the sale and repurchase prices. The securities serve as collateral for what is effectively a cash loan and, conversely, the cash serves as collateral for a securities loan. A key characteristic of repos is that they can be used either to obtain funds or to obtain securities. This latter feature is valuable to market participants because it allows them to obtain the securities they need to meet other contractual obligations, that is, to make delivery of a futures contract. In addition, repos can be used for leverage, to fund long positions in securities, and to fund short positions in order to hedge interest rate risks. Because repos are short-maturity collateralized instruments, repo markets have strong links with securities markets, derivatives markets, and other short-term markets such as interbank and money markets (see BIS 1999).

53. See de la Torre and Schmukler (2004) for an analysis of the issues of duration, currency, and jurisdiction in emerging markets within an integrated conceptual framework.

54. See IMF (2005), Tovar (2005), and UN-ECLAC (2005) for more detailed descriptions of theses issues.

55. The increased investor interest in local currency debt from emerging markets has led to the creation of indexes to track the performance of local currency bonds portfolios. In 2005 JPMorgan launched the Government Bond Index–Emerging Markets (GBI-EM), which tracks the performance of local currency bond markets in 19 emerging economies, including several Latin American countries (Brazil, Chile, Colombia, and Mexico).

56. See Glaessner (2003) for a more in-depth analysis of derivatives markets in emerging economies and their use in the implementation of economic policies.

57. Derivatives markets have traditionally measured their activity in terms of number of contracts traded. This generates difficulties when comparing volumes across exchanges, since each exchange defines contract sizes to suit its users and there is no reason why contracts from one exchange should be comparable to those in another exchange. Several alternative measures have been proposed to solve this issue (that is, notional value outstanding, trading velocity, and risk-equivalent values); however, because of data unavailability, comparisons are usually limited to the number of contracts outstanding. It is worth mentioning that when considering the notional value outstanding, the BM&F is still among the largest exchanges in

the world for exchange rate futures. On the other hand, the relative ranking of the MexDer is significantly lower in terms of notional value outstanding (see IOMA 2004 and Burghardt 2004 for more discussion on this issue).

58. Non–deliverable forwards (NDFs) are forward transactions whose settlement is made by a cash payment in U.S. dollars, so that no local currency changes hands. These types of contracts are mostly used for emerging market currencies, and the main participants in the market are large international banks. The most important currencies in the NDF market are the Argentine peso, the Brazilian real, the major Asian currencies, and the Hungarian forint. See Schmukler and Servén (2002).

59. See Alles (2001) for a general discussion of the elements of the legal framework that may prevent the development of structured finance in developing countries.

60. See Meddin (2004) for an overview of structured finance in emerging markets and the role it may play in fostering capital market development.

61. ABS transactions typically include consumer credits, auto loans, trade receivables, credit card receivables, or bank loans in the collateral pool. Future flow transactions are backed by expected, stable future flows arising from a financial asset or a firm. Mortgage-backed securites are the most common real-estate-related transactions.

62. In most countries this is because of the lack of development of private sector bond markets. In others, such as Mexico, regulations only allow the use of government securities as collateral for repo operations.

63. Retail investors, as opposed to institutional investors, are individuals who purchase small amounts of securities for their own holdings. Retail investors are also often called small or individual investors.

64. Gill, Packard, and Yermo (2005) argue, for instance, that because of over-regulation of pension fund investments, institutional investors in Latin America have—unlike their counterparts in OECD countries—not become an independent driving force behind financial innovation so far.

65. Overregulation of pension funds by the government might also weaken their insulation from political interference (Yermo 2003).

66. Some reforms that had a significant impact on securities market development, such as the creation of a credible indexation unit (Unidad de Fomento, UF), were implemented even before (the UF was created in 1967) and took a long time to mature (see Herrera and Valdes 2003, for a description of the Chilean experience with CPI indexation). The UF is an indexation unit that is adjusted on the basis of the previous month's change in the consumer price index.

67. Other Latin American countries, especially Brazil, have issued inflation-indexed securities. However, none has been as successful as Chile.

68. Each mortgage bond has to match the amount of a mortgage loan on the books of the issuing bank. The bank does not actually lend money directly to the borrower. Rather, it provides the borrower with the bond, which the bank then sells in the marketplace (normally taken at face value) on the borrower's behalf. The issuing bank charges a fee for its services. If, owing to prepayment, the associated loan is cancelled, then the issuing bank has to retire the bonds from the market in an equivalent amount.

69. The Cencosud issue was the first IPO to be launched simultaneously in Chile and in international markets. Also, instead of targeting institutional investors (pension funds in particular), as most issues in the Chilean market do, this issue targeted retail investors. As of September 2005, Cencosud had around 3,000 shareholders.

70. In 1984 Chile adopted a crawling exchange rate band, whose center or reference value was periodically adjusted to reflect the difference between domestic and foreign inflation rates. The band's width was gradually increased over time,

except for a temporary reversal in 1998. This system was abandoned in September 1999, when a floating exchange rate regime was adopted.

71. A 2003 assessment conducted by the World Bank found Chile to score well in its observance of the OECD Principles of Corporate Governance (14 of 23 principles were rated as "observed" or "largely observed"). This reflected, at least partially, improvements introduced by the "Ley de OPAs" (see World Bank 2003c). Also, see Linnenberg and Waitzer (2004) for a more detailed description of the reforms introduced by this law.

72. In 2002 the Chilean authorities initiated a strategy to normalize the yield curve by developing liquidity in government securities at key benchmark maturities (two, five, 10, and 20 years). This process has been quite successful, as banks have started to systematically trade these securities, especially those with maturities of two and five years.

73. See Glaessner (2003) for a more detailed discussion.

74. "Free float" can be defined as the percentage of a company's shares that are available for purchase in the market. It excludes stakes held by controlling shareholders, the company's management, the government, and strategic partners.

75. Note that business groups and conglomerates are the predominant corporate structure in Chile, with around 70 percent of nonfinancial listed companies belonging to one of about 50 conglomerates.

76. See Jeanneau and Perez Verdia (2005) for a detailed description of the initiatives adopted by the Mexican government to foster domestic bond market development.

77. Note that these data do not include bonds issued by the deposit insurance agency (Instituto para la Protección al Ahorro Bancario, IPAB), which amount to about 4 percent of GDP. The IPAB has been issuing floating rate bonds with government guarantees to finance its operations and the costs of the 1994–95 banking crisis.

78. See World Bank (2003c) for an assessment of corporate governance practices in Mexico and Capaul (2003) for a comparison of corporate governance in Mexico with other Latin American countries.

79. See Martinez and Werner (2002a) for a more detailed account of the 2001 financial sector reforms.

80. Debentures provide significant investor protection, in case of default, but are very costly to issue. On the other hand, medium-term notes are easy to issue but provide little investor protection. Also, medium-term notes are restricted to maturities between one and seven years and can only be repaid at maturity (bullet payment). Debentures, however, have no maximum or minimum maturities, and their amortization schedule is quite flexible.

81. A significant recent development in cross-border structured finance transactions has been the creation of transactions backed by local currency assets. In fact, all three cross-border transactions closed during 2005, representing a total of US$310 million, were take-out securitizations of residential construction loans. Currency mismatches in these transactions were mitigated through currency swaps.

82. The mortgage market in Mexico is dominated by public agencies. In 2004, INFONAVIT, the largest public housing agency, funded about 60 percent of all mortgages, while Sociedad Hipotecaria Federal provided funding for an additional 12 percent.

83. Sociedad Hipotecaria Federal was created to manage FOVI (Fondo de Operacion y Financiamiento Bancario a la Vivienda), a federal government fund previously managed by the central bank. SHF's second-tier lending to private mortgage originators will end by law in 2009, when its mission will be restricted to providing guarantee products.

84. INFONAVIT was created in 1972 to finance low-income housing. It is funded by private sector employers' contributions of five percent of their employees' gross wages. Following the pension reform, INFONAVIT has been integrated into the pension system. Funds are accumulated in individual accounts and have a minimum guaranteed return.

85. MexDer offers futures on individual equities, equity indexes, and foreign currencies, as well as options on equities, equity indexes, and exchange-traded funds. However, most of the trading on MexDer corresponds to interest rate futures, in particular contracts for the 28-day interbank equilibrium interest rate (TIIE).

86. The market has attracted only a handful of new listings in recent years, with less than 10 initial public offerings between 1998 and 2004.

87. Investment regulations require pension funds to invest at least 51 percent of their assets in inflation-indexed securities. Until December 2001 only federal government and central bank securities were eligible for investment under this rule, creating an investment floor for government securities. However, pension funds' holdings of government debt have significantly exceeded this floor, reaching about 80 percent of total assets at the end of 2005.

88. See World Bank (2002a) for a detailed description of the issues affecting liquidity in the Mexican securities markets

89. La Porta et al. (1998) analyze shareholder concentration in the 10 largest private nonfinancial firms in 49 countries and find that Mexico has the second highest concentration of all countries surveyed (after Greece), with the top three shareholders holding 64 percent of ownership on average. Regarding free float, although there are many difficulties in estimating it accurately, government officials estimate it to be between 12 percent and 15 percent (World Bank 2003c).

90. In 1989 regulatory changes were implemented to promote foreign investment without losing control to foreign investors, which led to the creation of dual shareholding structures. There are currently several classes of shares in the Mexican stock market: "A" shares are full voting shares reserved for Mexican investors; "B" shares have full voting rights and open ownership; "L" shares carry limited voting rights; and "O" shares are stocks of financial institutions with open ownership and full voting rights. According to Martinez and Werner (2002a), shares with restricted voting rights represent about 40 percent of market value and 45 percent of trading in the Mexican stock market.

91. There are different ways to "list" domestic stocks in international financial markets. A traditional way is to cross-list the share in another exchange. European companies tend to use this method of internationalization most often. A very popular way to internationalize among emerging market firms has been through depositary receipts, called American depositary receipts (ADRs) or Global depositary receipts (GDRs). These are foreign currency–denominated derivative instruments, issued by international banks such as the Bank of New York or Citibank, representing home securities held with a local custodian. Depositary receipt programs grow or shrink depending on demand, since the issuance of DRs and the conversion back to the underlying shares involves only a small transaction cost (see Levy Yeyati, Schmukler, and van Horen 2006).

92. As mentioned earlier, the comparisons on the degree of internationalization are based on measures such as the international issuance and trading activity of local firms. We do not analyze whether domestic or international investors are the ones participating in domestic and international markets. In fact, the foreign activity may well be driven by domestic investors. These distinctions are left for future research.

93. Note that investors in Latin American securities in foreign markets include not only foreign investors but also residents who have savings abroad.

94. Companies with international activity are those identified as having at least one active depositary receipt program at any time in the year, or having raised capital in international markets in the current or previous years, or trading on the London Stock Exchange, New York Stock Exchange, or NASDAQ.

95. Various publications have voiced concerns of markets becoming illiquid (for example, Bovespa 1996; *Financial Times* 1998; *Latin Finance* 1999; *The Economist* 2000; and the Federation des Bourses de Valeurs 2000).

96. For an analysis of the impact of internationalization on domestic stock markets see Moel (2001) and Levine and Schmukler (2006, forthcoming).

97. Given the fixed costs of going abroad, the need to meet a minimum size threshold, and information costs for investors, size might be an important factor for determining access to international equity markets. The empirical literature has found that larger firms, with higher growth opportunities and a higher share of foreign sales, are more likely to access international markets (see Pagano, Roell, and Zechner 2002 and Claessens and Schmukler 2006).

98. Generally, manipulation is defined as a series of transactions designed to raise or lower a price of a security or to give the appearance of trading for the purpose of inducing others to buy or sell.

99. See Claessens, Klingebiel, and Schmukler (2006) for an empirical analysis of the role of fundamentals in stock market development.

100. For a discussion on the similarities and differences between stock and bond markets see Herring and Chatusripitak (2001).

101. The data are averages from 1990 to 2004. See annex table 1 for a list of countries included in the analysis.

102. The data are averages between 1994 and 2004. See annex table 1 for the list of countries.

103. Note that in statistical analysis, even controlling for measures of macroeconomic volatility and the legal environment, GDP per capita is found to be positively and significantly associated with capital market development, suggesting that the income level captures aspects not measured by these explanatory variables (see, for example, Claessens, Klingebiel, and Schmukler forthcoming).

104. See, for example, Bencivenga and Smith (1998), Boyd, Levine, and Smith (2001), Boyd and Smith (2001), Huybens and Smith (1999), and IDB (1995).

105. The theoretical literature on credit market frictions, finance, and growth suggests that the relation between inflation and financial sector development may be characterized by thresholds (see, for example, Boyd and Smith 1998, and Huybens and Smith, 1998, 1999). Once inflation exceeds a critical level, subsequent increases in the rate of inflation may have no additional impact on financial sector activity. Boyd, Levine, and Smith (2001) confirm econometrically that higher levels of inflation are associated with smaller, less active, and less efficient banking systems and stock markets. They also highlight the nonlinear relation between inflation and financial sector performance.

106. In the case of bond markets, the evidence shows a positive relation between the deficit and government bond markets (almost as a matter of definition) and a nonsignificant relation between the deficit and private bond markets, consistent with the discussion above.

107. See Beck and Levine (2004) for a review.

108. See, for example, Claessens, Klingebiel, and Schmukler (2002); Johnson, McMillan, and Woodruff (2002); and La Porta et al. (1997, 1998, 2000, 2002).

109. See, for example, La Porta et al. (1997, 1998).

110. See, for example, Haber, Razo, and Maurer (2003); Pagano and Volpin (2001); Rajan and Zingales (2003a); and Roe (1994).

111. See, for example, Acemoglu, Johnson, and Robinson (2001, 2002); Diamond (1997); and Stulz and Williamson (2003).

112. Network effects are an intrinsic feature of securities trading: the benefits of participating in a given market increase with the number of participants (Economides 1993, 1996; Di Noia 1999). This generates positive feedback, because a liquid market attracts more participants, and each new participant brings additional trading opportunities and liquidity, benefiting all market participants and making the market more attractive to others. These network externalities imply a tendency toward concentration, explaining the durability of the dominant national trading markets (Domowitz and Steil 1999). There is also evidence of economies of scale in stock exchanges, especially regarding order execution (Malkamaki 1999).

113. Claessens, Djankov, and Klingebiel (2001) argue that stock markets in many transition economies might not be able to achieve the economies of scale necessary to compete with foreign markets. Furthermore, they suggest that as globalization and technological change increase the scale needed for exchanges to operate competitively, more countries may find it difficult to maintain an independent market. Regarding bond markets, Del Valle (2003) argues that many of the smaller economies in Latin America lack the size to support the necessary infrastructure to operate local markets and that authorities have to explore alternative mechanisms, such as private placements, access to international markets, and regional solutions. See Bossone, Honohan, and Long (2001) for a discussion of the main issues related to small financial systems and their policy implications.

114. See, for example, Jeanne (2000) and Krugman (1999).

115. See Chamon and Hausmann (2005); Eichengreen and Hausmann (1999, 2003); Eichengreen, Hausmann, and Panizza (2003), and Hausmann, Panizza, and Stein (2001).

116. This finding also confirms evidence from Acemoglu, Johnson, and Robinson (2001); Isham, Kaufmann, and Pritchett (1995); and many others regarding the role of institutions in determining the quality of (macro) economic management.

117. An explanation specific to foreign investors is that debt from nondemocratic governments may more easily be declared "odious" and be repudiated ex post (see Kremer and Jayachandran 2002). As a consequence, investors would ex ante be less willing to lend to such countries. For an earlier discussion on debt repudiation and its effects on sustainable debts, see Bulow and Rogoff (1989) and Eaton and Gersovitz (1981).

118. Similarly, Mehl and Reynaud (2005) focus on the "domestic original sin" and find that several factors, including macroeconomic policies, debt burdens, and the investor base, help to explain emerging economies' ability to borrow domestically in local currency, at long maturities and fixed interest rates.

119. See, for example, Burnside, Eichenbaum, and Rebelo (2001); Dooley (2000); McKinnon and Pill (1998); and Schneider and Tornell (2004). A related argument points to the idea that fixed exchange rate regimes might induce agents to underestimate the possibility of future currency changes, leading to excessive foreign exchange borrowing (Eichengreen 1994). See Frankel et al. (2001) for an exposition of the different arguments.

120. See, for example, Calvo (1996); de la Torre, Levy Yeyati, and Schmukler (2003); and Jeanne (2003).

121. To some degree, relevant answers to this inquiry can already be inferred from the discussion above, particularly when the explanatory variables have different signs.

122. The results for the exchange rate regime are consistent with evidence suggesting that after countries moved from fixed to floating exchange rate regimes, the sovereign and corporate sectors have responded by issuing more local currency debt in the very recent past. Tovar (2005) argues that the adoption of flexible exchange regimes by Latin American countries has facilitated the issuance of domestic currency debt in international markets. On the corporate side, Galiani, Levy Yeyati,

and Schargrodsky (2003) argue that Argentina's currency board contributed to the dollarization of firms' balance sheets by fueling beliefs in an implicit exchange rate guarantee that reduced firms' willingness to pay the cost of hedging their positions. In the case of Mexico, Martinez and Werner (2002b) propose a similar argument. They test it by analyzing the effects that the change from a fixed to a floating exchange rate regime in December 1994 had on the currency composition of corporate debt and on firms' currency mismatches. They find evidence supporting the view that this shift prompted firms to reduce their exposure to exchange rate risk. In the case of Brazil, Rossi (2004) finds that the number of firms exposed to currency risk is significantly lower during the period of floating exchange rate than during the fixed exchange rate regime.

123. See, for example, Cole and Kehoe (1996); Corsetti, Pesenti, and Roubini (1999); Eichengreen and Hausmann (1999); Feldstein (1999); Furman and Stiglitz (1998); Obstfeld (1998); Radelet and Sachs (1998); and Sachs, Tornell, and Velasco (1996).

124. The reliance of emerging countries on short-term debt has also been interpreted as a result of pre-commitment: short-term debt can serve as a commitment device for debtors in a context of time inconsistency (see, for example, Blanchard and Missale 1994; Calvo 1988; Jeanne 2000; and Rodrik and Velasco 1999). Tirole (2002) explains that short-term and foreign currency debt reduce the time inconsistency problems. De la Torre and Schmukler (2004) argue that because of the litigation option of a claim, the dominant strategy for creditors is to hedge against price risk by using short-term foreign currency–denominated debt, and take instead the greater exposure to default risk.

125. The term premium should be higher during financial crises, and debt issuance should shift toward shorter maturities when crises are the result of an increase in bondholders' risk aversion. On the other hand, debt issuance should move toward longer maturities when crises are the result of a decrease in the country's expected repayment capacity. All these predictions are supported by the evidence presented in Broner, Lorenzoni, and Schmukler (2004), which also develops a formal model.

126. Their sample corresponds to those emerging economies that borrowed heavily in foreign currency during that period, because these economies provide data for a large enough set of bonds of different maturities at each point in time. The analyzed countries are Argentina, Brazil, Colombia, Mexico, Russia, Turkey, Uruguay, and the República Bolivariana de Venezuela.

127. Also note that excess returns decrease with coupon size. This is expected, given that the term premiums are positive and duration is a decreasing function of coupon size.

128. Although these reforms were a significant part of the capital market reform programs implemented by most countries, this list is not exhaustive and does not attempt to cover all the policy initiatives oriented toward fostering stock market development that were implemented over the past decades.

129. See, for example, Alexander, Eun, and Janakiramanan (1987); Eun and Janakiramanan (1986); Errunza and Losq (1985); Stapleton and Subrahmanyam (1977); and Stulz (1999a).

130. See, for example, Bekaert and Harvey (2000); Henry (2000a, 2003); Kim and Singal (2000); and Edison and Warnock (2003).

131. See, for example, Bekaert, Harvey, and Lundblad (2005) and Henry (2000b, 2003).

132. Bhattacharya and Daouk (2002) carry out a comprehensive survey of insider trading laws, finding that these laws existed in 87 countries by 1998, but they had been enforced, as evidenced by prosecutions, in only 38 of them. They also find that the cost of equity does not change after the introduction of insider trading regulations, but decreases considerably after the first prosecution.

133. See Domowitz and Steil (1999) for a discussion of the impact of electronic trading on the exchange industry. Blennerhassett and Bowman (1998) report a fall in transaction costs after the move to electronic trading in the New Zealand Stock Exchange. Green et al. (2003) also find improvements in efficiency and liquidity following the introduction of screen-based trading in the Mumbai Stock Exchange.

134. Boutchkova and Megginson (2000) show that privatized firms are generally among the largest firms in local stock markets, even in many developed countries, and that they account for a large share of total market capitalization.

135. See Chiesa and Nicodano (2003) for a review of the theoretical arguments about the impact of privatization on stock market liquidity. Bortolotti et al. (2003) analyze the impact of share issue privatizations (also known as SIPs) in 19 developed countries and find that they are associated with improvements in turnover and liquidity.

136. The nature of the reforms differed across countries, with some countries shifting to fully funded systems of privately managed individual accounts, while others created multilayer systems, in which part of the pension system is pay-as-you-go, and there is also a distinct and separate privately managed funded component. See Rutkowski (1998, 2002) for a description of the reforms in transition economies. De Ferranti, Leipziger, and Srinivas (2002); Gill, Packard, and Yermo (2005); and Queisser (1998), among many others, review the experience of Latin American countries.

137. There is a large literature discussing the impact of structural pension reforms. See, for example, Feldstein (1998), Feldstein and Liebman (2002), Orszag and Stiglitz (2001), and World Bank (1994).

138. Walker and Lefort (2002) find evidence of a reduction in the cost of capital and higher trading volumes as a result of pension reform. Catalan, Impavido, and Musalem (2001) analyze the Granger causality between contractual savings (assets in pension funds and life insurance companies) and stock market development and find evidence that the growth in contractual savings causes increases in market capitalization and trading.

139. In a more general context, Loayza, Fajnzylber, and Calderón (2005) analyze whether the growth outcome of the reforms of the 1990s in Latin America can be interpreted as a disappointment. They estimate the expected impact of the reforms on economic growth using cross-country regressions and then compare the predicted growth rate of Latin American countries on the basis of the reforms with their observed growth during the 1990s. They find that most Latin American countries experienced growth rates consistent with the extent of the reforms and thus conclude that reforms had the predicted impact. However, the estimated payoffs of the reforms in many cases are quite small, suggesting that initial expectations may have been overly optimistic.

140. The literature on the determinants of capital flight (for example, Collier, Hoeffler, and Pattillo 2000; Schineller 1997; and Sheets 1996) has found that residents decide to invest their wealth abroad because of an adverse domestic investment climate, including macroeconomic instability and weak institutions.

141. The literature on "bonding" has expanded in recent years (see Benos and Weisbach 2004 for a review). One of the first articles in this literature is Coffee (1999), who argues that cross-listing in an exchange with better investor protection is a form of bonding, creating a credible and binding commitment by the issuer to protect the interests of minority shareholders. Reese and Weisbach (2002) find that after cross-listing in the United States, firms that come from countries with a weaker corporate governance framework are more likely to consecutively issue equity at home, since cross-listing improves investor protection for all shareholders, including those outside the United States. There are, however, skeptics of the

bonding view. For example, Licht (2003) and Siegel (2005) argue that the host regulators typically provide only limited protection against minority rights abuses by controlling shareholders in the firm's home country, and thus that the value from bonding is limited. More generally, many argue that the scope for "functional convergence" of corporate governance across countries is limited.

142. These results are consistent with the findings in Aggarwal, Klapper, and Wysocki (2005), who analyze portfolio holdings of emerging market equities by U.S. mutual funds and find that funds are more likely to invest in countries with stronger accounting standards, shareholder rights, and legal frameworks. Ladekarl and Zervos (2004) analyze the investment allocation process employed by portfolio investors in emerging markets and find that macroeconomic policies, corporate governance, and the legal and regulatory framework are important determinants of whether countries are considered "investable" or not. Wojcik, Clark, and Bauer (2004) also find that firms with better corporate governance practices are more likely to cross-list in the United States, consistent with the view that better fundamentals allow firms to access foreign markets.

143. Some examine the volume and liquidity of international firms in domestic markets; for example, see Hargis (2000); Noronha, Sarin, and Saudagaran (1996); and Pulatkonak and Sofianos (1999). Others study the impact of internationalization on stock prices; for example, see Alexander, Eun, and Janakiramanan (1988); Foerster and Karolyi (1999); and Miller (1999). Still others analyze asset size, growth, financing constraints, and the capital structure of firms; for example, see Pagano, Roell, and Zechner (2002) and Schmukler and Vesperoni (2006). See Karolyi (2006) for a review.

144. For concerns that local markets are becoming illiquid owing to internationalization, see Bovespa (1996), Federation des Bourses de Valeurs (2000), *Financial Times* (1998), *Latin Finance* (1999, 2004), and *The Economist* (2000). To overcome the illiquidity of domestic markets, policy makers are trying to come up with new solutions, such as the creation of Novo Mercado in Brazil or the establishment of regional stock exchanges (World Bank 2004b).

145. At the firm level, internationalization might signal firm quality. For example, internationalization might allow corporations to alleviate agency and informational asymmetry problems by "bonding" themselves into markets with greater disclosure requirements and stronger shareholder protection systems (Doidge, Karolyi, and Stulz 2004; Gozzi, Levine, and Schmukler 2006; Reese and Weisbach 2002; Siegel 2005). Or internationalization might reduce firms' cost of capital by allowing them to overcome barriers between markets. From this perspective, internationalization provides a signal about firm quality, as the market is better able to distinguish good firms from bad (those that do not internationalize). Cantale (1996) and Fuerst (1998) present models with information asymmetry and establish a signaling equilibrium in which firms with better prospects are able to distinguish themselves from firms with lower future profitability by cross-listing in markets with stricter regulatory environments.

146. See, for example, Aggarwal, Klapper, and Wysocki (2005), Bradshaw, Bushee, and Miller (2004), and Edison and Warnock (2004).

147. Turnover, and similar trade-based indicators, are frequently used to proxy for liquidity since (a) theory and evidence suggest a close association between turnover and bid-ask spreads, (b) many countries do not have bid-ask spread information, and (c) some research finds that turnover can be a better proxy for liquidity than bid-ask spreads because of problems with measuring spreads. Moreover, it is crucial to examine turnover, since theory and evidence identify a strong link between turnover and firm performance, industrial expansion, and national growth (see, for example, Beck and Levine 2002, 2004; Demirgüç-Kunt and Maksimovic 1998; and Levine and Zervos 1998a).

148. These results are consistent with previous research done at the aggregate level. Moel (2001) finds a negative association between the fraction of a country's firms that issue ADRs and total local market turnover. Karolyi (2004) also finds a negative link between ADR issuance and domestic stock market development.

149. The share of international firms in the domestic market is the number of international firms divided by the total number of firms listed in the domestic market (for each country and year). A firm is classified as international from the year it issues a depositary receipt, cross-lists, or raises capital abroad. If the firm terminates its depositary receipt program or delists from an international exchange, it is classified as domestic.

150. The evidence suggests that these results are not explained by reverse causality, whereby firms internationalize to flee from deteriorating domestic markets. As noted above, Levine and Schmukler (forthcoming) control for domestic market conditions. Moreover, they show that firms that internationalize without providing a mechanism to have their shares traded in public markets abroad experience an increase, not a decrease, in domestic trading activity, which runs counter to the fleeing argument. Furthermore, the results presented in the previous section show that firms from countries with good economic and institutional fundamentals are more likely to access and trade in international capital markets, which also runs counter to the view that firms from countries with poor local environments are the ones that internationalize.

151. For instance, firms that raise money through private placements in the United States by means of Rule 144A can only trade among qualified institutional buyers on the PORTAL system. Firms that issue Level I ADRs trade on the over-the-counter market, which is not an organized market or exchange, but rather a network of securities dealers. These markets tend to provide less liquidity than public exchanges and therefore are less likely to generate migration of trading abroad.

152. Specifically, for liquidity measures they use Amihud's (2002) illiquidity index, which equals the ratio of a stock's absolute returns to its value traded, and the proportion of days in a year when there are no changes in the price of a security.

153. See Schmukler (2004), among others, for a review.

154. There is some evidence that suggests that the converse is also true; namely, that the degree of internationalization in Latin America is higher than that predicted by macroeconomic and institutional fundamentals. While weak, the evidence also appears to suggest that, relative to other regions, capital market reforms in Latin America have had a pro-internationalization bias. However, these results could not be robustly confirmed because of data limitations and, hence, they are not fully discussed in this book.

155. Predicted values are estimated from a regression of the variables of interest on GDP per capita, fiscal deficit as a percentage of GDP, total equity flows (defined as portfolio equity flows plus foreign direct investment) as a percentage of GDP, and shareholder rights for a sample of 63 countries over the 1975–2004 period. The data displayed are the averages for the 1990–2004 period. See de la Torre, Gozzi, and Schmukler (forthcoming) for details.

156. In general terms, first-generation reforms concern those taken as part of the initial wave of efforts to regain macroeconomic stability while deregulating and privatizing the economy. In the financial sector, first-generation reforms focused mainly on liberalizing the domestic financial system (by, for instance, dismantling administered interest rates, unifying multiple exchange rate regimes, lifting credit ceilings, phasing out directed credit, reducing legal reserve requirements, privatizing public-sector commercial banks, and lowering functional barriers to banking) and on allowing freer cross-border capital mobility. Second-generation reforms concern the subsequent wave of reforms that are, by and large, much more

intensive in institution building. In the financial sector, these entail, for instance, strengthening prudential oversight and transparency, improving creditor rights systems, enhancing corporate governance practices and minority shareholder protection, and modernizing market infrastructures.

157. We discuss the issue of systemic risk in greater detail elsewhere. See de la Torre and Schmukler (2004).

158. Following the financial crises of the second half of the 1990s, initiatives to strengthen the international financial architecture resulted in an ambitious program to assess the degree of convergence of country practices with international standards. A number of new international standards were developed as a consequence. The International Monetary Fund and World Bank were entrusted with a leading role in implementing such programs—whose results are summarized in the so-called Reports on the Observance of Standards and Codes (ROSC). International standards that are relevant to the functioning of securities markets include the following: IOSCO Objectives and Principles of Securities Regulation; CPSS-IOSCO Recommendations for Securities Clearance and Settlement; OECD Principles of Corporate Governance, Accounting and Auditing Standards; and the World Bank Principles and Guidelines for Effective Insolvency and Creditor Rights Systems. For details see http://www.worldbank.org/ifa/rosc.html.

159. Observance of the international standards mentioned is often evaluated in the context of a fairly thorough diagnosis of a country's financial system, conducted jointly by the IMF and World Bank under the Financial Sector Assessment Program. For details see http://www1.worldbank.org/finance/html/fsap.html

160. See, for instance, Aghion, Bacchetta, and Banerjee (2004), who show theoretically that countries undergoing intermediate stages of financial development are likely to experience greater instability than countries in either advanced or early stages of financial development.

161. Consistent with this hypothesis, Kaminsky and Schmukler (2003) find that financial liberalization is associated with more pronounced boom-bust cycles in the short run but leads to more stable financial markets in the long run.

162. Renditions of this view, in the more general context of assessing the impact of reforms on economic development, can be found in Fernandez-Arias and Montiel (2001), Krueger (2004), Singh et al. (2005), and World Bank (1997).

163. Renditions of this view can be found, for instance, in Bhagwati (1998) and Stiglitz (2002).

164. A number of theoretical papers show that financial liberalization may be associated with crises (see, for example, Allen and Gale 2000; Bachetta and van Wincoop 2000; Calvo and Mendoza 2000; and McKinnon and Pill 1997). Empirically, several papers have found links between financial deregulation, boom-bust cycles, and banking and balance of payments crises (see, for example, Corsetti, Pesenti, and Roubini 1999; Demirgüç-Kunt and Detragiache 1999; Kaminsky and Reinhart 1999; and Tornell and Westermann 2005).

165. See Gavin and Hausmann (1996) for an excellent analysis of the macroeconomic roots of banking crises.

166. See, for example, Johnston and Sundararajan (1999) and McKinnon (1993).

167. See, for example, Ocampo (2003), Stiglitz (1999, 2000), and Tobin (2000).

168. Greenspan's argument that the capital markets can act as a "spare tire" when the "main tire" (the banking system) is flat illustrates this view (see Greenspan 1999).

169. See, for instance, Calvo and Reinhart (2000) and Hausmann et al. (1999).

170. This view is articulated, for instance, in Karacadag, Sundararajan, and Elliott (2003), who argue that there is a hierarchy of financial markets that reflects the complexity of the risks in each market and links among markets. On the basis

of this hierarchy, they propose a sequencing of market development and risk-mitigation measures.

171. Reversals in government debt management gains at times of financial turmoil, resulting in part from risk management problems in the private sector, particularly in the mutual fund industry, are illustrated by the cases of Brazil and Colombia, as discussed, for example, in World Bank (2003b) and World Bank (2002b), respectively.

172. A cogent and well-documented articulation of this type of criticism of the "get the sequence right" view is found in Rajan and Zingales (2003a). Kaminsky and Schmukler (2003) provide evidence on how reforms increase after financial liberalization. Braun and Raddatz (2004) show that trade liberalization, by increasing the strength of those sectors that benefit from better access to finance relative to those where increased availability of funds would dissipate incumbents' rents, can have a significant impact on financial development.

173. This view of financial development is consistent with the message in Caprio and Honohan (2001) that "it is the financial services themselves that matter [for growth] more than the form of their delivery" (p. 48).

174. De la Torre, Levy Yeyati, and Schmukler (2002) argue that these functions of the currency constitute two of the three components of the "blessed trinity" (strong contractual institutions is the third one), which empowers countries to seize the full benefits of the current wave of financial globalization.

175. This clarification is important because the missing market problem applies also to formally dollarized emerging countries, inasmuch as their equilibrium real exchange rate is subject to significant fluctuations—which can be the case even in countries that are small and open if their nontradable sectors account for a relatively large share of GDP. Even if the country in question remained formally dollarized, a market for financial contracts denominated in nontradable prices would be needed for debtors in the nontradable sector to avoid incurring unhedged real exchange rate exposure.

176. In de la Torre and Schmukler (2004), we note that the economics profession is moving toward a consensus on a three-pronged de-dollarization agenda, involving macroeconomic policy (i.e., exchange rate flexibility cum inflation targeting), prudential policy (for example, higher capital or provisioning requirements for dollar loans to debtors in the nontradable sector), and financial policy (i.e., the promotion of CPI-indexed contracts, possibly aided by CPI-indexed lending and borrowing by multilateral organizations). We also caution that enthusiasm for this agenda should be tamed, given the difficult thresholds that must be crossed for each of the three policy prongs to chip away financial dollarization in a sustainable manner. In de la Torre, Levy Yeyati, and Schmukler (2002), we sketch the reform priorities suitable for financial development of a highly dollarized system in a globalized context.

177. A cogent and fairly comprehensive discussion of reform issues concerning the international financial architecture is found in Eichengreen (1999).

178. A discussion of the issues, along with a specific proposal to create an Emerging Market Fund (EMF) is found in Calvo (2001).

179. A discussion of the issues, along with a specific proposal to create a Sovereign Debt Restructuring Mechanism (SDRM) is found in Krueger (2001).

180. See, for instance, Hausmann and Eichengreen (2002) and Levy Yeyati (2004).

181. A good way to gain a sense of this problem is to revise the highly convoluted regulations on "valuation" issued by securities markets regulators in countries with highly illiquid secondary markets.

182. As noted in chapter 2, the exception is Brazil, where derivatives markets for interest and exchange rates have grown to become much more liquid than the

underlying cash markets. However, this asymmetry appears to be an important source of vulnerability, as illustrated by the 2002–03 episode of financial turbulence, in which the unwinding of portfolios caused such volatility in asset prices that the government was compelled to shift risks to itself by becoming the main provider of hedges. See World Bank (2003b).

183. The retail investor base is miniscule in virtually all Latin American countries, as noted in chapter 2.

184. This helps explain why local stock markets and IPOs in the region appear to have been withering away (see chapter 2) despite the efforts to enhance corporate governance practices, as documented in Capaul (2003).

185. This sort of size threshold for issues is also needed to spread out the transaction costs of issuing, as discussed in Zervos (2004).

186. In de la Torre and Schmukler (2004), we discuss ways in which financial contracts are adapted (through dollarization, short-termism, and offshorization) to cope with systemic risk and, in the process, transform one form of systemic risk into another.

187. The hope actually goes beyond this in the minds of reformers that argue that fostering financial development at home is consistent with pension funds' fiduciary duties to the extent that domestic financial deepening promotes growth. See Corbo and Schmidt-Hebbel (2003).

188. For details see Gill, Packard, and Yermo (2005).

189. For a detailed discussion of these finding and associated issues, see Rocha (2004).

190. Indexes used to benchmark the performance of emerging market sovereign bond funds include the EMBI indexes reported by JPMorgan Chase and the Brady Bond Index published by Salomon Brothers. Local currency debt funds are normally benchmarked to the ELMI index, calculated also by JPMorgan Chase. An index commonly used to benchmark emerging market equity funds is the Morgan Stanley Capital International (MSCI) index and the emerging market indexes produced by Lehman Brothers and Merrill Lynch. According to the MSCI Web site, over 90 percent of the U.S. institutional investors' investments in international equities are benchmarked to MSCI indexes.

191. Following over 30 structured interviews with market participants, Ladekarl and Zervos (2004) conclude that securities issued in amounts under US$150–200 million "remain unattractive to many large emerging market investors" (p. 23). Claessens and Schmukler (2006), using a large sample of firms from 53 countries, show that the size of the firm is an important determinant of the probability of accessing international financial markets.

192. Many have recommended the regional integration of securities markets as a preferred route to overcome the constraints imposed by small size—a view that tends to be popular among many in the international financial institutions. As discussed in the annex to this chapter, however, several good reasons cast doubts on the proposition that regional integration of capital markets would be superior to the alternative of a deeper and better integration with the developed financial centers.

193. Exchanges have traditionally been considered national monopolies, with competition limited to that among exchanges within the same country. Competition has usually led to the concentration of trading in only a few exchanges at the national level. In the case of the United States, for example, technological and regulatory changes reduced the geographic barriers that protected local exchanges and led to a gradual consolidation, with the number of exchanges falling from more than 100 in the late 19th century to 18 by 1940, 11 by 1960, and seven by 1980 (Arnold et al. 1999). Similar processes have taken place in other countries, such as the United Kingdom, where all regional exchanges where absorbed by the London

Stock Exchange by 1973. In contrast, the regional stock exchanges in Germany are still quite active, although there has been a tendency toward concentration in recent years (see Klagge and Martin 2005 for a comparison of the stock markets systems in the United Kingdom and Germany).

194. Malkamaki (1999) finds evidence of significant economies of scale in stock exchange activities, especially regarding order execution.

195. Lower transaction costs and higher liquidity, as well as a larger investor base, can lead to reductions in firms' costs of capital (see Amihud and Mendelson 1986; Brennan and Subrahmanyam 1996; and Merton 1987).

196. Cybo-Ottone, Di Noia, and Murgia (2000) identify nearly 70 cross-border deals among European exchanges between 1996 and 1999.

197. Most of the merger activity has occurred at the national level, with mergers between stock and derivative exchanges in the same country, and between regional exchanges. Cross-border mergers have been rare.

198. There is a formal agreement among the three main exchanges in CARICOM (Caribbean Community and Common Market) to allow the cross-listing and trading of stocks. The Argentine, Brazilian, and Uruguayan stock exchanges have signed an agreement to interconnect their operations in the future. Conversations are under way among the Andean countries toward allowing cross-listings, integrating their infrastructures (for example, securities custody), and electronically linking their exchanges.

199. Frankel (1996) argues that the existence of a high currency risk premium can also hinder the integration of equity markets.

200. Alternatively, some argue that, to the extent that SME risk can be pooled, say, through a mutual or investment fund, the participations in such a fund could be more easily placed with institutional investors in a regional market, as compared to a local market. This argument, however, would militate even more strongly in favor of a globally integrated capital market, where the institutional investor base would be immensely larger.

201. Frankel (1996) argues that integration with global equity markets is better for economic welfare than regional integration alone and that regional integration might be a second-best solution.

References

Acemoglu, D., P. Aghion, and F. Zilibotti. 2006. "Distance to Frontier, Selection, and Economic Growth." *Journal of the European Economic Association* 4 (1): 37–74.

Acemoglu, D., S. Johnson, and J. A. Robinson. 2001. "The Colonial Origins of Comparative Development: An Empirical Investigation." *American Economic Review* 91 (5): 1369–1401.

———. 2002. "Reversal of Fortunes: Geography and Institutions in the Making of the Modern World Income Distribution." *Quarterly Journal of Economics* 117 (4): 1133–92.

Aggarwal, R., L. Klapper, and P. D. Wysocki. 2005. "Portfolio Preferences of Foreign Institutional Investors." *Journal of Banking and Finance* 29 (12): 2919–46.

Aghion, P., P. Bacchetta, and A. Banerjee. 2004. "Financial Development and the Instability of Open Economies." *Journal of Monetary Economics* 51 (6): 1077–1106.

Alexander, G., C. Eun, and S. Janakiramanan. 1987. "Asset Pricing and Dual Listing on Foreign Capital Markets: A Note." *Journal of Finance* 42 (1): 151–58.

———. 1988. "International Listings and Stock Returns: Some Empirical Evidence." *Journal of Financial and Quantitative Analysis* 23 (2): 135–51.

Allen, F. 1990. "The Market for Information and the Origin of Financial Intermediaries." *Journal of Financial Intermediation* 1 (1): 3–30.

Allen, F., and D. Gale. 2000. "Bubbles and Crises." *Economic Journal* 110: 236–55.

Alles, L. 2001. "Asset Securitization and Structured Financing: Future Prospects and Challenges for Emerging Market Countries." IMF Working Paper WP/01/147, International Monetary Fund, Washington, DC.

Amihud, Y. 2002. "Illiquidity and Stock Returns: Cross-Section and Time-Series Effects." *Journal of Financial Markets* 5 (1): 31–56.

Amihud, Y., and H. Mendelson. 1986. "Asset Pricing and the Bid-Ask Spread." *Journal of Financial Economics* 17 (2): 223–49.

Arestis, P., P. O. Demetriades, and K. B. Luintel. 2001. "Financial Development and Economic Growth: The Role of Stock Markets." *Journal of Money, Credit, and Banking* 33 (1): 16–41.

Arnold, T., P. Hersch, J. H. Mulherin, and J. Netter. 1999. "Merging Markets." *Journal of Finance* 53 (3): 1083–1107.

Bacchetta, P., and E. van Wincoop. 2000. "Capital Flows to Emerging Markets: Liberalization, Overshooting and Volatility." In *Capital Flows and the Emerging Economies–Theory, Evidence, and Controversies*, ed. S. Edwards. Chicago: University of Chicago Press.

Banerjee, A., and A. Newman. 1993. "Occupational Choice and the Process of Development." *Journal of Political Economy* 101 (2): 274–98.

Batten, J., and Y. Kim. 2001. "Expanding Long-Term Financing Through Bond Market Development: A Post-Crisis Policy Task." In *Government Bond Market Development in Asia*, ed. K. Yun-Hwan. Manila: Asian Development Bank.

Beck, T., and A. de La Torre. 2006. "The Basic Analytics of Access to Financial Services." Working Paper, World Bank, Washington, DC.

Beck, T., A. Demirgüç-Kunt, L. Laeven, and R. Levine. 2005. "Finance, Firm Size, and Growth." Policy Research Working Paper 3485, World Bank, Washington, DC.

Beck, T., A. Demirgüç-Kunt, and R. Levine. 2001a. "Law, Politics, and Finance." Policy Research Working Paper 2585, World Bank, Washington, DC.

———. 2001b. "The Financial Structure Database." In *Financial Structure and Economic Growth*, ed. A. Demirgüç-Kunt and R. Levine. Cambridge, MA: MIT Press.

———. 2006. "Finance, Inequality and Poverty: Cross-Country Evidence." Mimeo, University of Minnesota (Carlson School of Management), Minneapolis, MN.

Beck, T., A. Demirgüç-Kunt, and V. Maksimovic. 2005. "Financial and Legal Constraints to Firm Growth: Does Size Matter?" *Journal of Finance* 60 (1): 137–77.

Beck, T., A. Demirgüç-Kunt, and M. S. Martinez Peria. Forthcoming. "Reaching Out: Access to and Use of Banking Services across Countries." *Journal of Financial Economics*.

Beck, T., and R. Levine. 2002. "Industry Growth and Capital Allocation: Does Having a Market- or Bank-Based System Matter?" *Journal of Financial Economics* 64 (2): 147–80.

———. 2004. "Stock Markets, Banks and Growth: Panel Evidence." *Journal of Banking and Finance* 28 (3): 423–42.

Bekaert, G., and C. R. Harvey. 2000. "Foreign Speculators and Emerging Equity Markets." *Journal of Finance* 55 (2): 565–613.

Bekaert, G., C. R. Harvey, and C. Lundblad. 2005. "Does Financial Market Liberalization Spur Growth?" *Journal of Financial Economics* 77 (1): 3–55.

Beckaert, G., C. R. Harvey, C. T. Lundblad, and S. Siegel. Forthcoming. "Global Growth Opportunities and Market Integration." *Journal of Finance*.

Bencivenga, V. R., and B. D. Smith. 1992. "Deficits, Inflation and the Banking System in Developing Countries: The Optimal Degree of Financial Repression." *Oxford Economic Papers* 44 (4): 767–90.

Bencivenga, V. R., B. D. Smith, and R. M. Starr. 1995. "Transactions Costs, Technological Choice, and Endogenous Growth." *Journal of Economic Theory* 67 (1): 53–177.

Benos, E., and M. S. Weisbach. 2004. "Private Benefits and Cross-Listings in the United States." *Emerging Markets Review* 5 (2): 217–40.

Bhagwati, J. 1998. "The Capital Myth." *Foreign Affairs* 77 (3): 7–12.

Bhattacharya, U., and H. Daouk. 2002. "The World Price of Insider Trading." *Journal of Finance* 57 (1): 75–108.

BIS (Bank for International Settlements). 1999. "Implications of Repo Markets for Central Banks." Committee on the Global Financial System Publications No. 10, Basel, Switzerland.

———. 2005. "The Role of Ratings in Structured Finance: Issues and Implications." Committee on the Global Financial System Publications No. 23, Basel, Switzerland.

Blackburn, K., and V. T. Y. Hung. 1998. "A Theory of Growth, Financial Development, and Trade." *Economica* 65 (257): 107–24.

Blanchard, O., and A. Missale. 1994. "The Debt Burden and Debt Maturity." *American Economic Review* 84 (1): 309–19.

Blennerhassett, M., and R. G. Bowman. 1998. "A Change in Market Microstructure: The Switch to Electronic Screen Trading on the New Zealand Stock Exchange." *Journal of International Financial Markets, Institutions and Money* 8 (3–4): 261–76.

Borensztein, E., B. Eichengreen, and U. Panizza. 2006. "Debt Instruments and Policies in the New Millennium: New Markets and New Opportunities." IDB Working Papers 1020, IDB, Washington, DC.

Bortolotti, B., F. de Jong, G. Nicodano, and I. Schindele. 2003. "Privatization and Stock Market Liquidity." Working Paper 105 Fondazione Eni Enrico Mattei, Milan, Italy.

Bossone, B., P. Honohan, and M. Long. 2001. "Policy for Small Financial Systems." Financial Sector Discussion Paper 6, World Bank, Washington, DC.

Boutchkova, M. K., and W. L. Megginson. 2000. "Privatization and the Rise of Global Capital Markets." *Financial Management* 29: 31–76.

Bovespa. 1996. "Nova York Ataca e os Mercados Reagem." *Revista Bovespa* April–June.

Boyd, J. H., R. Levine, and B. D. Smith. 2001. "The Impact of Inflation on Financial Sector Performance." *Journal of Monetary Economics* 47 (2): 221–48.

Boyd, J. H., and E. C. Prescott. 1986. "Dynamic Coalitions, Growth, and the Firm." Staff Report 100, Federal Reserve Bank of Minneapolis.

Boyd, J. H., and B. Smith. 1998. "Capital Market Imperfections in a Monetary Growth Model." *Economic Theory* 11 (2): 241–73.

Bradshaw, M. T., B. J. Bushee, and G. S. Miller. 2004. "Accounting Choice, Home Bias, and U.S. Investment in Non-U.S. Firms." *Journal of Accounting Research* 42: 795–841.

Braun, M., and C. Raddatz. 2004. "Trade Liberalization and the Politics of Financial Development." Policy Research Working Paper 3517, World Bank, Washington, DC.

Brennan, M. J., and A. Subrahmanyam. 1996. "Market Microstructure and Asset Pricing: On the Compensation for Illiquidity in Stock Returns." *Journal of Financial Economics* 41 (3): 441–64.

Broner, F., G. Lorenzoni, and S. Schmukler. 2004. "Why Do Emerging Markets Borrow Short Term?" Working Paper 3389, World Bank, Washington, DC.

Bulow, J., and K. Rogoff. 1989. "Sovereign Debt: Is to Forgive to Forget?" *American Economic Review* 79 (1): 43–50.

Burgess, R., and R. Pande. 2005. "Can Rural Banks Reduce Poverty? Evidence from the Indian Social Banking Experiment." *American Economic Review* 95 (3): 780–95.

Burghardt, G. 2004. "World Futures Volume Soars to New Highs . . . Again." *Futures Industry* March/April.

Burnside, C., M. Eichenbaum, and S. Rebelo. 2001. "Hedging and Financial Fragility in Fixed Exchange Rate Regimes." *European Economic Review* 45 (7): 1151–93.

Calvo, G. 1996. *Money, Exchange Rates, and Output*. Cambridge, MA: MIT Press.

———. 2001. "Globalization Hazard and Weak Government in Emerging Markets." "Presidential Address" to the Latin American and Caribbean Economic Association (LACEA), Montevideo, Uruguay, October 18.

Calvo, G., and E. G. Mendoza. 2000. "Rational Contagion and Globalization of the Securities Market." *Journal of International Economics* 51 (1): 79–113.

Calvo, G., and C. Reinhart. 2000. "When Capital Flows Come to a Sudden Stop: Consequences and Policy." In *Key Issues in Reform of the International Monetary and Financial System*, ed. P. K. Kenen and A. K. Swoboda. Washington, DC: International Monetary Fund.

Cameron, R. 1967. "Scotland, 1750–1845." In *Banking in the Early Stages of Industrialization: A Study in Comparative Economic History*, ed. R. Cameron, 60–99. New York: Oxford University Press.

Cantale, S. 1996. "The Choice of a Foreign Market as a Signal." Mimeo, Tulane University, New Orleans, LA.

Capaul, M. 2003. "Corporate Governance in Latin America." Mimeo, Regional Study, Chief Economist's Office, Latin America and the Caribbean Region, World Bank.

Caprio, G., and P. Honohan. 2001. *Finance for Growth: Policy Choices in a Volatile World*. New York: Oxford University Press; Washington, DC: World Bank.

Catalan, M., G. Impavido, and A. R. Musalem. 2001. "Contractual Savings or Stock Market Development: Which Leads?" *Journal of Applied Social Science Studies* 120: 445–87.

Chamon, M., and R. Hausmann. 2005. "Why Do Countries Borrow the Way They Borrow?" In *Other People's Money: Debt Denomination and Financial Instability in Emerging Market Economies*, ed. B. Eichengreen and R. Hausmann. Chicago: University of Chicago Press.

Chiesa, G., and G. Nicodano. 2003. "Privatization and Financial Market Development: Theoretical Issues." Working Paper 1.2003, Fondazioni Eni Enrico Mattei (FEEM), Milan, Italy.

Chong, A., A. Galindo, and A. Micco. 2004. "Creditor Protection and SME Finance." Mimeo, Inter-American Development Bank.

Chordia, T., R. Roll, and A. Subrahmanyam. 2000. "Commonality in Liquidity." *Journal of Financial Economics* 56 (1): 3–28.

Chowdhry, B., and V. Nanda. 1991. "Multimarket Trading and Market Liquidity." *Review of Financial Studies* 4 (3): 483–511.

Claessens, S., S. Djankov, and D. Klingebiel. 2000. "Stock Markets in Transition Economies." Financial Sector Discussion Paper 5, World Bank Washington, DC. Forthcoming in *Financial Transition in Europe and Central Asia: Challenges of the New Decade*, ed. Alex Fleming, Lajos Bokros, and Cari Votava. Washington, DC: World Bank.

Claessens, S., D. Klingebiel, and S. Schmukler. 2002. "The Future of Stock Markets in Emerging Economies: Evolution and Prospects." *European Business Organization Law Review* 3: 403–38. Also published in *Brookings-Wharton Papers on Financial Services 2002*, ed. R. Litan and R. Herring, 167–202. Washington, DC: Brookings Institution Press.

———. 2006. "Stock Market Development and Internationalization: Do Economic Fundamentals Spur Both Similarly?" *Journal of Empirical Finance* 26 (3): 316–50.

———. Forthcoming. "Government Bonds in Domestic and Foreign Currency: The Role of Institutional and Macroeconomic Factors." *Review of International Economics*.

Claessens, S., and L. Laeven. 2003. "Financial Development, Property Rights, and Growth." *Journal of Finance* 58: 2401–36.

Claessens, S., R. Lee, and J. Zechner. 2003. "The Future of Stock Exchanges in European Union Accession Countries." Report commissioned by the Corporation of London.

Claessens, S., and S. Schmukler. 2006a. "Accessing International Equity Markets: What Firms from Which Countries Go Abroad?" Mimeo, World Bank, Washington, DC.

———. 2006b. "International Financial Integration through Equity Markets: Which Firms from Which Countries Go Global?" Mimeo, World Bank, Washington, DC.

Coffee, J. 1999. "The Future as History: The Prospects for Global Convergence in Corporate Governance and Its Implications." *Northwestern University Law Review* 93 (3): 641–708.

———. 2002. "Racing Towards the Top?: The Impact of Cross-Listings and Stock Market Competition on International Corporate Governance." *Columbia Law Review* 102 (7): 1757–1831.

Cole, H. L., and T. J. Kehoe. 1996. "A Self-Fulfilling Model of Mexico's 1994–95 Debt Crisis." Staff Report 210, Federal Reserve Bank of Minneapolis.

Collier, P., A. Hoeffler, and C. Pattillo. 2000. "Flight Capital as Portfolio Choice." *World Bank Economic Review* 15: 55–80.

Corbo, V., and K. Schmidt-Hebbel. 2003. "Efectos Macroeconómicos de la Reforma de Pensiones en Chile." Paper presented at the International Federation of Pension Funds Administrators Conference, "Reformas a los Sistemas de Pensiones: Sus Efectos y Retos." Panama, July 10–11.

Corsetti, G., P. Pesenti, and N. Roubini. 1999. "What Caused the Asian Currency and Financial Crisis?" *Japan and the World Economy* 11 (3): 305–73.

Coughenour, J. F., and M. M. Saad. 2004. "Common Market Makers and Commonality in Liquidity." *Journal of Financial Economics* 73: 37–69.

Coval, J., and T. Moskovitz. 1999. "Home Bias at Home: Local Equity Preference in Domestic Portfolios." *Journal of Finance* 54: 2045–73.

Cybo-Ottone, A., C. Di Noia, and M. Murgia. 2000. "Recent Development in the Structure of Securities Markets." In *Brookings-Wharton Papers on Financial Services*, ed. R. Litan and R. Herring. Washington, DC: Brookings Institution Press.

Davis, H. A. 2005. "The Definition of Structured Finance: Results from a Survey." *Journal of Structured Finance* 11: 5–10.

De Ferranti, D., D. Leipziger, and P. S. Srinivas. 2002. "The Future of Pension Reform in Latin America." *Finance and Development* 39: 39–43.

de la Torre, A., J. C. Gozzi, and S. Schmukler. 2006a. "Innovative Experiences in Access to Finance: Market Friendly Roles for the Visible Hand?" Policy Research Working Paper 3963, World Bank, Washington, DC.

———. 2006b. "Stock Market Development under Globalization: Whither the Gains from Reforms?" Working Paper, World Bank, Washington, DC.

———. Forthcoming. "Capital Market Development: Whither Latin America?" In *Strengthening Global Financial Markets*, IASE/NBER Volume, ed. M. Garcia and S. Edwards. Chicago: University of Chicago Press.

de la Torre, A., E. Levy Yeyati, and S. Schmukler. 2002. "Financial Globalization: Unequal Blessings." *International Finance* 5 (3): 335–57.

———. 2003. "Living and Dying with Hard Pegs: The Rise and Fall of Argentina's Currency Board." *Economia* 3 (2): 43–107.

de la Torre, A., and S. Schmukler. 2004. "Coping with Risks through Mismatches: Domestic and International Financial Contracts for Emerging Economies." *International Finance* 7 (3): 349–90.

Del Valle, C. 2003. "Developing Bond Markets: A Comprehensive View." In *Focus on Capital: New Approaches to Developing Latin American Capital Markets*, ed. K. Dowers and P. Masci. Washington, DC: Inter-American Development Bank.

Demirgüç-Kunt, A., and E. Detragiache. 1999. "Financial Liberalization and Financial Fragility." In *Financial Liberalization: How Far, How Fast?*, ed. G. Caprio, P. Honohan, and J. Stiglitz. Cambridge, U.K.: Cambridge University Press.

Demirgüç-Kunt, A., and R. Levine. 2001. "Bank-Based and Market-Based Financial Systems: Cross-Country Comparisons." In *Financial Structure and Economic Growth: A Cross-Country Comparison of Banks, Markets, and Development*, ed. A. Demirgüç-Kunt and R. Levine, 81–140. Cambridge, MA: MIT Press.

Demirgüç-Kunt, A., and V. Maksimovic. 1998. "Law, Finance, and Firm Growth." *Journal of Finance* 53: 2107–37.

Department for International Development. 2004. "The Importance of Financial Sector Development for Growth and Poverty Reduction." Policy Division Working Paper 030, London.

Devereux, M. B., and G. W. Smith. 1994. "International Risk Sharing and Economic Growth." *International Economic Review* 35: 535–50.

Di Noia, C. 1999. "The Stock Exchange Industry: Network Effects, Implicit Mergers, and Corporate Governance." Quaderni di Finanza No. 33, National Commission for Corporations and Stock Exchanges (CONSOB).

Diamond, J. 1997. *Guns, Germs, and Steel: The Fates of Human Societies*. New York: W. W. Norton.

Doidge, C. A., A. Karolyi, and R. M. Stulz. 2004. "Why Are Firms that List in the U.S. Worth More?" *Journal of Financial Economics* 71 (2): 205–38.

Domowitz, I., J. Glen, and A. Madhavan. 1998. "International Cross-Listing and Order Flow Migration: Evidence from an Emerging Market." *Journal of Finance* 53 (6): 2001–27.

Domowitz, I., and B. Steil. 1999. "Automation, Trading Costs, and the Structure of the Securities Trading Industry." In *Papers on Financial Services*, ed. R. Litan and A. Santomero. Washington, DC: Brookings Institution.

Dooley, M. 2000. "A Model of Crises in Emerging Markets." *Economic Journal* 110 (460): 256–72.

Dowers, K., F. Gomez-Acebo, and P. Masci. 2003. "Developing a Strategy for Reforming Capital Markets in Latin America and the Caribbean." In *Focus on Capital: New Approaches to Developing Latin American Capital Markets*, ed. K. Dowers and P. Masci. Washington, DC: Inter-American Development Bank.

Eaton, J., and M. Gersovitz. 1981. "Debt with Potential Repudiation: Theoretical and Empirical Analysis." *Review of Economic Studies* 48 (2): 289–309.

Economides, N. 1993. "Network Economics with Application to Finance." *Financial Markets, Institutions and Instruments* 2 (5): 89–97.

———. 1996. "The Economics of Networks." *International Journal of Industrial Organization* 14 (6): 673–99.

The Economist. 2000. "Latin America's Stock Markets: High and Dry." February 19.

Edison, H., and F. E. Warnock. 2003. "A Simple Measure of the Intensity of Capital Controls." *Journal of Empirical Finance* 10 (1): 81–103.

———. 2004. "U.S. Investors' Emerging Market Equity Portfolios: A Security Level Analysis." *Review of Economics and Statistics* 86 (3): 691–704.

Eichengreen, B. 1994. *International Monetary Arrangements for the 21st Century*. Washington, DC: Brookings Institution.

———. 1999. *Towards a New International Financial Architecture: A Practical Post-Asia Agenda*. Washington, DC: Institute for International Economics.

Eichengreen, B., and R. Hausmann. 1999. "Exchange Rates and Financial Fragility." NBER Working Paper 7418, National Bureau of Economic Research, Cambridge, MA.

———. 2003. *Debt Denomination and Financial Instability in Emerging Market Economies*. Chicago: University of Chicago Press.

Eichengreen, B., R. Hausmann, and U. Panizza. 2003. "Original Sin: The Pain, the Mystery, and the Road to Redemption." In *Debt Denomination and Financial Instability in Emerging Market Economies*, ed. B. Eichengreen and R. Hausmann. Chicago: University of Chicago Press.

———. 2005. "The Mystery of Original Sin." In *Other People's Money: Debt Denomination and Financial Instability in Emerging Market Economies*, ed. B. Eichengreen and R. Hausmann. Chicago: University of Chicago Press.

Eichengreen, B., and N. Sussman. 2000. "The International Monetary System in the Very Long Run." In *World Economic Outlook Supporting Studies*, 52–85.

Errunza, V. R., and E. Losq. 1985. "International Asset Pricing Under Mild Segmentation: Theory and Test." *Journal of Finance* 40: 105–24.

Errunza, V., and D. Miller. 2000. "Market Segmentation and the Cost of Capital in International Equity Markets." *Journal of Financial and Quantitative Analysis*. 35 (4): 577–600.

Eun, C. S., and S. Janakiramanan. 1986. "A Model of International Asset Pricing with a Constraint on the Foreign Equity Ownership." *Journal of Finance* 41: 897–914.

Federation des Bourses de Valeurs. 2000. *Price Discovery and the Competitiveness of Trading Systems*, Report to the FIBV Annual Meeting, Paris, October.

Feldstein, M. 1998. *Privatizing Social Security*. Chicago: Chicago University Press.

———. 1999. "Self-Protection for Emerging Market Economies." NBER Working Paper 6907, National Bureau of Economic Research, Cambridge, MA.

Feldstein, M., and J. Liebman. 2002. "Social Security." In *The Handbook of Public Economics*, ed. A. Auerbach and M. Feldstein. Vol. 4. Amsterdam: Elsevier Science.

Fernandez, V. 2002. "The Derivatives Markets in Latin America with an Emphasis on Chile." Working Paper 128, Center for Applied Economics, Universidad de Chile.

Fernandez-Arias, E., and P. Montiel. 2001. "Reform and Growth in Latin America: All Pain, No Gain?" *IMF Staff Papers* 48 (3): 522–46.

Financial Times. 1998. "ADRs Prove a Double-Edged Sword." April 6.

Foerster, S., and G. A. Karolyi. 1999. "The Effects of Market Segmentation and Investor Recognition on Assets Prices: Evidence from Foreign Stock Listing in the U.S." *Journal of Finance* 54 (3): 981–1014.

Frankel, J. A. 1996. "Exchange Rates and the Single Currency." In *European Equity Markets: The State of the Union and an Agenda for the Millennium*, ed. B. Steil. Copenhagen: European Capital Markets Institute.

Frankel, J., E. Fajnzylber, S. Schmukler, and L. Servén. 2001. "Verifying Exchange Rate Regimes." *Journal of Development Economics* 66 (2): 351–86.

French, K. R., and J. M. Poterba. 1991. "Investor Diversification and International Equity Markets." *American Economic Review* 81 (2): 222–26.

Fuerst, O. 1998. "A Theoretical Analysis of the Investor Protection Regulations Argument for Global Listing of Stocks." Mimeo, Yale University, New Haven, CT.

Furman, J., and J. E. Stiglitz. 1998. "Economic Crises: Evidence and Insights from East Asia." Paper presented to the Brookings Panel on Economic Activity, Washington, DC, September.

Galetovic, A. 1996. "Specialization, Intermediation and Growth." *Journal of Monetary Economics* 38 (3): 549–59.

Galiani, S., E. Levy Yeyati, and E. Schargrodsky. 2003. "Financial Dollarization and Debt Deflation under a Currency Board." *Emerging Markets Review* 4 (4): 340–67.

Galor, O., and J. Zeira. 1993. "Income Distribution and Macroeconomics." *Review of Economic Studies* 60 (1): 35–52.

Gavin, M., and R. Hausmann. 1996. "The Roots of Banking Crises: The Macroeconomic Context." In *Banking Crises in Latin America*. Washington, DC: Inter-American Development Bank.

Gavin, M., R. Hausmann, and L. Leiderman. 1995. "Macroeconomics of Capital Flows to Latin America: Experience and Policy Issues." IDB Working Paper 310, Inter-American Development Bank, Washington, DC.

Gill, I., T. Packard, and J. Yermo. 2005. *Keeping the Promise of Social Security in Latin America*. Washington, DC: World Bank; Stanford, CA: Stanford University Press.

Glaessner, T. 2003. "Derivatives in Implementation of Economic Policy within Emerging Economies: Getting Back to Basics." Paper presented at the first "Derivatives and Financial Markets Conference" organized by the Brazilian Mercantile & Futures Exchange, Campos de Jordao, Brazil.

Goldsmith, R. W. 1969. *Financial Structure and Development*. New Haven, CT: Yale University Press.

Gozzi, J. C., R. Levine, and S. Schmukler. 2006. "Internationalization and the Evolution of Corporate Valuation." Policy Research Working Paper Series 3933,

World Bank, Washington, DC. Previously released as NBER Working Paper 11023, National Bureau of Economic Research, Cambridge, MA.

Green, C., R. Mannos, V. Murinde, and J. Suppakitjarak. 2003. "The Impact of Microstructure Innovations in Emerging Markets Stock Markets: Evidence from Mumbai, India." Mimeo, Loughborough University, Leicestershire, U.K.

Greenspan, A. 1999. "Do Efficient Financial Markets Contribute to Financial Crises?" Paper presented at "Financial Markets Conference of the Federal Reserve Bank of Atlanta," Sea Island, Georgia, October 17.

Greenwood, J., and B. Jovanovic. 1990. "Financial Development, Growth, and the Distribution of Income." *Journal of Political Economy* 98 (5): 1076–1107.

Grinblatt, M., and M. Keloharju. 2001. "How Distance, Language, and Culture Influence Stockholdings and Trades." *Journal of Finance* 56 (3): 1053–74.

Guiso, L., P. Sapienza, and L. Zingales. 2004. "Does Local Financial Development Matter?" *Quarterly Journal of Economics* 119 (3): 929–69.

Haber, S. H. 1991. "Industrial Concentration and the Capital Markets: A Comparative Study of Brazil, Mexico, and the United States, 1830–1930." *Journal of Economic History* 51 (3): 559–80.

———. 1997. "Financial Markets and Industrial Development: A Comparative Study of Governmental Regulation, Financial Innovation and Industrial Structure in Brazil and Mexico, 1840–1940." In *How Latin America Fell Behind: Essays in the Economic History of Brazil and Mexico, 1800–1914*, ed. S. Haber, 146–78. Stanford, CA: Stanford University Press.

Haber, S., A. Razo, and N. Maurer. 2003. "The Politics of Property Rights: Political Instability, Credible Commitments, and Economic Growth in Mexico." Cambridge, U.K.: Cambridge University Press.

Halling, M., M. Pagano, O. Randl, and J. Zechner. 2005. "Where Is the Market? Evidence from Cross-Listings." Centre for Economic Policy Research (CEPR) Discussion Paper 4987, London.

Handbook of World Stock, Derivative and Commodity Exchanges. 2001. London MondoVisione.

Hargis, K. 2000. "International Cross-Listing and Stock Market Development in Emerging Economies." *International Review of Economics and Finance* 9: 101–22.

Hasbrouck, J., and D. J. Seppi. 2001. "Common Factors in Pricing, Order Flows and Liquidity." *Journal of Financial Economics* 59 (3): 383–411.

Häusler, G., D. J. Mathieson, and J. Roldos. 2004. "Trends in Developing Country Capital Markets around the World." In *The Future of Domestic Capital Markets in Developing Countries*, ed. R. Litan, M. Pomerleano, and V. Sundarajan. Washington, DC: Brookings Institution Press.

Hausmann, R., and B. Eichengreen. 2002. "How to Eliminate Original Financial Sin." *Financial Times,* November 22.

Hausmann, R., M. Gavin, C. Pages-Serra, and E. Stein, 1999. "Financial Turmoil and the Choice of Exchange Rate Regime." IDB Working Paper 400 Washington, DC.

Hausmann, R., and U. Panizza. 2003. "On the Determinants of Original Sin: An Empirical Investigation." *Journal of International Money and Finance* 22: 957–90.

Hausmann, R., U. Panizza, and E. Stein. 2001. "Why Do Countries Float the Way They Float?" *Journal of Development Economics* 66 (2): 387–414.

Henry, P. B. 2000a. "Stock Market Liberalization, Economic Reform, and Emerging Market Equity Prices." *Journal of Finance* 55 (2): 529–64.

———. 2000b. "Do Stock Market Liberalizations Cause Investment Booms?" *Journal of Financial Economics* 58 (1–2): 301–34.

———. 2003. "Capital Account Liberalization, the Cost of Capital, and Economic Growth." *American Economic Review* 93 (2): 91–96.

Herrera, L., and R. Valdes. 2003. "Dedollarization, Indexation and Nominalization: The Chilean Experience." Paper presented at the IDB/World Bank "Conference on Financial Dedollarization: Policy Options," Washington, DC, December 1–2.

Herring, R., and N. Chatusripitak. 2000. "The Case of the Missing Market: The Bond Market and Why It Matters for Financial Development." Wharton Financial Institutions Center Working Paper, University of Pennsylvania, Philadelphia.

Huberman, G. 2001. "Familiarity Breeds Investment." *The Review of Financial Studies* 14 (3): 659–80.

Huybens, E., and B. Smith. 1998. "Financial Market Frictions, Monetary Policy, and Capital Accumulation in a Small Open Economy." *Journal of Economic Theory* 81 (2): 353–400.

———. 1999. "Inflation, Financial Markets, and Long-Run Real Activity." *Journal of Monetary Economics* 43 (2): 283–315.

IDB (Inter-American Development Bank). 1995. *Overcoming Volatility Report on Economic and Social Progress in Latin America*. Washington, DC: IDB.

———. 2002. *Beyond Borders: The New Regionalism in Latin America*. Washington, DC: IDB.

———. 2005. *Unlocking Credit: The Quest for Deep and Stable Bank Lending*. Baltimore: Johns Hopkins University Press.

IFC (International Finance Corporation). 2000. *Building Local Bond Markets: An Asian Perspective*. Washington, DC: IFC.

IMF (International Monetary Fund). 2002. *Global Financial Stability Report— Market Developments and Issues*. Washington, DC: IMF.

———. 2005. *Global Financial Stability Report*. Washington, DC: IMF.

IOMA (International Options Market Association). 2004. *Derivatives Market Survey 2003*.

Isham, J., D. Kaufmann, and L. Prichett. 1995. "Governance and Returns on Investment: An Empirical Investigation." Policy Research Working Paper 1550, World Bank, Washington, DC.

Jeanne, O. 2000. "Foreign Currency Debt and the Global Financial Architecture. *European Economic Review* 44 (4–6): 719–27.

———. 2003. "Why Do Emerging Economies Borrow in Foreign Currency?" IMF Working Paper 03/177, International Monetary Fund, Washington, DC.

Jeanneau, S., and C. Perez Verdia. 2005. "Reducing Financial Vulnerability: The Development of the Domestic Government Bond Market in Mexico." *BIS Quarterly Review* (December): 95–107.

Johnson, S., J. McMillan, and C. Woodruff. 2002. "Property Rights and Finance." *American Economic Review* 92 (5): 1335–56.

Johnston, B. R., and V. Sundararajan. 1999. *Sequencing Financial Sector Reforms: Country Experiences and Issues*. Washington, DC: International Monetary Fund.

Kaminsky, G. L., and C. M. Reinhart. 1999. "The Twin Crises: The Causes of Banking and Balance-of-Payments Problems." *American Economic Review* 89 (3): 473–500.

Kaminsky, G. L., and S. Schmukler. 2003. "Short-Run Pain, Long-Run Gain: The Effects of Financial Liberalization." NBER Working Paper 9787, National Bureau of Economic Research, Cambridge, MA.

Karacadag, C., V. Sundararajan, and J. Elliott. 2003. "Managing Risks in Financial Market Development: The Role of Sequencing." IMF Working Paper 03/116, International Monetary Fund, Washington, DC.

Karolyi, G. A. 2004. "The Role of American Depositary Receipts in the Development of Emerging Equity Markets." *Review of Economics and Statistics* 86 (3): 670–90.

———. 2006.. "The World of Cross-Listings and Cross-Listings of the World: Challenging Conventional Wisdom." *Review of Finance* 10 (1): 99–152.

Kim, E. H., and V. Singal. 2000. "Opening Up of Stock Markets: Lessons from Emerging Economies." *Journal of Business* 73 (1): 25–66.

King, R. G., and R. Levine. 1993a. "Finance and Growth: Schumpeter Might Be Right." *Quarterly Journal of Economics* 108 (3): 717–38.

———. 1993b. "Finance, Entrepreneurship, and Growth: Theory and Evidence." *Journal of Monetary Economics* 32 (3): 513–42.

Klagge, B., and R. Martin. 2005. "Decentralised versus Centralised Financial Systems: Is There a Case for Local Capital Markets?" *International Journal of Management Reviews* 7 (3): 135–65.

Kremer, M., and S. Jayachandran. 2002. "Odious Debt." NBER Working Paper 8953, National Bureau of Economic Research, Cambridge, MA.

Krueger, A. 2001. "A New Approach to Sovereign Debt Restructuring." Address at the Indian Council for Research on International Economic Relations, Delhi, India, December 20.

———. 2004. "Meant Well, Tried Little, Failed Much: Policy Reforms in Emerging Market Economies." Remarks at the Roundtable Lecture at the Economic Honors Society, New York University, New York, March 23.

Krugman, P. 1999. "Balance Sheets, the Transfer Problem, and Financial Crises." *International Tax and Public Finance* 6 (4): 459–72.

Ladekarl, J., and S. Zervos. 2004. "Housekeeping and Plumbing: The Investability of Emerging Markets." Policy Research Working Paper 3229, World Bank, Washington, DC.

Lane, P., and S. Schmukler. Forthcoming. The International Financial Integration of China and India. In *Dancing with Giants: China, India, and the Global Economy*, ed. L. Alan Winters and Shahid Yusuf. Washington, DC: World Bank.

Lang, M., V. Lins, and D. Miller. 2003. "ADRs, Analysts, and Accuracy." *Journal of Accounting Research* 41 (2): 317–45.

La Porta, R., F. Lopez-de-Silanes, A. Shleifer, and R. W. Vishny. 1997. "Legal Determinants of External Finance." *Journal of Finance* 52 (3): 1131–50. Washington, DC: World Bank.

———. 1998. "Law and Finance." *Journal of Political Economy* 106 (6): 1113–55.

———. 2000. "Investor Protection and Corporate Governance." *Journal of Financial Economics* 58 (1–2): 3–27.

———. 2002. "Investor Protection and Corporate Valuation." *Journal of Finance* 57: 1147–70.

————. 2006. "What Works in Securities Laws?" *Journal of Finance* 61 (1): 1–32.

Latin Finance. 1999. "The Incredible Shrinking Markets." September.

Lee, R. 1999. *What Is an Exchange? The Automation, Management and Regulation of Financial Markets.* Oxford, U.K.: Oxford University Press.

Levine, R. 1991. "Stock Markets, Growth, and Tax Policy." *Journal of Finance* 46 (4): 1445–65.

————. 1997. "Financial Development and Economic Growth: Views and Agenda." *Journal of Economic Literature* 35 (2): 688–726.

————. 2002. "Bank-Based or Market-Based Financial Systems: Which Is Better?" *Journal of Financial Intermediation* 11 (1): 398–428.

————. 2005. "Finance and Growth." In *Handbook of Economic Growth*, ed. P. Aghion and S. Durlauf. Amsterdam: Elsevier.

Levine, R., N. Loayza, and T. Beck. 2000. "Financial Intermediation and Growth: Causality and Causes." *Journal of Monetary Economics* 46 (1): 31–77.

Levine, R., and S. Schmukler. 2006. "Internationalization and Stock Market Liquidity." *Review of Finance-Journal of the European Finance Association* 10 (1): 153–87.

————. Forthcoming. "Migration, Spillovers, and Trade Diversion: The Impact of Internationalization on Domestic Stock Market Liquidity." *Journal of Banking & Finance.*

Levine, R., and S. Zervos. 1998a. Capital Control Liberalization and Stock Market Development. *World Development* 26 (7): 1169–84.

————. 1998b. "Stock Markets, Banks, and Economic Growth." *American Economic Review* 88 (3): 537–58.

Levy Yeyati, E. 2004. "Dollars, Debts, and the IFIs: Dedollarizing Multilateral Lending." Mimeo, Universidad Torcuato Di Tella, Buenos Aires, Argentina.

Levy Yeyati, E., S. Schmukler, and N. van Horen. 2006. "International Financial Integration through the Law of One Price." Working Paper 3897, World Bank, Washington, DC.

Levy Yeyati, E., and F. Sturzenegger. 2003. "To Float or to Fix: Evidence on the Impact of Exchange Rate Regimes on Growth." *American Economic Review* 93 (4).

Licht, A. 1998. "Stock Market Integration in Europe." Harvard Institute for International Development, CAER II Discussion Paper No. 15, Consulting Assistance on Economic Reform, Cambridge, MA.

Licht, A. N. 2003. "Cross-Listing and Corporate Governance: Bonding or Avoiding?" *Chicago Journal of International Law* 4 (1): 141–63.

Linnenberg, D., and E. J. Waitzer. 2004. "Corporate Governance Reforms in Chile." Paper presented at the "Fourth International Conference on Finance," Universidad de Santiago de Chile, January 7–9.

Lins, K., D. Strickland, and M. Zenner. 2005. "Do Non-U.S. Firms Issue Equity on U.S. Stock Exchanges to Relax Capital Constraints?" *Journal of Financial and Quantitative Analysis* 40 (1): 109–33.

Loayza, N., P. Fajnzylber, and C. Calderón. 2005. *Economic Growth in Latin America and the Caribbean: Stylized Facts, Explanations, and Forecasts.* Washington, DC: World Bank.

Loser, C., and M. Guerguil. 2000. "The Long Road to Financial Stability." *Finance and Development* 37 (1, March): 1–12.

Love, I. 2003. "Financial Development and Financing Constraint: International Evidence from the Structural Investment Model." *Review of Financial Studies* 16 (3): 765–91.

Lucas, R. E., Jr. 1988. "On the Mechanics of Economic Development." *Journal of Monetary Economics* 22 (1): 3–42.

Malkamaki, M. 1999. "Are There Economies of Scale in Stock Exchange Activities?" Discussion Papers 4/99, Bank of Finland, Helsinki.

Martinez, L., and A. Werner. 2002a. "Capital Markets in Mexico: Recent Developments and Future Challenges." Paper prepared for the seminar organized by Banco de Mexico, "Estabilidad Macroeconómica, Mercados Financieros y Desarrollo Económico," November 12–13.

———. 2002b. "The Exchange Rate Regime and the Currency Composition of Corporate Debt: The Mexican Experience." *Journal of Development Economics* 69 (2): 315–34.

McAndrews, J., and C. Stefanadis. 2002. "The Consolidation of European Stock Exchanges." *Current Issues in Economics and Finance* (Federal Reserve Bank of New York) 1 (6).

McCauley, R., and E. Remolona. 2000. "Size and Liquidity of Government Bond Markets." *BIS Quarterly Review* (November).

McKinnon, R. I. 1973. *Money and Capital in Economic Development.* Washington, DC: Brookings Institution.

McKinnon, R. 1993. *The Order of Economic Liberalization, Financial Control in the Transition to a Market Economy.* Baltimore: John Hopkins University Press.

McKinnon, R., and H. Pill. 1997. "Credible Economic Liberalizations and Overborrowing." *American Economic Review* 87 (2): 189–93.

———. 1998. "International Overborrowing: A Decomposition of Credit and Currency Risks." *World Development* 26 (7): 1267–82.

Meddin, L. 2004. "Structured Finance in the Emerging Markets." In *Global Securitisation Review 2004/2005,* Euromoney Institutional Investor PLC, London.

Mehl, A., and J. Reynaud. 2005. "The Determinants of 'Domestic' Original Sin in Emerging Market Economies." Working Paper 560, European Central Bank, Frankfurt, Germany.

Merton, R. 1987. "A Simple Model of Capital Market Equilibrium with Incomplete Information." *Journal of Finance* 42 (3): 483–510.

———. 1992. "Financial Innovation and Economic Performance." *Journal of Applied Corporate Finance* 4 (4): 461–81.

Merton, R. C., and Z. Bodie. 1995. "A Conceptual Framework for Analyzing the Financial Environment." In *The Global Financial System: A Functional Perspective,* ed. D. B. Crane et al., 3–31. Boston: Harvard Business School Press.

———. 2004. "The Design of Financial Systems: Towards a Synthesis of Function and Structure." Working Paper Number 10620, National Bureau of Economic Research, Cambridge, MA.

Mihaljek, D., M. Scatigna, and A. Villar. 2002. "Recent Trends in Bond Markets." *BIS Papers* No. 11: 13–41.

Miller, D. 1999. "The Market Reaction to International Cross-Listings: Evidence from Depositary Receipts." *Journal of Financial Economics* 51 (1): 103–23.

Missale, A., and O. Blanchard. 1994. "The Debt Burden and Debt Maturity." *American Economic Review* 84 (1): 309–19.

Moel, A. 2001. "The Role of American Depositary Receipts in the Development of Emerging Markets." *Economia* 2 (1): 209–73.

Noronha, G., A. Sarin, and S. Saudagaran. 1996. "Testing for Microstructure Effects of International Dual Listings Using Intraday Data." *Journal of Banking and Finance* 20 (6): 965–83.

Obstfeld, M. 1994. "Risk-Taking, Global Diversification, and Growth." *American Economic Review* 84 (5): 1310–29.

Obstfeld, M. 1998. "The Global Capital Market: Benefactor or Menace?" *Journal of Economic Perspectives* 12 (Fall): 9–30.

Obstfeld, M., and A. M. Taylor. 2005. *Global Capital Markets: Integration, Crisis, and Growth*. Cambridge, U.K.: Cambridge University Press.

Ocampo, J. A. 2003. "Capital-Account and Counter-Cyclical Prudential Regulations in Developing Countries." In *From Capital Surges to Drought: Seeking Stability for Emerging Markets*, ed. R. French-Davis and S. Griffith-Jones. London: Palgrave Macmillan.

Orszag, P., and J. Stiglitz. 2001. "Ten Myths of Pension Reform." In *New Ideas about Old-Age Security*, ed. R. Holzmann and J. Stiglitz. Washington, DC: World Bank.

Pagano, M., A. Roell, and J. Zechner. 2002. "The Geography of Equity Listing: Why Do European Companies List Abroad?" *Journal of Finance* 57 (6): 2651–94.

Pagano, M., and P. Volpin. 2001. "The Political Economy of Finance." *Oxford Review of Economic Policy* 17 (4): 502–19.

Patro, D. 2000. "Return Behavior and Pricing of American Depositary Receipts." *Journal of International Financial Markets, Institutions and Money* 10 (1): 43–67.

Perotti, E., and L. Laeven. 2002. "Confidence Building in Emerging Stock Markets." Working Paper, University of Amsterdam.

Perotti, E., and P. Van Oijen. 2001. "Privatization, Political Risk, and Stock Market Development in Emerging Economies." *Journal of International Money and Finance* 20 (1): 43–69.

Pulatkonak, M., and G. Sofianos. 1999. "The Distribution of Global Trading in NYSE-listed Non-U.S. Stocks." NYSE Working Paper 99-03, New York Stock Exchange, New York.

Queisser, M. 1998. "Pension Reform: Lessons from Latin America." Policy Brief 15, OECD Development Center, Paris.

Radelet, S., and J. Sachs. 1998. "The Onset of the East Asian Financial Crisis." Working Paper, Harvard Institute for International Development, Cambridge, MA.

Rajan, R. G., and L. Zingales. 1998. "Financial Dependence and Growth." *American Economic Review* 88 (3): 559–86.

———. 2001. "Financial Systems, Industrial Structure, and Growth." *Oxford Review of Economic Policy* 17 (4) 467–82.

———. 2003a. "The Great Reversals: The Politics of Financial Development in the Twentieth Century." *Journal of Financial Economics* 69 (1): 5–50.

———. 2003b. *Saving Capitalism from the Capitalists*. New York: Crown Business Division of Random House.

Reese, W. A., Jr., and M. S. Weisbach. 2002. "Protection of Minority Shareholder Interests, Cross-Listing in the United States, and Subsequent Equity Offerings." *Journal of Financial Economics* 66 (1): 65–104.

Robinson, J. 1952. "The Generalization of the General Theory." In *The Rate of Interest, and Other Essays*, 67–142. London: Macmillan.

Rocha, R. 2004. "Chile: The Pensions Sector." Technical Background Paper to the Chile FSAP. Mimeo.

Rodrik, D., and A. Velasco. 1999. "Short-Term Capital Flows." Annual "World Bank Conference on Development Economics," Washington, DC, April.

Roe, M. J. 1994. *Strong Managers, Weak Owners: The Political Roots of American Corporate Finance*. Princeton, NJ: Princeton University Press.

Rossi, J. L., Jr. 2004. "Corporate Foreign Vulnerability and the Exchange Rate Regime: Evidence from Brazil." Mimeo, Yale University, New Haven, CT.

Roubini, N. 2001. "Key Macroeconomic Issues to Consider in the Development of Regional Capital Market Integration." Remarks prepared for an IDB panel "Promoting Capital Market Integration in Latin America and the Caribbean," Washington, DC, February 5.

Rousseau, P. L., and P. Wachtel. 1998. "Financial Intermediation and Economic Performance: Historical Evidence from Five Industrial Countries." *Journal of Money, Credit and Banking* 30 (4): 657–78.

———. 2000. "Equity Markets and Growth: Cross-Country Evidence on Timing and Outcomes, 1980–1995." *Journal of Business and Finance* 24 (12): 1933–57.

Rutkowski, M. 1998. "A New Generation of Pension Reforms Conquers the East: A Taxonomy in Transition Economies." *Transition* 9 (4): 16–19.

———. 2002. "Pensions in Europe: Paradigmatic and Parametric Reforms in EU Accession Countries in the Context of EU Pension System Changes." *Journal of Transforming Economies and Societies* 9 (1): 2–26.

Sachs, J., A. Tornell, and A. Velasco. 1996. "Financial Crises in Emerging Markets: The Lessons from 1995." *Brookings Papers on Economic Activity* 1: 147–215.

Saint-Paul, G. 1992. "Technological Choice, Financial Markets and Economic Development." *European Economic Review* 36 (4): 763–81.

Schinasi, G., and R. T. Smith. 1998. "Fixed Income Markets in the United States, Europe, and Japan: Some Lessons for Emerging Markets." IMF Working Paper 173/98, International Monetary Fund, Washington, DC.

Schineller, L. M. 1997. "An Econometric Model of Capital Flight from Developing Countries." International Finance Discussion Paper 579, Federal Reserve Board, Washington, DC.

Schmukler, S. 2004. "Financial Globalization: Gain and Pain for Developing Countries." *Federal Reserve Bank of Atlanta Economic Review* (Second Quarter): 39–66.

Schmukler, S., and L. Servén. 2002. "Pricing Currency Risk under Currency Boards." *Journal of Development Economics* 69 (2): 367–391. Longer version appeared as "Pricing Currency Risk: Facts and Puzzles from Currency Boards," NBER Working Paper 9047, National Bureau of Economic Research, Cambridge, MA.

Schmukler, S., and E. Vesperoni. 2001. Globalization and Firms' Financing Choices: Evidence from Emerging Economies." In *Financial Structure and Economic Growth*, ed. A. Demirgüç-Kunt and R. Levine, 347–75. Cambridge, MA: MIT Press.

———. 2006. "Financial Globalization and Debt Maturity in Emerging Economies." *Journal of Development Economics* 79 (1): 183–207.

Schneider, M., and A. Tornell. 2004. "Bailout Guarantees, Balance Sheet Effects, and Financial Crises." *Review of Economic Studies* 71 (3): 883–913.

Shah, A., and S. Thomas. 2001. "Securities Markets Infrastructure for Small Countries." Mimeo, World Bank, Washington, DC.

Shaw, E. 1973. *Financial Deepening in Economic Development.* New York: Oxford University Press.

Sheets, N. 1996. "Capital Flight from the Countries in Transition: Some Theory and Empirical Evidence." International Finance Discussion Paper 514, Federal Reserve Board Washington, DC.

Siegel, J. 2005. "Can Foreign Firms Bond Themselves Effectively by Renting U.S. Securities Laws?" *Journal of Financial Economics* 75 (2): 319–60.

Singh, A., A. Belaisch, C. Collyns, P. De Masi, R. Krieger, G. Meredith, and R. Rennhack. 2005. "Stabilization and Reform in Latin America: A Macroeconomic Perspective on the Experience since the Early 1990s." IMF Occasional Paper 238, International Monetary Fund, Washington, DC.

Smith, K., and G. Sofianos. 1997. "The Impact of a NYSE Listing on the Global Trading of Non-U.S. Stocks." NYSE Working Paper 97-02, New York Stock Exchange, New York.

Sonakul, C. M. 2000. "Keynote Address." Presented at the ADB conference "Government Bond Market and Financial Sector Development in Developing Asian Economies," Manila, March 20–26.

Stapleton, R. C., and M. G. Subrahmanyam. 1977. "Market Imperfections, Capital Market Equilibrium and Corporation Finance." *Journal of Finance* 32 (2): 307–19.

Stern, N. 1989. "The Economics of Development: A Survey." *Economic Journal* 99 (397): 597–685.

Stiglitz, J. 1999. "Bleak Growth for the Developing World." *International Herald Tribune*, April 10–11.

———. 2000. "Capital Market Liberalization, Economic Growth, and Instability." *World Development* 28 (6): 1075–86.

———. 2002. *Globalization and Its Discontents.* New York: W. W. Norton.

Stulz, R. M., 1999a. "Globalization of Equity Markets and the Cost of Capital." NBER Working Paper 7021, National Bureau of Economic Research, Cambridge, MA.

Stulz, R. 1999b. "Globalization of Equity Markets and the Cost of Capital." *Journal of Applied Corporate Finance* 12 (3): 8–25.

Stulz, R., and R. Williamson. 2003. "Culture, Openness, and Finance." *Journal of Financial Economics* 70 (3): 313–49.

Tesar, L., and I. Werner. 1995. "Home Bias and High Turnover." *Journal of International Money and Finance* 14 (4): 467–92.

Tirole, J. 2002. *Financial Crises, Liquidity and the International Monetary System.* Princeton, NJ: Princeton University Press.

Tobin, J. 2000. "Financial Globalization." *World Development* 28 (6): 1101–04.

Tornell, A., and F. Westermann. 2005. *Boom-Bust Cycles and Financial Liberalization.* Cambridge, MA: MIT Press.

Tovar, C. 2005. "International Government Debt Denominated in Local Currency: Recent Developments in Latin America." *BIS Quarterly Review* (December): 109–18.

UN-ECLAC. 2005. *Balance Preliminar de las economías de América Latina y el Caribe:* UN Economic Commission for Latin America and the Caribbean, Santiago, Chile.

Velli, J. 1994. "American Depositary Receipts: An Overview." *Fordham International Law Journal* 17 (1): 38–57.

Walker, E. 1998. "The Chilean Experience Regarding Completing Markets with Financial Indexation." Working Paper, Central Bank of Chile, Santiago.

Walker, E., and F. Lefort. 2002. "Pension Reform and Capital Markets: Are There Any (Hard) Links?" Social Protection Discussion Paper 24082, World Bank, Washington, DC.

Williamson, John. 1990. "What Washington Means by Policy Reform?" In *Latin American Adjustment: How Much Has Happened?*, ed. John Williamson. Washington, DC: Institute for International Economics.

Wojcik, D. G. L. Clark, and R. Bauer. 2004. "Corporate Governance and Cross-Listing: Evidence from European Companies." Working Paper, University of Oxford, Oxford, U.K.

World Bank. 1994. "Averting the Old Age Crisis: Policies to Protect the Old and Promote Growth." World Bank Policy Research Report, Oxford University Press, New York.

———. 1997. *The Long March: A Reform Agenda for Latin America and the Caribbean in the Next Decade.* Washington, DC: World Bank.

———. 1998. *World Development Report.* Washington, DC: World Bank.

———. 2002a. *Financial Sector Assessment, Mexico.* Washington, DC: World Bank.

———. 2002b. "Reform Roadmap: Strategic Choices in Developing Colombia's Debt Market." Mimeo.

———. 2003a. *Global Development Finance: Striving for Stability in Development Finance.* Washington, DC: World Bank.

———. 2003b. "Program Document for Proposed Second Programmatic Fiscal Reform Loan." Report 25880-BR, World Bank, Washington, DC.

———. 2003c. *Report on the Observance of Standards and Codes (ROSC): Corporate Governance Country Assessment Mexico.* Washington, DC: World Bank.

———. 2004a. *Global Development Finance 2004—Harnessing Cyclical Gains for Development.* Washington, DC: World Bank.

———. 2004b. *Whither Latin American Capital Markets?* Washington, DC: World Bank.

———. 2005. *Doing Business in 2006.* Washington, DC: World Bank.

———. 2006. *Global Development Finance 2006: The Development Potential of Surging Capital Flows.* Washington, DC: World Bank.

Wright, R. E. 2002. *The Wealth of Nations Rediscovered: Integration and Expansion in American Financial Markets, 1780–1850.* Cambridge, U.K.: Cambridge University Press.

Wurgler, J. 2000. "Financial Markets and the Allocation of Capital." *Journal of Financial Economics* 58 (1–2): 187–214.

Xu, Z. 2000. "Financial Development, Investment, and Growth." *Economic Inquiry* 38 (2): 331–44.

Yermo, J. 2003. "Pension Reform and Capital Market Development: Background Paper for Regional Study on Social Security Reform." Office of the Chief Economist, Latin America and the Caribbean, World Bank, Washington, DC.

Zervos, S. 2004. "The Transaction Costs of Primary Market Issuance: The Case of Brazil, Chile and Mexico." Mimeo, World Bank, Washington, DC.

Index

In the index, *f* refers to figure, *n* refers to note, and *t* refers to table.